Commentaries on Aristotle's

On Sense and What Is Sensed and

On Memory and Recollection

❖o❖

THOMAS AQUINAS IN TRANSLATION

ST. THOMAS AQUINAS

Commentaries on Aristotle's *On Sense and What Is Sensed* and *On Memory and Recollection*

translated with introductions and notes by
Kevin White and Edward M. Macierowski

The Catholic University of America Press
Washington, D.C.

Library of Congress Cataloging-in-Publication Data
Thomas, Aquinas, Saint, 1225?–1274.
    [In Aristotelis libros De sensu et sensato, De memoria et
reminiscentia commentarium. English]
    Commentaries on Aristotle's "On sense and what is sensed"
and "On memory and recollection" / translated with an
introduction and notes by Kevin White and Edward M.
Macierowski.—1st ed.
       p. cm.—(Thomas Aquinas in translation)
    Includes bibliographical references.
    ISBN 0-8132-1379-7 (cloth : alk. paper)—
ISBN 0-8132-1382-7 (pbk. : alk. paper)
    1. Aristotle. De sensu et sensibilibus. 2. Senses and
sensation—Early works to 1800. 3. Aristotle. De memoria et
reminiscentia. 4. Memory (Philosophy)—Early works to 1800.
I. White, Kevin, 1952– II. Macierowski, E. M., 1948– III. Title.
IV. Series.
B444.T4613 2005
121'.35—dc22

                                       2003023086

"In consulting the excellent commentary of St. Thomas Aquinas on the *Parva Naturalia* of Aristotle, I was struck at once with its close resemblance to Hume's Essay on association. The main thoughts were the same in both, the *order* of the thoughts was the same, and even the illustrations differed only by Hume's occasional substitution of more modern examples. I mentioned the circumstance to several of my literary acquaintances, who admitted the closeness of the resemblance, and that it seemed too great to be explained by mere coincidence; but they thought it improbable that Hume should have held the pages of the angelic Doctor worth turning over. But some time after Mr. Payne, of the King's mews, shewed Sir James Mackintosh some odd volumes of St. Thomas Aquinas, partly perhaps from having heard that Sir James (then Mr.) Mackintosh had in his lectures passed a high encomium on this canonized philosopher, but chiefly from the fact, that the volumes had belonged to Mr. Hume, and had here and there marginal marks and notes of reference in his own hand writing. Among these volumes was that which contains the *Parva Naturalia,* in the old Latin version, swathed and swaddled in the commentary afore mentioned!"

—Samuel Taylor Coleridge, *Biographia literaria*, Chapter V

CONTENTS

PREFACE AND ACKNOWLEDGMENTS

If there are two people, one of whom writes one part of a book and the other another part, then "we wrote that book" is not literally correct, but a synecdoche, inasmuch as the whole stands for the parts.

Summa theologiae III, Q.67, a.6, ad 3

The present volume consists of English translations of the commentaries by Thomas Aquinas on the first two books of Aristotle's *Parva naturalia: De sensu et sensato* and *De memoria et reminiscentia*. The translations are based on the critical edition of the commentaries published by René-Antoine Gauthier, O.P., in 1985 in Volume 45.2 of the Leonine Commission's edition of Aquinas's *opera omnia*. Gauthier's edition includes critical texts of the Latin versions that Aquinas had of the Aristotelian works, as well as an informative introduction in French and valuable notes to the text in Latin. It is hoped that the present translations may be useful to readers interested in Aquinas's thought, in the history of Aristotelianism, or in important pre-modern discussions of sensation and its objects and of memory and recollection. In imitation of the Leonine format, the words of the Aristotelian text that are repeated in the commentaries have been italicized. The translators would like to express their gratitude to the Leonine Commission for its kind permission to use the Leonine text.

A possible source of confusion should be clarified. In the dominant traditional ordering of Aristotle's works, *De sensu et sensato*, the sequel to *De anima*, is followed by *De memoria et reminiscentia*. Aquinas accepted this ordering and followed it in his commentaries on the three works. Toward the beginning of his commentary on *De sensu et sensato*, however, apparently under the influence of Averroes, he characterizes *De memoria et reminiscentia* as the second "treatise" of the "book" *De sensu et sensato* (see pp. 17, 24 below), and Gauthier's edition accordingly presents a single commentary on two treatises of one book. But at the beginning of his commentary on *De memoria et reminiscentia,* Aquinas provides a commentator's prologue, apparently signaling the beginning of a distinct commentary on a distinct work, and he now calls *De memoria et reminiscentia* a "book" (see p. 184 below). In keeping with Aquinas's second thoughts, and with traditional Aristotelian and Thomistic scholarship, the present volume distinguishes two translations by two translators of two Thomistic commentaries on two Aristotelian works.

I would like to thank Chad Engelland and Travis Cooper, who, at different stages, helped prepare the manuscript of the commentary on *On Sense and What Is Sensed* for publication.

Kevin White

I'd like to add a note of thanks to my wife, Carol, who has more than matched the job description of a good wife at the end of the book of Proverbs, and to our five new adopted children, Jacob, Jeremiah, Janea, David, and Hailey, who have added spice and energy to our lives.

Edward M. Macierowski

ST. THOMAS AQUINAS

Commentary on Aristotle's
On Sense and What Is Sensed

Translated by Kevin White

TRANSLATOR'S INTRODUCTION

The best way for the modern reader to approach this medieval commentary on an ancient text by Aristotle is to start by reading the ancient text—which is apparently a sequel to Aristotle's *On the Soul*—on its own, outlining its structure, paraphrasing and summarizing, and noting any comments and questions that occur. The commentary can then be read with the greatest possible appreciation of its distinctive procedures and interests, in dramatic contrast to those of Aristotle. At that point, the reader with even slight familiarity with Aquinas's work may wish to turn at once to his prologue (p. 14), which begins with a provocative quotation from *On the Soul* about things, the intellect, and separation from matter; Aquinas himself can take it from there. On the other hand, the reader who requires preliminary historical information about and a foretaste of the commentary may find the following brief introduction useful.

1. Origins of the Commentary

The standard modern edition of the Greek text of Aristotle's nine little books on psychological and physiological topics collectively called *Parva naturalia* was published in 1955 by Sir David Ross.[1] The edition includes material by Ross—an introduction, divisions of the text, paraphrases of and comments on the divisions—which amounts to a commentary that, with respect to its treatment of the first two books, may be taken as a modern counterpart to the two medieval commentaries translated in the present volume. Ross begins by discussing the thirteenth-century term *parva naturalia,* which seems to have been coined shortly after Aquinas's death and which means, roughly, "little books in natural philosophy," although, as Ross says, "Aristotle sums up the contents better when, in 436a6–8, he refers to 'the phenomena common to soul and body.'"[2] Ross goes on to discuss the listing of these works in the ancient catalogues of Aristotle's writings and their place in his development, arguing that, although they seem meant to be read after *On the Soul,* all of them were composed before at least the second book of the latter.[3]

3

After his death in 322 B.C., Aristotle's works were transmitted to the Hellenistic, Byzantine, and Arabic worlds. Some or all of the *Parva naturalia* were occasionally the subject of commentaries, notably the Greek commentary on *On Sense and What Is Sensed* by Alexander of Aphrodisias (fl. A.D. 200) and the Arabic "compendium" of *Parva naturalia* by Averroes (A.D. 1126–98). In the Latin world, after a long period in which Aristotle was known only in some of his logical writings, most of his other works, including *Parva naturalia,* were translated from Arabic versions in the latter half of the twelfth century.[4]

The standard introduction to Aquinas's life, times, and works is Jean-Pierre Torrell's *Saint Thomas Aquinas, Volume 1: The Person and His Work,*[5] the twelfth chapter of which is an excellent introduction to Aquinas's Aristotelian commentaries. Aquinas was born in 1224 or 1225, about a quarter of a century after the University of Paris was founded. In 1210, 1215, and 1231, prohibitions were issued against the teaching of Aristotle's works at Paris, with particular reference to his writings in natural philosophy, but in the 1230s and 1240s some of the Aristotelian corpus, including *On Sense and What Is Sensed,* was included in two introductions to philosophy composed in Paris. Roger Bacon, who taught at Paris during the 1240s, and who later claimed to have been the first to lecture on Aristotle there, wrote a commentary on *On Sense and What Is Sensed* that may date from this period. In 1252, at about the time Aquinas arrived in Paris for his first stay in the Faculty of Theology, as a student during 1252–56 and a master during 1257–59, the English Nation of the Faculty of Arts included *On the Soul* in its official program of study; in 1255 the Faculty of Arts issued a comprehensive new program based on all available writings of Aristotle, which thus replaced the centuries-old tradition of liberal arts; the program indicates that *On Sense and What Is Sensed* was to be taught in six weeks and *On Memory and Recollection* in two. The available instruments for study of the *Parva naturalia* were the twelfth-century translations of them out of the Arabic and the compendium of Averroes, which had been translated in the early thirteenth century. Between 1254 and 1260 Aquinas's former teacher Albert the Great composed commentary-paraphrases of the *Parva naturalia* in Germany or Italy; Aquinas immediately had Albert's *On Sleep and Wakefulness,* and probably his *On Sense and What Is Sensed* and *On Memory and Recollection* as well, copied out for his own use.

In 1259 Aquinas's Dominican order sent him to Orvieto, and in 1265 it assigned him to what seems to have been a school of his own in Rome,[6] where he began two of his greatest and most original projects: the *Summa theologiae* and a series of twelve commentaries on works by Aristotle, of which the first, composed in 1267–68, was on *On the Soul,* and the second and third on *On Sense and What Is Sensed* and *On Memory and Recollection.* New impetus had just been given to study of *Parva naturalia* by William of Moerbeke's recent translations, directly from the Greek, both of the *Parva naturalia* and of Alexander of Aphrodisias's commentary on *On Sense and What Is Sensed;* Aquinas's commentaries on the first two books of the *Parva naturalia* seem to have been the first to make use of these translations. He may have begun these commentaries in Rome, but he finished them only after returning to the Parisian Faculty of Theology in the fall of 1268 for another teaching period, which lasted until 1272. During this period he acquired a number of followers in the Faculty of Arts, young teachers of Aristotelian texts who were impressed by his ability as an expositor of those texts, as a letter from them to the master of the Dominican order after Aquinas's death in 1274 indicates. One of them, Peter of Auvergne, composed commentaries of his own on *On Sense and What Is Sensed* and *On Memory and Recollection,* in which he borrows heavily and without acknowledgement from the corresponding commentaries of Aquinas. The extent of these borrowings might seem, from a modern point of view, to open him to the charge of plagiarism, but they should probably be understood in light of his renown as Aquinas's "most faithful disciple."[7]

2. The Title

The original title of Aristotle's work is *Peri aisthēseōs kai aisthētōn,* in which even those who know no Greek may hear two words related to *aesthēsis,* which means "sensation" or "perception"—or rather both, since the word, like its Latin translation, *sensus,* combines the two meanings. *Aesthēsis* is the root of English words that refer to sensation such as "anesthetic," as well as the root of "aesthetics," the name of the modern philosophical discipline concerned with judgments of beauty and the fine arts. The transition in the word "aesthetics" from the meaning of perception in general to the connotation of perception of beauty was established by the eighteenth-century follower of Christian Wolff, Alexander Baumgarten. Immanuel Kant's usage reflects both the old and the new aspects of the word: the "Transcendental Aesthetic" in his *Critique of Pure Reason* discusses the faculty of sensibility; the "Critique of Aesthetic Judgment" in his *Critique of Judgment* discusses judgments of beauty. Aristotle would no doubt be surprised by the modern extension of the Greek word, but perhaps he and Aquinas would hear distant echoes of remarks of their own in the connections modern aesthetics makes between sensation, judgment, and pleasure.

The Latin translation of Aristotle's title, *De sensu et sensato,* may evoke another association for the modern reader, namely the title of J. L. Austin's *Sense and Sensibilia* (1962),[8] which itself alludes to Jane Austen's *Sense and Sensibility* (1811). Austen's title, which might be paraphrased as "Good Sense versus Sentimental Sensitivity," suggests a confrontation between reasonableness and romanticism, or, as Aquinas might have said, between reason and the passions of sense-appetite; Austin's work criticizes earlier twentieth-century British philosophers for the view that we never directly perceive or sense material objects, but only sense-data or our ideas, a criticism with which Aristotle and Aquinas would be in sympathy. It might, accordingly, be objected that I should have translated Aristotle's title as *On Perception and What Is Perceived,* to make clear that Aristotle and Aquinas are primarily concerned with perceptual consciousness of things, not sense-data, but it seemed best, especially in the title, to stay as etymologically close as possible to the crucial original term.

The original title of the commentary is *Sentencia libri De sensu et sensato,* the redundancy of which might be captured in English by "The Sense (i.e., The Meaning) of the Book on Sense and the Sensed." Some overtones that the word *sentencia* had for Aquinas can be gathered from twelfth-century uses of it by Hugh of St. Victor and Peter Lombard. The former distinguished three levels of interpretation of a text: the *littera,* or order of words; the *sensus,* or meaning that the *littera* offers at first sight; and the *sentencia* (or *sententia*), a deeper meaning requiring exposition and interpretation.[9] The latter compiled a collection of views or opinions of the Church Fathers that he called the book of their *sententiae;* Aquinas's commentary on this book quotes a Latin translation of the Arabic writer Avicenna to explain that *sententia* in this context means "a definite and very determinate conception."[10] The editor of the Latin text of our commentary says that *sentencia* as used in the titles of Aquinas's commentaries means a simple doctrinal summary, to be distinguished from an *expositio*, or minute analysis of the letter of the text.[11] But our commentary is much more than a summary, and it contains a good bit of minute textual analysis. It repeats almost all of the words in the text and adds to them in varying degrees, providing synonyms, paraphrases, reasons behind or implications of them, and passages that introduce or follow up a section of text with extensive material supplied entirely by the commentator. The first of these passages is Aquinas's prologue.[12]

3. The Order of Theoretical Sciences

The reader who has taken the trouble to first read Aristotle's text by itself will be struck by the methodic and thematic concern with order that the commentary brings to it. This double concern with order is a prominent feature of Aquinas's work in general, in which it is related to such neoplatonic themes as hierarchy, measure, participation, degrees of likeness, and metaphoric nearness to and distance from a measure. In his metaphysics and theology these themes are brought to bear on the hierarchy of being and on God as the first measure of things.[13] Many of them appear on a smaller scale in the present commentary, which nowhere mentions God and is not primarily concerned with being, although the reader should be alert for occasional appearances of an underlying metaphysical concern. The theme of order shows up at once in Aquinas's prologue, which illustrates his compositional practice of subordinating a large amount of material to a single principle.[14]

Before starting on the prologue, it is a good idea to read the first page or so of the commentary on *On the Soul,* for two reasons. One is to appreciate the elaborateness of Aquinas's prologue to *On Sense and What Is Sensed,* which, like his much briefer prologue in the earlier commentary on *On the Soul,* introduces Aristotle's writings on living things, but in greater detail, suggesting that he is here making up for an earlier sketchiness. The other reason is to note the earlier commentary's remark, based in Ciceronian rhetoric, that anyone who writes a prologue does three things: he makes the audience well disposed, ready to be taught, and attentive; this remark summarizes the understanding of prologues that Aquinas had throughout his career.[15]

The prologue is quite indifferent to the kinds of historical considerations with which Ross begins, being exclusively concerned with the *theoretical* relation of the books of the *Parva naturalia* to other works of Aristotle. It proceeds in a way that is typical of Aquinas's prologues to Aristotle: it starts with an epigrammatic quotation from a work other than the one about to be commented on; the quotation then provokes an explanation, which leads to a discussion that identifies the *intentio*, that is, the proposed subject-matter, of the text to be commented on, and explains the place of the text in the order of Aristotle's writings. Here the epigram is from *On the Soul*: "just as things are separable from matter, so also is what pertains to intellect." Aquinas immediately explains with the axiomatic principle that anything is intelligible inasmuch as it is separable from matter, and he then applies this principle to things and to intellect. With respect to things, he distinguishes what is by nature separate from matter, and so is actually intelligible in itself, from what has to be abstracted from material conditions and made actually intelligible by our agent intellect. With respect to intellect, he argues that because the habits of a power are specifically distinguished by differentiation in the power's proper object, it follows that the sciences, which are habits of the intellect, are distinguished by differentiation in the intellect's object, namely "the separable from matter" (pp. 14–15). The elements of this argument are notions in Aristotle's works, notably *On the Soul* and *Ethics*, that Aquinas develops extensively in his own writings. A soul, which is the form and actuality of a living body and cause of the activities of life, has accidents or features called powers, that is, capacities or abilities for kinds of actions, each power and corresponding act having a formal object; a habit is a kind of quality, an acquired and settled disposition of a power that inclines what has the power to act in one way rather than another; intellect is a power for knowing or considering what is immaterial; a science is a habit of intellect that disposes one to consider some aspect of the immaterial. Because of its frequent occurrence in the commentary (indeed, throughout Aquinas's works), we should underline the apparently humble notion "consideration," which Aquinas elsewhere defines as "the act of the intellect in looking at the truth of a thing."[16]

Very quickly, then, the prologue arrives at a generalization—sciences are distinguished by differentiations in the separable from matter—which it next uses as an ordering principle for a survey, in five stages, of

theoretical sciences and of Aristotle's works in theoretical philosophy
(pp. 15–17).

1. Most generally, theoretical sciences are divided into metaphysics,
which considers what is separate from matter in being and nature;
mathematics, which considers what is separate from matter in nature
but not in being; and natural philosophy, which considers what includes
sensible matter in its nature.[17]

2. On the principle that what is more universal is more separate from
matter than what is less so, natural philosophy is divided into consideration of what is most common to natural things, namely movement and
its principles, and subsequent "concretions" or "applications" of these to
special kinds of moving things, some of which have life.

3. Consideration of living things is divided into three: consideration
of the soul by itself in abstraction; application of soul to body in a general way; and application to individual species of animals and plants.

4. Division of the general application of soul to body, which concerns
features common to all living things, or to all or many animals, is made
in terms of Aristotle's distinction in *On the Soul* of four levels of living
things on the basis of the number of their powers: plants have only "nutritive" or vital power; imperfect animals also have power of sensation;
perfect animals have nutritive and sensitive powers, but also power of
forward movement; human beings have all these and intellective power. All of the powers can be considered in the general application of soul
to body except the last, intellect, the one that is not the "actuality" of a
bodily organ. Accordingly, the books of the *parva naturalia* are divided
into three: those concerned with living things as such, those concerned
with power of movement, and those concerned with power of sensation.

5. This last group is divided into two: the acts of external and internal
sense-powers are the subjects of *On Sense and What Is Sensed* and of *On
Memory and Recollection* respectively; and the contrast between sensing
and not-sensing produced by the difference between being awake and
sleeping is the subject of *On Sleep and Wakefulness.*

The prologue culminates in a determination of the order of the books
or sciences mentioned in points 4 and 5 above: after the consideration of
the soul by itself in *On the Soul,* there follow first the books on the sensi-

tive part, then those on the motive part, and finally those on merely living things. Two principles are introduced to form an argument that the
present book must *immediately* follow the consideration of the soul by itself in *On the Soul*. The major premise is a neoplatonic principle of order:
"one should pass through the more similar to the dissimilar." The minor
premise concerns the subject of the text to be discussed: "sensing itself
pertains more to soul than to body" (p. 17). Early in the text Aristotle
will argue that the events common to soul and body—imagination,
memory, sleep and waking, youth and old age, breath, life and death,
sickness and health—may all be understood in relation to sensation,
which thus provides a focus for them all (p. 436blf.). Aquinas goes him
one better here by suggesting why it does so, namely because it, of all
such phenomena (including movement and nourishment) stands out as
being most "psychic," least "somatic." Occurring as it does as the end of
the prologue, just before analysis of the text begins, the point seems especially important, setting a sort of keynote for the commentary as a
whole.

4. The Order of Learning

The remainder of the commentary is devoted to discussion of the
words of the text. The basic procedure, which is complemented by
the above-mentioned additions to the text, is to divide and subdivide,
descending from large sections to chapters (not to be confused with
chapter-divisions in modern editions of the Aristotelian text), then to
what we would call paragraphs and sentences, until individual words
(where "the letters" emerge into the foreground) can be considered
with attention. The procedure is in a way the mirror image of Aquinas's
procedure in the *Summa theologiae*, where he manifests the construction
of the work as he goes along, explaining its divisions into parts, questions, and articles. Both in taking apart the books of others and in build-
ing up his *Summa*, then, he shows the same concern with making clear
the order of parts, and of the parts of parts, in the whole.

One of the divisions in the commentary is worth pointing out. Immediately after the discussion of colors, at the beginning of Chapter 8 the
text says that odors and flavors are to be treated next, but flavors first,
because they are more manifest to us (Chapter 8, 440b28–31). The commentary introduces a kind of scholastic objection: it might seem that

odor should be discussed immediately after color, since both are perceived through an external medium. This objection appears to appeal to the principle mentioned in the prologue that one should proceed through the similar to the dissimilar, but Aquinas responds with what seems to be a higher principle, namely that "the order of learning" *(ordo disciplinae)* requires that one proceed from the more to the less manifest (p. 75). The phrase "order of learning" is familiar to readers of Aquinas from its prominent occurrence in the prologue of the *Summa theologiae,* where he complains that beginners in theology are not being taught according to this order, but in keeping with the requirements of commenting on books or opportunities of disputation. By implicitly promising to follow this order in the *Summa,* Aquinas offers it as a new kind of theological book. The much less well known occurrence of the phrase in Chapter 8 of our commentary not only explains what "order of learning" means, but also insinuates that Aristotle follows it as a matter of course. To be sure, Aquinas understands theological and philosophical learning to be quite distinct. But he seems to think that the same kind of order should be followed in each, and that while he needs to introduce it into theological writing, he need only discover it in the philosophical works of Aristotle.

5. The Commentary's Principal Divisions of
On Sense and What Is Sensed

Aquinas's principal divisions of *On Sense and What Is Sensed* are as follows.

1. There are a prologue and a treatise (Chapter 1–18).

2. The treatise is divided into three: a résumé and development of what was said about sense-powers in *On the Soul* (Chapter 1); the main business of application of the soul's sense-powers to the bodily dimension (Chapters 2–13); and some concluding questions (Chapters 14–18).

3. Application to the bodily is made with reference first to organs (Chapters 2–4), then to objects (Chapter 5–13) of the senses.

4. Application with reference to objects was already made in *On the Soul,* but in terms of how they affect the sense-powers. What is considered here is rather what each kind of sense-object is in itself. But objects of touch are not considered here, because either they are elemental properties like wet and dry, and as such are considered in *On Generation*

and Corruption, or they are features of kinds of bodies, such as hard and soft, and as such are considered in the *Meteorology.* Nor is the object of hearing considered here, because in the case of sound there is no distinction between explanation of how it is produced and explanation of how it affects the sense of hearing, and it was already explained from the latter point of view in *On the Soul* (pp. 54–55). This leaves three kinds of sense-object to be considered in themselves: colors (Chapter 5–7), flavors (Chapters 8–10), and odors (Chapters 11–13). Each of the three is defined generically, then divided into species.

5. There are three concluding questions. The first is about sensible objects: Are they, like the bodies in which they inhere, infinitely divisible (Chapter 14)? The second is about alteration of a sense-power by its object: Does light first come to a mid-point in the medium before it reaches the power of sight, or does it cross the medium instantaneously (Chapter 15)? The third is about sense-power: Can two senses, such as sight and hearing, perceive simultaneously (Chapters 16–18)?

6. Philosophy and Science

There is a fair bit of pre-modern "science" in both the text and the commentary. Neither Aristotle nor Aquinas, of course, had our distinction between the philosophical and the scientific, and in reading the commentary we should be careful not to be too quick to dismiss the text and commentary to the status of something attractively exotic or unattractively obsolete, but also not to confuse what is indeed outmoded cosmology, physics, chemistry, or biology with a properly philosophical metaphysics, mathematics, philosophy of nature, or psychology that has a permanent claim on our interest. I propose, as a hypothesis the reader may wish to test, that the commentary to a great extent saves the text from dismissal on grounds of obsolescence by highlighting the philosophical dimension that is in it and by adding philosophical considerations of its own.

Evidence for this hypothesis can be found in passages such as the following: the neoplatonic presentation of memory and anger as approximations to reason in the prologue (pp. 19–20); the distinction between animal prudence and human prudence, and the contrast between sight and hearing as sources of learning, in Chapter 1 (pp. 19–20); the argument against Democritean materialism in Chapter 3 (p. 41); the explanation of how to define an accident in Chapter 5 (p. 58), and of the nature of measure in Chapter 6 (p. 63–64); the questions on accidents and on action in Chapter 9 (pp. 82–84); the distinctions between generation and instantaneous production, and between properties and adventitious qualities in Chapter 15 (pp. 128, 131–32); and the distinction between perception of parts in a whole and perception of separated parts in Chapter 17 (p. 148). Even when such passages are based on remarks in other works of Aristotle or in Alexander's commentary, they are contributions by Aquinas to what he takes to be the commentator's job of actualizing the potential intelligibility of the text.

Finally, the reader should note two points of central importance for Aquinas's understanding of sensation: his development of the Aristotelian theme of a "sense-judgment" (Ch. 18, p. 156); and his introduction of the Averroistic notion of an "intentional" being or existence that sensible things take on in the media of sense-perception and in the sense-powers (Ch. 4, p. 47; Ch. 18, p. 156).[18]

436A1–B8

436a1 *Since it was determined about soul in itself, and each virtue from the point of view of it, the next thing is to make a consideration about animals, and everything that has life, as to what are their proper and what their common operations. Accordingly let the things that were said about soul be underlying, and let us speak about the rest, and first about what is first.*

436a6 *The greatest both of the common and of the proper features of animals are seen to be common to both body and soul.*

436a8 *For instance, sense and memory, and anger and desire, and appetite as a whole, and with these pleasure and pain. For almost all of these are present in all animals. And with these, some things that are common to everything that participates in life, and some to some of the animals. Of these, the greatest are four pairs in number, namely wakefulness and sleep, and youth and old age, and inhalation and exhalation, and life and death. About these it must be considered what each of them is and for what causes it occurs. But it also belongs to the student of nature to discover first principles concerning health and sickness.*

436a18 *For it is impossible for either health or sickness to occur in what lacks life. Therefore, in general, in the case of most students of nature, and of the physicians who pursue the art more philosophically, the former finish with what belongs to medicine, but the latter begin medicine with what belongs to nature.*

436b1 *That all the abovementioned are common to soul and body is not unclear. For with respect to all, some take place together with the sense-power, some through the sense-power. And with respect to certain ones, some exist as affections of it, some as conditions, some as protections and benefits, and some as destructions and privations. And that sense is present in the soul by means of the body is clear both through discussion and apart from discussion.*

Commentary

As The Philosopher says in *On the Soul* III, "just as things are separable from matter, so also is what pertains to intellect":[1] for everything is intelligible inasmuch as it is separable from matter. Hence what is by nature separate from matter is of its very self intelligible in actuality; but what is abstracted by us from conditions of matter is made intelligible in actuality by the light of our agent intellect. And because the habits of a power are specifically distinguished according to differentiation of that which is the per se object of the power, the habits of the sciences, by which intellect is perfected, are necessarily distinguished according to differentiation of "the separable from matter," and so the Philosopher in *Metaphysics* VI distinguishes genera of science according to different manners of separation from matter: what is separate from matter according to being and nature pertains to the metaphysician; what is separate from matter according to nature and not according to being pertains to the mathematician; and what includes sensible matter in its nature pertains to the natural philosopher.[2]

And just as different genera of science are distinguished according as things are in different ways separable from matter, so also in individual sciences, and especially in natural science, the parts of a science are distinguished according to different manners of separation and concretion. And because universals are more separate from matter, in natural science one proceeds from universals to what is less universal, as the Philosopher teaches in *Physics* I.[3] And so he began the teaching of natural science with what is most common to all natural things, namely movement and principles of movement, and from there proceeded by way of concretion or application of common principles, to determinate mobile things, some of which are living bodies.

Concerning these he also proceeded in a similar way, dividing this consideration into three parts. First he considered soul in itself, in an abstraction, as it were; second he has a consideration of what belongs to soul according to a concretion or application to body, but in general; third he has a consideration that applies all this to individual species of animals and plants, determining what is proper to each species. Thus, the first consideration is contained in the book *On the Soul*; the third consideration is contained in books that he wrote on animals and plants; the intermediate consideration is contained in books that he wrote on some things that pertain in common either to all animals, or to several kinds of them, or even to all living things, and the present intention involves these books.

Hence it must be considered that in *On the Soul* II Aristotle determined four levels of living things. The first consists of those that have only the nutritive part of soul, by which they are alive, namely plants. But there are some living things that, together with this, also have a sense-power but without progressive movement, namely imperfect animals, for instance shellfish. And there are some that have in addition forward local movement, namely perfect animals such as the horse and the cow. And some in addition have intellect, namely human beings. For although the appetitive part is held to be a fifth genus of powers of soul, it does not constitute a fifth level of living things, because it always accompanies the sensitive part. Now among these powers, intellect is the actuality of no part of a body, as is proved in *On the Soul* III,[4] and so it cannot be considered by a concretion or application to a body or to any bodily organ, for its greatest concretion is in soul and its highest abstraction is in separate substances. This is why Aristotle did not write, in addition to the book *On the Soul*, a book *On Intellect and the Intelligible*, but if he had done so, it would not pertain to natural science, but rather metaphysics, to which consideration of separate substances belongs. But all other parts of soul are actualities of parts of a body, and so there can be a special consideration of them by application to a body or bodily organs beyond the consideration made of them in the book "On the Soul."

Accordingly this intermediate consideration must be divided into three parts. One includes what pertains to a living thing inasmuch as it is living. This is contained in the following: the book that he wrote *On Life and Death*, in which he determines about "Inhalation and Exhalation," by which life is preserved in some living things, and about "Youth and Old Age," by which the stages of life are differentiated; likewise the book entitled *On Causes of Length and Shortness of Life*, and the book that he wrote *On Health and Disease*, which also pertain to the disposition of life; and also the book he is said to have written *On Nutrition and the Nourishing*. We do not yet have these last two books.

Another part of the consideration pertains to the moving part of soul. This is contained in two books: the book *On the Cause of Movement of Animals*; and the book *On the Progression of Animals*, in which there is a determination about the parts of animals adapted for movement.

The third part of the consideration pertains to the sensitive part of soul, concerning which consideration can be made, first, of what pertains to the act of the internal or of the external sense-power, and to this extent consideration of the sensitive part is contained in the present book, which is entitled *On Sense and What Is Sensed*, that is, "On the Sensitive Part and the Sensible Object," in which is also contained the treatise "On Memory and Recollection."[5] Again, what causes the difference between sensing and not-sensing that is brought about by sleep and wakefulness also pertains to consideration of the sensitive part, and this is determined in the book entitled *On Sleep and Wakefulness*.

But because one should pass through the more similar to the dissimilar, the order of these books seems reasonably to be such that after the book *On the Soul*, in which it is determined about soul in itself, there immediately follows the present book *On Sense and What Is Sensed*, because sensing itself pertains more to soul than to body. Next in order should be the book *On Sleep and Wakefulness*, which imply binding and freeing of the sense-power. Then follow the books that pertain to the moving part, which is next closest to the sensitive part. And last in order are the books that pertain to the general consideration of a living thing, because this consideration to the greatest extent involves bodily disposition.

❖o❖

436a1 Accordingly the present book, which is entitled *On Sense and What Is Sensed*, is first divided into two parts: a prologue, and the treatise, which begins where he says *About sense and sensing* (Chapter 1, 436b8).

On the first point he does two things. First he makes clear his intention, showing what is to be treated. Second he gives the reason why it is necessary to treat of such things, where he says *The greatest* (436a6).

Accordingly he first says that *it was* already *determined about soul in* its very *self* in the book *On the Soul*, that is, where he defined soul. Again, it was subsequently determined about *each virtue*—that is, power—of it, I mean *from the point of view of it*.[6] For since powers of soul, apart from intellect, are actualities of parts of a body, there can be consideration of them in two ways: in one way according as they pertain to soul as certain powers or "virtues" of it, and in another way from the point of view of body. Accordingly it was determined about powers of soul themselves *from the point of view of* soul *itself* in the book *On the Soul*, but now *the next thing is to make a consideration about animals, and everything that has life*—

which he adds because of plants—namely, by determining *what are their proper operations*—that is, proper to particular species of animals and plants—*and what are common*—that is, common to either all living things, or all animals, or many kinds of animals. *Accordingly let the things that were said about soul be underlying,* or supposed—that is, let us use them in what follows as suppositions that have already been explained. *And let us speak about the rest, and first about what is first*—that is, first about what is common and after about what is proper: for that is the order required in natural science, as was determined at the beginning of the book *The Physics.*[7]

436a6 Then, when he says *The greatest,* he shows the necessity of this subsequent consideration.

If the proper as well as common operations of animals and plants were proper to soul itself, the consideration of soul would suffice for this purpose; but because they are common to soul and body, it is necessary, after the consideration of soul, to determine about them so that it may be known what kinds of bodily dispositions are required for these operations or affections. And so the Philosopher here shows that all of them are common to soul and body.

On this point he does three things. First he presents what he intends. Second he enumerates the features with which the intention is concerned, where he says *For instance, sense and memory* (436a8). Third he proves the proposal, where he says *That all the abovementioned* (436b1).

Accordingly he says first that *of the features* that pertain to *animals* and plants, those that are *greatest*—that is, the outstanding ones—whether they are *common* to all animals or several, or *proper* to individual species, *are seen,* even at very first sight, *to be common to soul and body.* Hence they require another consideration beyond the one about soul taken absolutely.

436a8 Then, when he says *For instance, sense and memory,* he enumerates the features with which the intention is concerned.

First he presents what pertains to the sensitive part, namely *sense and memory.* He makes no mention of the other sense-powers, namely imagination and the estimative power, because these are not distinguished from sense from the point of view of the thing known, since they are of present things, or of things taken as present. But memory is so distinguished by the fact that it is of past things inasmuch as they are past.[8]

Second he presents what pertains to the locomotive part. Now the proximate principle of movement in animals is sensitive appetite, which is divided into two powers, namely "irascible" and "concupiscible," as was said in *On the Soul* III.[9]

Accordingly he mentions *anger,* which pertains to the irascible power, and *desire,* which pertains to the concupiscible. It is from these two passions, as from what is more evident, that the two powers are named: for the concupiscible power is named from "desire" and the irascible power from "anger" *(ira).*[10] But because there are other passions of the soul pertaining to the appetitive power, he adds *and appetite as a whole,* to include everything that pertains to the appetitive power. But all passions of the soul, whether they are in the irascible or the concupiscible power, are followed by pleasure and pain, as is said in *Ethics* II.[11] And so he adds, *and with these, pleasure and pain,* the final and ultimate passions, as it were.

He adds that *these* features that have been enumerated are *almost all* found *in all* kinds of *animals.* He says "almost all" because most of them, namely sense, desire, appetite, and pleasure and pain, are found in all animals, perfect as well as imperfect. For imperfect animals have, of the senses, only touch; they also have imagination, desire, and pleasure and pain, although these are indeterminate in them; and they are moved in an indeterminate way, as was said in *On the Soul* III.[12] But memory and anger are not found in them at all, but only in perfect animals.

The reason for this is that not everything belonging to a lower genus, but only what is highest or more perfect, achieves a participation of likeness in what is proper to a higher genus.[13]

Now the sense-power differs from intellect and reason because intellect or reason is of universals, which are everywhere and always, but the sense-power is of individuals, which are here and now. And so sense, according to its proper nature *(ratio)* is apprehensive only of what is present. But if there is a power of the sensitive part that extends to something not present, this is according to participation by likeness in reason or intellect. Hence memory, which is able to know things past, belongs only to perfect animals, being something supreme in sensitive knowledge.

Likewise, the sensitive appetite that follows from sense is, according to its proper nature *(ratio)* appetite for what is pleasant according to sense, and this appetite pertains to the concupiscible power that is common to all animals. But if an animal tends by appetite to something laborious, such as fighting or something similar, this contains a likeness to rational appetite, to which it is proper to desire some things for the sake of an end that are not in themselves desirable. And so anger, which is appetite for retribution, belongs only to perfect animals, because of an approach to the genus of what is rational.

436a11 Then he presents what pertains in any way to the nature of life.

He says that *with* the foregoing, other features are found in animals, *some* of which *are common to everything that participates in life,* that is, not only animals but also plants; but some pertain only *to some* kinds of *animals.* And the outstanding *of these* are listed in four pairs. The first pair he presents is *wakefulness and sleep,* which are found in all animals, but not in plants. The second is *youth and old age,* which are found in animals as well as plants, for the life of anything subject to death and birth is divided into different ages. The third is *inhalation and exhalation,* which are found in certain kinds of animals, namely all that have lungs. The fourth is *life and death,* which are found in all living things in this lower world. And he says that *about* all of *these it must be considered what each of them is, and* what is its cause.

436a17 Because he said that the abovementioned features are the "greatest," he adds something about some that are not so outstanding, namely health and disease, which are not both found in all individuals of the genera in which they exist by nature, as does happen with the abovementioned, but which are by nature found in all living things, animals as well as plants.

He says that *it also* pertains *to* the natural philosopher *to discover first* and universal *principles* of *health and sickness.* Consideration of particular principles pertains to the physician, the artisan who makes health, as it pertains to any operative art to consider particulars about its own business, because operations take place in particulars.

436a18 He proves in two ways that the former consideration does pertain to the natural philosopher, where he says *For it is impossible* (436a18).

First he does so by argument. *Health or sickness* can be found only *in what* has *life*, from which it is clear that the living body is the proper subject of health and disease. But the principles of a subject are also the principles of its proper attribute *(passio)*. Hence, since it pertains to the natural philosopher to consider the living body and its principles, he must also consider the principles of health and disease.

Second he proves the same thing by a sign or example that he concludes to from an argument that he presents. *Most* natural philosophers *finish* their study *with what belongs to medicine,* and likewise most *physicians*—that is, those *who pursue the art* of medicine *more philosophically,* not only applying experience, but inquiring into causes—*begin* their consideration of medicine with what is natural. From this it is clear that consideration of health and disease is common to both physicians and natural philosophers.

The reason for this is that health is sometimes caused by nature alone, and because of this it pertains to the consideration of the natural philosopher, to whom it belongs to consider the workings of nature; but sometimes it is caused by art, and in this respect it is considered by the physician. But because the art causes health not principally, but by as it were helping nature and ministering to it, the physician necessarily gets the principles of his science from the natural philosopher as from one who is prior, as a ship's captain gets his principles from an astronomer. This is the reason why physicians who pursue their art well start with what belongs to natural philosophy.

But anything artificial that is made by art alone, for instance a house or a boat, in no way pertains to the natural philosopher's consideration, just as what is made by nature alone in no way pertains to the consideration of art except inasmuch as art makes use of a natural thing.

436b1 Then, when he says *That all the abovementioned,* he proves the proposal, namely *that all the abovementioned are common to soul and body.*

He uses the following argument. All the abovementioned pertain to the sense-power. But the sense-power is common to soul and body, for sensing pertains to the soul through the body. Therefore all the abovementioned are common to soul and body.

He makes the first premise clear by an induction, as it were. Of the abovementioned features, *some take place together with the sense-power,* namely those that pertain to sensitive apprehension, such as sense, imagination, and memory. Some take place *through the sense-power,* for instance those that pertain to the appetitive power, which is moved by the apprehension of sense-power. Of the others, which pertain even more clearly to the body, some are *affections* of the sense-power, namely sleep, which is a binding of sense-power, and wakefulness, which is its freeing; some are *conditions* of the sense-power, namely youth and old age, which have to do with whether the sense-power is in good condition or is weak; some are *protections* of *and benefits* to the sense-power, namely breathing, life, and health; and some are *destructions and privations* of it, namely death and sickness.

He says that the second premise, that sense is common to soul and body, *is clear* both by argument and without argument.

The argument is ready to hand. Since a sense-power is affected by something sensible, as was shown in the book *On the Soul,*[14] and sensible things are bodily and material, what is affected by the sensible is necessarily bodily.

Even without argument this is clear from experience, because if the bodily organs are disturbed, the operation of the sense-power is impeded; and if they are removed, the sense-power is completely removed as well.

CHAPTER 1

436B8–437A19

436b8 *About sense and sensing—what it is and why this affection occurs in animals—something was said before in the discussions On the soul.*

436b10 *Any animal as animal necessarily has sense-power, for by this we determine that something is an animal or non-animal.*

436b12 *Taking each of them by itself, touch and taste accompany all necessarily, touch for the cause stated in the discussions On the soul, but taste because of food: for by this it distinguishes the pleasant (good-tasting) and unpleasant (bad-tasting)[1] with respect to food, so as to avoid the latter, but pursue the former. And in general, flavor is the affection of the nutritive part of soul.*

436b18 *But the senses that go through what is external—such as smell, hearing, sight—are in those of them that advance. And they are in all that have them because of health, so that, pre-sensing, they might pursue food, but avoid what is bad and harmful.*

437a1 *And they are in those that have prudence for the sake of the "well": for they announce many differences, from which there arises in them discernment of what can be contemplated and what can be done.*

437a3 *Of these, sight is better for what is necessary and of itself, but hearing for understanding and by accident.*

437a5 *For the power of sight announces many and many kinds of differences, because all bodies participate in color. Hence the common objects are also better perceived by this; I call size, shape, movement, and number "common." But hearing announces only differences of sound, but to a few also those of voice.*

437a11 *But by accident hearing contributes a greater share to prudence. For discussion, being audible, is a cause of learning, not in itself, but by accident; for it consists of words, and each of the words is a symbol. Hence of those deprived from birth of one of the two senses, the blind are wiser than deaf-mutes.*

437a18 *The power that each sense has has now been discussed.*

Commentary

436b8 Having presented a prologue in which he has shown his intention, here the Philosopher begins to follow up his proposal.

First he determines about what pertains to the external sense-power. Second he determines about certain things pertaining to inner sensitive cognition, namely memory and recollection, where he says *About memory and remembering* (449b4); for the treatise On memory and recollection is part of the present book according to the Greeks.[2]

On the first point he does three things. First he takes up some things that were said about the sense-power in the book On the soul and that are to be used as suppositions, as was said above.[3] Second, he determines the truth that he intends about the workings of the senses and of sensible objects, where he says *At present some inquire* (Chapter 2, 437a19). Third, he solves certain difficulties about the foregoing, where he says *But someone will raise an objection* (Chapter 14, 445b3).

On the first point he does two things. First he states what was said about the sense-power in the book On the soul. Second he takes up some of these points, where he says *Any animal as animal* (436b10).

Accordingly he first says that *in* the book *On the soul, something was said about sense and sensing*—that is, about the sensitive power and its act. Two things were said about them, namely *what* each of them *is, and* the cause *why* they occur *in animals.* He calls sensing an *"affection" (passio)* because the action of sense comes about in a being-affected *(paciendo),* as was proved in *On the Soul* II.[4] Near the end of *On the Soul* II he showed what sense is and why animals sense by the fact that animals are able to receive the forms of sensible things without matter.[5]

436b10 Then, when he says *Any animal as animal,* he takes up three things that were said about sense in the book *On the Soul.* The first pertains to sense in general. The second pertains to the senses that are common to all animals; he takes this up where he says *Taking each of them by itself* (436b12). The third pertains to the other senses, which are found in perfect animals; he takes this up where he says *But the senses that go through what is external* (436b18).

Accordingly he first says that every *animal,* inasmuch as it is *animal, necessarily has* some *sense-power: for* the nature *(ratio)* of *animal,* by which it is distinguished from what is *non-animal,* consists in its being sensitive.

❖o❖

The reason is this. An animal reaches the lowest level of knowing things, which surpass things that lack knowledge by being able to contain several beings in themselves, by which their power is shown to be more open and to extend to more things. And inasmuch as a knower has a more universal grasp of things, its power is more absolute, immaterial, and perfect. Now the sensitive power that is in animals is certainly open to what is outside, but only in the singular. Hence it also has an immateriality inasmuch as it is receptive of forms of sensible things without matter, but it has the lowest immateriality in the order of knowers, inasmuch as it can receive these forms only in a bodily organ.

436b12 Then, when he says *Taking each of them by itself,* he presents what pertains to the senses that are common and necessary to animals.

On this point it must be considered that the senses that are common and necessary to every animal are those that apprehend what is necessary to an animal. Now there are two ways in which something sensible is necessary to an animal: in one way inasmuch as the animal is a mixed body, composed of the four elements, and thus there is necessary to it the required balance of hot and cold, moist and dry, and other such differences of mixed bodies; and something else is necessary to the animal inasmuch as its body is a living thing capable of being nourished, and thus suitable food is necessary to it. By the contraries of these an animal is destroyed. And although the first is necessary to every mixed body, and the second is also necessary to plants, an animal has something more than these in being able to have knowledge of what is necessary, for the reason already stated, according to the level of its nature. Accordingly, in order for it to apprehend what is necessary or harmful to it according to its nature *(ratio)* as a mixed body, it has the sense of touch, which apprehends the above-mentioned differences; and in order for it to apprehend suitable nourishment, the sense of taste is necessary to it, by which it apprehends what tastes good and bad, which are signs of suitable and unsuitable nourishment.

This is why he says that *touch and taste necessarily accompany all* animals. Concerning *touch, the cause* was given *in* the book *On the soul,* namely that touch is cognitive of the things of which an animal is composed. *But taste* is necessary to an animal *because of food,* because by taste an animal *distinguishes the pleasant and unpleasant,* or *good-tasting and badtasting,* in *food, so as to pursue* one of these as suitable and *avoid* the other as harmful. *And flavor* as a whole *is the affection of the nutritive part of soul*—not that it is the object of the nutritive power, but that it is directed to the act of the nutritive power as its end, as was said.

But Alexander says in the commentary that in some manuscripts in Greek the text reads: "flavor is the affection *of the tasting part* of the nutritive part of the soul."[6] For flavor is apprehended by taste, which is ordered to nourishment.

436b18 Then when he says *But the senses that go through what is external,* he follows up on the senses that are only in perfect animals.

First he gives the general cause of these senses being in all animals of this kind. Second he gives the special cause of their being in the more perfect of them, where he says *And they are in those that have prudence* (437a1).

❖ᗯ❖

On the first point it must be known that animals are called "perfect" in which there is not merely a sensitive part without forward movement, as in oysters, but which in addition have a moving part with respect to forward movement. And it must be considered that such animals surpass imperfect, that is, immobile animals as the latter surpass plants and other mixed bodies: for plants and inanimate bodies have no awareness of what is necessary to them; immobile animals have knowledge of what is necessary only inasmuch as it is immediately presented to them; but forward-moving animals also receive knowledge of what is necessary from a distance, and so they more closely approach intellectual knowledge, which is not confined to the here and now.

And just as in all animals taste is ordered to knowing the necessary pertaining to nourishment inasmuch as it is immediately presented, so smell is ordered to knowing it from a distance as well. For odor and flavor have an affinity, as will be said below,[7] and just as by flavor the suitability of food taken in is known, so by odor the suitability of food at a distance is known. But the other two senses, sight and hearing, are ordered to knowing from a distance everything necessary or harmful to an animal, whether in its nature *(ratio)* as a mixed body or in its nature as a living body capable of being nourished, for it is clear that by sight and hearing animals avoid whatever is harmful and pursue what is healthy.

knows at a distance

❖ᗯ❖

And so he says that *the senses that* are actualized *through external* media, as was said in *On the Soul* II,[8] namely *smell, hearing,* and *sight, are in those* among the animals *that advance*—that is, move with forward movement—*in all* of them for one general cause, namely *because of health*—that is, so that they might know what is necessary from a distance, just as by taste and touch they know it when present. And he adds: *so that, pre-sensing*—that is, sensing from a distance—*they might pursue* suitable *food* and *avoid* whatever is *bad and harmful.* For instance, a sheep flees a wolf as something harmful, but a wolf pursues a sheep that is seen, heard, or smelled, as suitable food.

437a1 Then, when he says *And they are in those that have prudence,* he gives another, specific cause why these senses are in some more perfect animals.

First he presents this cause. Second he compares the senses with reference to the causes mentioned, where he says *Of these, sight is better* (437a3).

❖०❖

On the first point it must be considered that prudence is directive in what is to be done. Universal prudence is directive with respect to anything to be done whatsoever, and so it is in none of the animals except human beings, who have reason, which is able to know universals. But there are certain particular prudences in other animals for certain predetermined acts, for instance in the ant, which in summer gathers food on which it lives in winter.

Now the above-mentioned senses, but especially hearing and sight, are advantageous to animals for particular prudences of this kind, and to human beings for universal prudence, in order that something might be done *well.* But smell seems to be wholly subservient to the need for nourishment, and not at all to prudence, and so this sense is extremely weak in all those who have perfect prudence, as is said in the book On the soul.[9]

He shows how the above-mentioned senses serve prudence by the fact that they show *many differences* among things, *from which* the human being goes on to discern *what can be contemplated and what can be done.* For by sensible effects the human being is raised to consideration of what is intelligible and universal; and also by what is sensible—that is, by what he has heard and seen—he is instructed about what is to be done. Other animals do not participate in any contemplation, although they do participate in action in a particular way, as is said in *Ethics* X.[10]

These two senses announce many differences because their objects are found in bodies as consequences of what is common to all bodies, both lower and higher. For color is a consequence of light and the transparent *(dyaphanum),* which lower bodies have in common with the heavenly body; and sound is a consequence of local movement, which is also found in both kinds of body. But odor is a consequence only of the mixed bodies by which an animal is naturally nourished.

437a3 Then, when he says *But of these, sight is better,* he compares sight and hearing with reference to the above-mentioned causes.

First he presents the comparison. Second he proves it, where he says *For the power of sight* (437a5).

On the first point he says that *sight* surpasses hearing in two ways. In one way with respect to *what is necessary,* for instance in seeking food and avoiding what is harmful, things that are apprehended with more certainty by sight, which is altered by things themselves, than by hearing, which is altered by sounds, which are consequences of the movements of some things. In another way sight is also *of itself* superior to hearing, because it is more able to know, and able to know more things, than is hearing. But *hearing* surpasses sight inasmuch as it serves *understanding,* although this is *by accident,* as will be shown below.

437a5 Then he clarifies what he said, where he says *For the power of sight announces.*

First that sight is in itself better. Second that hearing is better accidentally, where he says *But by accident hearing contributes* (437a11).

Accordingly he first says that sight is in itself better because the *power* of sight by its apprehension *announces* to us *many differences* among things *and* among various *kinds* of things. This is *because* its object, which is the visible, is found in all bodies: for a thing becomes visible by the transparent being illuminated in actuality by a shining body, and the lower bodies have this in common with the higher ones. And so he says that *all bodies participate in color,* the higher as well as the lower ones, because in all bodies either there is color itself in its proper nature *(ratio),* in the case of bodies in which there is a bounded transparent; or there are at least the principles of color, which are the transparent and light. And so more things are manifested by sight than by hearing.

Also, the *common* sensibles *are better* known *by this* sense, because inasmuch as sight has a power of knowing that is more universal and extends to more things, it is more effective in knowing, because the more universal any power is, the more powerful it is. And those are called *"common"* sensibles that are known not by one sense only, as are the proper sensibles, but by several, for instance *size, shape, movement,* and *number.* For the qualities that are the proper objects of the senses are forms in a continuum, and so the continuum itself, inasmuch as it is the subject of these qualities, must move the sense-power not accidentally, but as the per se and common subject of all sensible qualities. And all the so-called common sensibles do in some way pertain to the continuum: whether with respect to measurement of it, in the case of size; or with respect to division of it, in the case of number; or with respect to limitation of it, in the case of shape; or with respect to distance and nearness, in the case of motion.

But *hearing* announces to us only *differences* among sounds, which are *hearing* not found in all bodies, and are not expressive of the many diversities of things. *But to a few* animals hearing does show differences *of voice.* Voice *voice* is sound projected with an imagining from an animal's mouth, as is said in On the soul II,[11] and so the voice of an animal as such naturally indicates the animal's inner feeling *(passio),* as the barking of dogs indicates their anger. Thus the more perfect animals know one another's inner feelings from voices, a knowledge that is not in imperfect animals.

Therefore hearing of itself knows only differences among sounds, such as high and low and so on, or differences among voices inasmuch as they are indicative of various feelings. And so the knowledge of hearing does not of itself extend to as many differences among things as does that of sight.

437a11 Then when he says *But by accident hearing contributes,* he shows that hearing is accidentally better for understanding.

He says that *hearing contributes* much *to prudence.* Here "prudence" is taken to mean any intellectual knowledge, not just "right reason about possible action," as it is described in *Ethics* VI.[12] But this is *by accident,* because *discussion,* which is *audible, is a cause of learning not* of *itself*—that is, not by differences themselves among sounds—*but by accident,* that is, inasmuch as *words of* which discussion *(sermo)*—that is, speech *(locutio)*—is composed are symbols—that is, signs—of meanings *(intentiones)* understood, and consequently of things. Thus a teacher teaches a student inasmuch as, through discussion, he signifies what his intellect conceives to the student. And a human being can know more by learning from someone else, for which hearing is useful, even though accidentally, than he can by discovering for himself, for which sight is especially useful.

Hence it is that, among *those deprived from birth of one of the two senses—* that is, sight or hearing—*the blind,* who lack sight, *are wiser than deaf-mutes,* who lack hearing. He adds "mutes" because everyone who is deaf from birth is necessarily mute, for he cannot learn to form the signifying words that signify by convention, and so he stands in relation to the speech of the whole human race as one who has never heard a particular language stands in relation to that language. But it is not necessary, conversely, that every mute be deaf, for it can happen that someone is mute from some other cause, for instance obstruction of the tongue.

437a18 Finally, adding an epilogue, he concludes that *the power that each* sense *has has been discussed.*

CHAPTER 2

437A19–438A5

437a19 *At present some inquire about the organs of the body in which these are actualized with reference to the elements of bodies. But not being able to adapt them to four, since there are five, they are concerned about the fifth.*

437a22 *But all of them have sight be made of fire, because they do not know the cause of a certain affection: when the eye is squeezed and moved, fire seems to shine. This happens in darkness, or when the eyelids are lowered, which also makes it dark.*

437a26 *But this presents another difficulty. For if something visible cannot escape the notice of one who is sensing and seeing, it will be necessary that the eye always be seeing fire. Why then does it not happen when it is at rest?*

437a30 *Now the cause of this—both for the objection and for the view that sight is made of fire—is to be understood as follows. Smooth things naturally shine in darkness, but they do not produce light; and the so-called black part and center of the eye is smooth. And what appears, appears to an eye that is moved because what happens is that what is one becomes as though it were two, and the speed of the movement makes it seem that what sees and what is seen are different. Hence it does not happen unless quickly.*

437b5 *This happens in darkness, for a smooth thing in darkness naturally shines, as do certain heads of fish, and the ink of the cuttle-fish. And when the eye is gently moved, it does not happen that what sees and what is seen seem simultaneously to be one and two. But in the other case, the eye itself sees itself, as it does in refraction.*

437b10 *If it were fire, as Empedocles says, and as is written in the Timaeus,[1] and seeing took place by a light going out, the way it does from a lamp, why does sight not also see in darkness?*

437b14 *To say that in going out it is "extinguished" in darkness is completely foolish.*

437b15 *For what is "extinction" of light? What is hot and dry is extinguished by either moisture or cold, as can be seen in the case of the embers of a fire, and flame. But neither appears to be the case with light.*

437b19 *If it were the case, but the light escapes our notice because of "weakness," it would have to be extinguished by day, and in water, and it would be more darkened where there is ice, for flame and burning bodies are affected in this way. But no such thing happens in this case.*

437b23 *Empedocles seems to think, as was said before, that seeing takes place by light going out. For he says:*

> As when someone contemplating going out on a winter night
> Prepares a lamp, he kindles a light of burning fire
> In such a way as to block the force of all winds,
> For he deflects the breath of blowing winds.
> But the light breaks out: however farther it expands
> It illuminates with rays subdued by a covering—
>   Likewise ancient light guarded in membranes—fine linens—
> Pours out around in a circle through the pupil,
> Which will reveal a depth of water flowing around.
> But the light comes out, however farther it expands.

Sometimes, then, he says that seeing is like this, but sometimes that it takes place by emanations from what is seen.

Commentary

437a19 After The Philosopher has summarized what is necessary for the present consideration of sensitive powers themselves, now he proceeds to his principal proposal in this book by applying the consideration of sense-powers to what is bodily.

First with respect to sense-organs. Second with respect to sensible objects, where he says *Concerning sensible objects* (Chapter 5, 439a6).

On the first point he does two things. He assigns sense-organs to elements, first disproving arguments of others; second determining what might more probably be the case, where he says *If, then, what happens in these cases* (Chapter 4, 438b16).

On the first point he does two things. First he touches in general on the way in which the Ancients assigned sense-organs to elements. Second he focuses specifically on the organ of sight, about which many were mistaken, where he says *But all of them have sight be made of fire* (437a22).

Accordingly he first says that previous philosophers asked, *with reference to the elements of bodies,* What are the kinds of bodily *organs in which,* and by which, the operations of the sense-powers are exercised?

They did so because, as was said in *On the Soul* I, they held that like is known by like, and hence they held that the soul itself has the same nature as the principles of things, so that thereby it might know all things, being as it were conformed to all things, since all things share in the principles.[2]

For the same reason they assigned sense-organs to elements of bodies, because all bodily things are known through sense-organs. But immediately one difficulty occurred to them: there are *five* senses and *four* elements. And so they looked for something to which they could assign the organ of the *fifth* sense.

Now between air and water there is an intermediary, denser than air but finer than water, which is called "smoke" or "vapor," and some held that it is also a first principle, to which they assigned the organ of smell, since odor is perceived by means of a smoky evaporation. And they assigned the other four senses to the four elements: touch to earth, taste to water (since flavor is perceived by means of moisture), hearing to air, and sight to fire.

437a22 Then, when he says *But all of them have sight be made of fire,* he proceeds specifically to the organ of sight, which they assigned to fire.

First he disproves the cause they gave for their position. Second he disproves the position itself, where he says *If it were fire* (437b10).

On the first point he does three things. First he presents the cause that moved some to assign the organ of sight to fire. Second he raises a difficulty, where he says *But this presents another difficulty* (437a26). Third he determines the truth about both points, where he says *Now the cause of this* (437a30).

Accordingly he first says that *all* who assign the organ of *sight* to *fire* do so *because they do not know the cause of a certain affection* that occurs in the eye: if *the eye* is pressed *and* forcefully *moved,* it *seems* that *fire shines.* If the eyelids are open, this happens only when the surroundings are dark; it also happens when the surroundings are bright if *the eyelids* are first closed, because thus one *makes it dark* to the closed eye. They thought that this affection is a clear sign that the organ of sight pertains to fire.

437a26 Then, when he says *But this presents another difficulty,* he raises a difficulty about the foregoing.

For it is clear that a sense-power apprehends a sensible thing that is present, and hence that sight apprehends a *visible* thing that is present;

and fire, because of its light, is something visible. Therefore, if fire is always present to sight, that is, to the organ of sight, since it exists in it, it seems that sight should *always be seeing fire.*

But this does not follow from the principles that Aristotle has established, for he holds that a sense-power is in potentiality to a sensible thing, and that it must be altered by the thing through a medium. According to him, then, a sensible thing placed on top of a sense-power is not perceived, as is said in *On the Soul* II,[3] so that if the organ of sight were made of fire, for this very reason sight would not see fire.

But according to the other philosophers sight and the other senses perceive sensible things inasmuch as they actually are of the same kind as—that is, like—the sensible things, because they have the same nature as the principles of things, as was said. According to them, then, just because the organ of sight is made of fire, it follows that it sees fire in the way described.

But then there remains the difficulty that Aristotle here introduces: *Why* does an eye *at rest not* see fire, as does an eye that is moved?

437a30 Then, when he says *Now the cause of this,* he gives *the cause* of the above-mentioned appearance, by which the difficulty raised is solved, and it is shown how foolish of them it was to think *that sight is made of fire.*

On this point it must be understood that *smooth*—that is, polished and clean—bodies have, from a property of their nature, a certain shine, one that does not occur in rough and uneven bodies because some parts rise above others and overshadow the latter. And although such bodies in a way *shine* in themselves, they do *not* have enough shine to be able to make a medium bright in actuality, as do the sun and such bodies.

Now it is clear that *the center of the eye,* which is *called the black part* of the eye, is as it were *smooth* and polished. Hence it has a shine by reason of its smoothness, not from the nature of fire, as the others thought. This already removes any need to assign the organ of sight to fire, since the cause of the brightness that appears can be attributed to something other than fire.

But whether it is caused by fire or the pupil's smoothness, there remains a difficulty common to both positions: why an eye that is moved sees this shining, but an eye at rest does not.

So he gives the cause of this, and says that shining of this kind *appears to an eye that is moved because what happens* through the movement of the eye *is that what is one becomes as though it were two.* For the shining and seeing pupil is one and the same in subject: but inasmuch as it shines, it projects its shine outward; and inasmuch as it sees, it apprehends the shining by, as it were, receiving it from without.

When the eye is still, therefore, it emits the shine outward, and so sight does not receive the shine in such a way as to see it. But when it is quickly moved, its black part is brought, before the brightness fades, to the "external" place to which the pupil emitted its brightness. Thus the pupil, having been quickly brought to the second place, receives its own brightness as if from without, and so it seems *that what sees and what is seen are different,* although they are the same in subject. So this appearance of the shining *does not happen unless* the eye is *quickly* moved, because if it is moved slowly, the impression of the shining will fade from the "external" place the shining went to before the pupil gets there.

But it seems that no speed of movement would suffice for this to happen. For however rapid local movement may be, it must be in time. But emission of shine at the presence of a shining body, and its cessation at the absence of it, occur instantaneously. Therefore it does not seem possible, however quickly the eye is moved, for the pupil to reach the "external" place before the shining, which came there from the pupil existing in the other place, ceases.

According to Alexander in the commentary, we must say in response that the pupil is a body, divisible into parts. Hence if the eye is quickly moved, when part of the pupil begins to reach the other place, the shining is still coming there from the rest of the body of the pupil that has not yet gotten to that place. This is why the pupil begins to see a shining that is, as it were, shining from elsewhere. A sign of this is that the shining does not seem to fade: rather, when it passes, the sight of it ceases abruptly.[4]

437b5 He also gives the reason why this kind of operation *happens in darkness* and not in light, namely because the shining of *smooth* bodies is so small that it is obscured by great brightness, although it is seen in darkness. This also happens with other things that have a small amount of light, and for this reason are seen in darkness but not in light, for instance *certain heads of fish, and* the dark fluid of the fish called *the cuttlefish.* He adds that if *the eye is gently*—that is, slowly—*moved,* the above-mentioned appearance *does not happen* by *what sees and what is seen* seeming *simultaneously to be one and two,* as was said. But *in the other case*—that is, when the eye is quickly moved—then *the eye sees itself,* being as it were affected by itself in its other position. This also happens *in "refraction"*—that is, reflection—for instance when an eye sees itself in a mirror from which, as from without, the form of the eye returns to the eye itself by way of reflection, just as, in the above-mentioned appearance the shining of the eye returns to the eye itself, as was said.

437b10 Then when he says *If it were fire,* he proceeds to disprove the position itself: first inasmuch as those philosophers assigned sight to fire; second inasmuch as they held that sight sees by extromission, where he says *It is altogether irrational* (Chapter 3, 438a25).

On the first point he does three things. He presents first the opinion of Plato; second the opinion of Empedocles, where he says *Empedocles seems to think* (437b23); and third the opinion of Democritus, where he says *Democritus says correctly* (Chapter 3, 438a5).

On the first point he does two things. First he raises an objection against Plato. Second he disproves Plato's response, where he says *To say that in going out* (437b14).

Concerning the first point it must be known that *Empedocles,* and Plato *in the Timaeus,* agreed on two things: one is that the organ of sight pertains to *fire;* the second is that vision occurs by *a light going out* from the eye as *from a lamp.* From these two positions the Philosopher concludes that *sight* should *see in darkness,* just as it does in light: for light can be emitted from a lamp to light up the medium in the dark; and so, if the eye saw by emission of light, it would follow that the eye should also be able to see in the dark.

437b14 Then, when he says *To say that in going out,* he disproves the response of Plato, who says in the Timaeus that when light goes out from the eye, if it encounters light in the medium it is preserved by it as by something like itself, and because of this vision occurs; but if it does not encounter light, but *darkness,* then because of the unlikeness of darkness to light, the light *going out* from the eye *is "extinguished,"* and so the eye does not see. But Aristotle says that to give this cause *is foolish*.

437b15 And he proves this where he says *For what is "extinction" of light?*

For no reason can be given why the *light* of the eye is "extinguished" by darkness. The Platonists said that there are three species of fire, namely light, flame, and ember.[5] Since fire is naturally *hot and dry,* it *is extinguished by either cold or moisture,* and this clearly happens *in the case of embers and flame.* But *neither* is a cause of extinction in the case of *light,* for it is destroyed neither by cold nor by moisture. Therefore it is incorrect to say that light is extinguished in the way fire is.

But Alexander says in the commentary that there is another reading, as follows:

> **437b15** . . . *as is seen in fire in embers and flame. But neither seems to belong to* **darkness**. *For it is neither moisture nor cold by which the "extinction" occurs.*[6]

And on this reading Aristotle's argument seems to be more to the point: the fire-light that appears *in embers and flames* is found to be extinguished by cold and moisture; *but darkness* is *neither* something *cold nor* something *moist;* therefore the fire-light that goes out from the eye cannot be extinguished by darkness.

437b19 Someone might say that the fire-light going out from the eye is not "extinguished" in darkness, but that, because it is not "strengthened" by external light, and so is weak, it *escapes our notice,* and that this is why vision does not occur.

But Aristotle disproves this where he says *If it were the case.*

On this point it must be known that fire-light is "extinguished" or darkened in two ways: in one way with respect to a property of light, namely that a little light is extinguished by the presence of a greater light; in another way with respect to a property of fire, which is extinguished in water.

Accordingly if *the* weak *light* going out from the eye were made of fire, it *would have to be extinguished* in daylight, because of the greater brightness; *and in water,* because of its contrariety to fire; *and* the light of the visual power would be even *more* darkened *where there is ice, for* we see that this is what happens in the case of *flame and burning bodies.* But it does not *happen* in the case of sight, and so it is clear that the abovementioned response is foolish.

437b23 Then, when he says *Empedocles seems to think,* he relates the opinion of Empedocles, the disproof of which has already been touched on.

He says that *Empedocles seems to think, as was said, that* vision occurs *by light going out.*

And he gives the words of Empedocles, which were composed in meter. Empedocles said that what happens in vision is like *when someone* thinking of *going out* along a road *on a winter night*—that is, when wind is blowing—*prepares a lamp. He kindles a light of burning fire,* and to *block the force of all winds* he puts the light kindled in a lantern, and by this means *he deflects* the blowing of breathing *winds*—that is, he prevents their blowing from reaching the light of the fire. *But the light* contained within goes *out,* and *however farther* outward *it expands, it illuminates* the air more, but in such a way that *the rays* going out are *subdued*—that is, weakened—*by a covering* on the lamp, for instance skin or some such thing; for the air is not as brightly illuminated by the lamp as it would be by unshielded fire.

And he says that something similar happens in the eye, in which *ancient light*—that is, light there since the eye's formation—is *guarded*—that is, safely preserved—for sensing, *in membranes*—that is, corneas of the eye—through which, as if through *fine linens,* light *pours out* around in all directions *through the pupil.* These corneas *reveal,* by the rays emitted through them, *a depth of water flowing around* the fire kindled in the pupil, water for nourishing, or rather tempering, the fire gathered in the depth. And so *the light reaches out, however farther it expands,* starting from inside.

Alternatively, his mention of "around in a circle" should be understood with reference to the roundness of the pupil.

It should be noted that he said, significantly, "with rays subdued by a covering," to indicate the reason why a thing is not seen in darkness, namely that the light going out is weakened by passing through the above-mentioned coverings, so that it cannot completely illuminate the air.

Having presented the words of Empedocles, he adds that *sometimes* he said that vision occurs by emission of light, as was said, *but sometimes* he said that vision occurs by certain bodies emanating from visible things and coming to sight. And perhaps his opinion was that the two are united for vision.

CHAPTER 3

438A5–B2

438a5 *Democritus says correctly that it is water, but not correctly that he thought that the appearance is the seeing itself. For this occurs because the eye is smooth. And it is not in that, but in what is doing the seeing. For the affection is a reflection. But it seems that it was not yet clear to him about appearances and reflection.*

438a10 *But it is inconsistent that it also did not occur to him to wonder why only the eye sees, and none of the other things in which "idols" appear.*

438a12 *For it is indeed true that sight is made of water, but seeing does not occur according as it is water, but according as it is transparent, which is something common to it and air. But water is more preservable than air and denser, which is why the pupil and eye are made of water.*

438a17 *This is manifested in the very workings. For when eyes are destroyed, water can be seen flowing out. And in completely new-formed ones, there is extreme cold and brightness. And in those that have blood, the white of the eye is fat and thick, to keep the moisture unfrozen; and so the eye is the part of the body that feels cold least, for no-one has ever felt cold inside the eyelids. The eyes of bloodless animals are made of hard skin, and this provides protection.*

438a25 *It is altogether irrational that sight should see by something going out, whether it extends all the way to the stars, or, as some say, it goes only so far and "coalesces."*

438a27 *For in the latter case it is better for it to be united at the beginning, that is, in the eye.*

438a29 *But this is also foolish. For what is it for light to be "united" to light? Or how is it possible, since not just anything is united with anything? And how is the inner light united with the outer, since the membrane is between?*

Commentary

438a5 After the opinions of Plato and Empedocles, here, in the third place, The Philosopher follows up the opinion of Democritus.

On this point he does three things. First he shows what Democritus said correctly and what he said incorrectly. Second he follows up what he said incorrectly, where he says *But it is inconsistent* (438a10). Third he follows up what he said correctly, where he says *For it is indeed true that sight is made of water* (438a12).

Accordingly he first says that *Democritus* spoke *correctly* in assigning sight to *water, but* he spoke incorrectly in saying *he thought that* vision *is* nothing but *the appearance* in the pupil of the thing seen. *For* such an appearance *occurs* in the pupil because of the bodily disposition of the eye, that is, *because the eye is smooth,* that is, polished and clean, as it were. So it is clear that seeing itself is *not* located *in* the appearance of this form in the eye, *but in what is doing the seeing,* that is, in what has the power of sight: for the eye is a seeing thing not because it is smooth, but because it has the power of sight. *For* that *affection*—the appearing of the form of the thing seen in the eye—*is a reflection;* that is, it is caused by the reflection or rebound of the form from a polished body.

We see something like this happen in a mirror also. For when the alteration of the transparent caused by a visible body reaches a body that is not transparent, the alteration can go no further, but is somehow turned back, like a ball thrown at a wall and bounced back, and because of this rebound the form of the thing seen goes back in the opposite direction. Thus in a mirror one can see oneself, or even some other thing not directly presented to one's sight.

This takes place only if two things coincide. One is that the body be smooth on its surface, and therefore somewhat bright, as was explained above;[1] the form reflected in it is manifested by this moderate brightness. The other is that the body be terminated within at some point so that the above-mentioned alteration does not go beyond; thus we see that this kind of appearance does not occur, unless glass is covered with lead or something similar to block its transparency, so that the alteration does not go beyond.

Now both of these coincide in the eye: it is moderately bright because of its smoothness, as was established above,[2] and it has something in its depth that terminates its transparency. So it is clear that this event of the form of the thing seen appearing in the eye happens merely because of reflection, which is a bodily affection caused by the determinate disposition of a body.

But *it was not yet clear* to Democritus about these reflections and about
the forms that appear in mirroring bodies because of reflection. Vision
itself, according to the truth of the matter, is not a bodily affection:
rather, its principal cause is a power of soul. But Democritus held that
soul is something bodily, and so it is no wonder that he called an operation of soul nothing but a bodily affection.

It should be known, however, that the above-mentioned appearance
is a cause of vision with respect to initial reception of the form. For vision is an act of soul only through a bodily organ, and so it is no wonder
that it has a cause from the point of view of a bodily affection, but in
such a way that the bodily affection is not the same thing as the vision:
rather, it is a cause of it with respect to the initial "impact," if I may so
call it, of the visible form on the eye. The subsequent reflection contributes nothing to the eye's seeing of the thing seen through the form
appearing in it, but rather contributes to the form's being able to appear
to someone else; thus the eye that sees the thing by means of the form
that appears in it does not see this form itself.

438a10 Then, when he says *But it is inconsistent,* he follows up what
Democritus said incorrectly.

He says that since Democritus held that vision is nothing but the
above-mentioned appearance, it seems very *inconsistent* that the following difficulty did not occur to him: Why do *other* bodies *in which* forms—
which he called *"idols"*—of visible things *appear* as in a mirror not see,
but *only the eye?* From this it is clear that the above-mentioned appearing
is not the whole essence *(ratio)* of vision, but that there is something else
in the eye that causes vision, namely the power of sight.

438a12 Then, when he says *For it is indeed true that sight is made of water,* he follows up what Democritus said correctly.

First he presents the truth. Second he clarifies it by signs, where he
says *This is manifested* (438a17).

Accordingly he first says that what Democritus said in assigning the
organ of *sight* to *water is true.* However, it must be known that vision is
assigned to water *not according as it is water, but* by reason of transparency,
which water and *air* have in *common:* for a visible object is something

that moves the transparent, as is said in the book *On the Soul.*[3] However, vision is assigned to water rather than to air for two reasons. First, *water* can be preserved better *than air* (air is easily dispersed), and so it is more suitable for the preservation of sight than is air, and nature always does what is better. Second, water is *denser* than air, and by reason of its density it allows the form of a thing seen to appear in it by reflection, which is proper to the organ of sight. What is proper to the medium of sight is to be transparent, which is common to air and water. So he concludes that *the eye and pupil* are to be assigned to *water* rather than to air.

The heavenly body is also transparent, but because it does not enter into the composition of the human body, he passes over it here.

438a17 Then, when he says *This is manifested,* he shows that the organ of sight is made of water by three signs that are *manifested in the very workings.*

The first is that if the *eyes* are destroyed, there visibly appears *water flowing out of them.*

The second is that the *new-formed* eyes of embryos—eyes that, as it were, still retain much of the power *(virtus)* of their origin—have abundant *cold and brightness,* both of which are connatural to water.

The third sign is that *in* animals *that have blood,* in which there is the possibility of generating, so to speak, fat from the blood, the pupil is surrounded by *the white of the eye,* which has fatness and oiliness so that its heat will keep the water-*moisture* of the pupil from freezing, which would diminish the transparency of the water, and thus impede vision. *And so,* by reason of the above-mentioned fat, *the eye,* because of its heat, does not freeze: *for no-one* has *ever* suffered cold in the whole of what is contained *inside the eyelids.* In *animals that are bloodless,* in which there is no fat, nature made *eyes of hard skin* to protect the water-moisture that is in the pupil.

438a25 Then, when he says *It is altogether irrational,* he goes on to disprove what some held, namely that vision occurs by extromission, which was the reason for their assigning sight to fire. Thus, once the latter is eliminated, the former will be too.

On this point he does two things. First he presents two opinions of those who held that we see by extromission. Second he disproves the second opinion, where he says *For in the latter case* (438a27).

Accordingly he first says that it seems *irrational* that *sight* should *see by something going out* from it, which was held to occur in two ways.

In one way such that what goes out from the eye extends all the way to the thing seen, from which it would follow that even when we see the stars, what goes out from sight *extends all the way to the stars.*

This involves an obvious impossibility. Since "going out" pertains only to bodies, it would follow that some body going out from the eye would reach all the way to the stars, which is clearly illogical, for many reasons.

First because it would follow that there are several bodies in the same place, both because what goes out from the eye would be in the same place as the air, and because these things going out from eyes would have to be multiplied in the same medium according to multiplicity of those who are seeing through the same medium.

Second because any projection of a body is stronger at the beginning but weaker at the end, which is why flame proceeding from a burning body tends towards an apex. But here the contrary happens, for the mathematicians, whose position this is, say that the apex of the body going out from the eye is inside the eye and the base at the thing seen.

Third because the size of an eye is insufficient for a body going out from it to be big enough to reach all the way to the stars, however much the body might be rarefied, for there is a limit to the rarefaction of natural bodies; besides, the more rarefied it became, the more easily it would be destroyed.

Again, the body emitted from the eye would have to be either air or fire. There is no need for air to be emitted from the eye because it is abundant outside the eye. And if it were fire we would also see at night; on the other hand, we would not be able to see through the medium of water; and we would only be able to see upwards, where the movement of fire tends.

But it cannot be said that the bodily thing that goes out from the eye is light, because light is not a body, as was proved in the book *On the Soul.*[4]

The other opinion is that of Plato, who held that light going out from the eye does not go all the way to the thing seen, but *only so far,* that is, some determinate distance, namely to where it *"coalesces"* with the external light; and that vision occurs by reason of this coalescence, as was said before.[5]

438a27 Then, when he says *For in the latter case,* he passes over the first opinion as clearly unreasonable, and disproves the second in two ways.

First because it posits something uselessly and unnecessarily, which is just what he says: that it would be *better* to say that the inner light is *united* with the outer at the surface of the eye itself rather than outside at some distance. This is because if there is no outer light in the intermediate space, the inner light will be extinguished by darkness according to Plato's opinion, as was said above.[6] But if light reaches all the way to the eye, it is better for the two to be united immediately, because what can occur without a medium is better than what occurs through a medium, since it is better for something to occur by means of fewer things than more.

438a29 Second, where he says *But this is also foolish,* he disproves the union of inner light with outer even on the supposition that it occurs at the beginning, i.e. in the eye itself. He does this in three ways.

First because "being united and separated" is proper to bodies, each of which has subsistence per se, but not to qualities, which exist only in a subject. Hence, since light is not a body but an accident, it is meaningless to say that *light* is *"united"* to *light,* unless what is meant is that a luminous body is united to a luminous body. Howver, it is possible for light to be intensified in the air by multiplication of luminous bodies, as heat is intensified by increase in the cause of heat, although this is not by addition, as is clear from *Physics* IV.[7]

Second he disproves the point as follows: even granted that both lights are bodies, it would still not be *possible* for them to be united, since they are not of the same nature. *For not just any* body is naturally united with just any body, but only those that are in some way homogenous.

Third, since an intervening body, namely *the membrane*—that is, the cornea of the eye—comes *between the inner and the outer* light, there cannot be a union of the two lights.

CHAPTER 4

438B2–439A5

438b2 *That it is impossible to see without light was said elsewhere. But whether it is light or air that is between the thing seen and the eye, the movement through it causes seeing.*

438b5 *It is reasonable that what is inside be made of water, for water is transparent. And it seems that, as what is outside is not without light, so also what is inside. Therefore it must be transparent. Therefore it is necessarily water, because it is not air.*

438b8 *For the soul, or the sensitive part of soul, is not at the limit of the eye, but clearly inside. Hence the inside of the eye needs to be transparent and receptive of light.*

438b11 *This is also clear from what happens. For when some are wounded in war about the temples in such a way that the passages of the eye are cut off, they experience a darkening as when a lamp is extinguished, because the transparent thing called the pupil is, like a torch, cut off.*

438b16 *If, then, what happens in these cases is as we have said, it is clear that, if one must, following this method, attribute and assign each one of the sensitive parts to one of the elements, one should think that eyesight is of water, what is perceptive of sounds is of air, and smelling is of fire.*

438b21 *For what smelling is in actuality the olfactory part is in potentiality. For a sensible object makes a sense-power act, and so the latter necessarily exists first in potentiality. But odor is smoky evaporation. But smoky evaporation is from fire.*

438b25 *For this reason the proper sensitive part of smell is in a place around the brain: for the potentially hot is the matter of what is cold.*

438b27 *And the generation of the eye also has the same mode: for it stems from the brain, and the brain is coldest and moistest of all parts of the body.*

438b30 *But the tactile part is of earth, and the tasting part is a kind of touch.*

439a1 *And so the sensitive part for these, namely taste and touch, is near the heart: for the heart is opposite the brain, and is the warmest of the parts.*

439a4 *Let it be determined in this way about the sensitive parts of the body.*

Commentary

438b2 After the Philosopher has disproved the opinion of those who hold that vision occurs by extromission, here he determines the truth.

On this point he does three things. First he makes clear how vision occurs according to his own thought. Second, on this basis, he gives the cause of something mentioned above concerning the organ of sight, where he says *It is reasonable* (438b5). Third he shows the cause by a sign, where he says *This is also clear* (438b11).

Accordingly he first takes up something that *was said in* the book *On the Soul, that it is impossible to see without light.*[1] For because vision occurs through a medium that is transparent, vision requires light, which makes a body be transparent in actuality, as was said in the book *On the Soul.*[2] And so, *whether* the medium that is *between the thing seen and the eye is air* that is illuminated in actuality, *or* whether it is *light*—light existing not in itself, since it is not a body, but in something else that is a body, such as glass or water—*the movement* that occurs *through* this medium causes vision.

❖⚬❖

This movement should not be taken to be local movement, as if, as Democritus and Empedocles held, it were a movement of bodies emanating from the thing seen to the eye, because then it would follow that the bodies that are seen would be reduced by this emanation until they were totally worn away. It would also follow that the eye would be injured by the continuous striking of these bodies. Again, it would not be possible for a whole body to be seen by anyone, but only as much as could be taken in by the pupil.

Rather, this is "movement" according to alteration: the alteration is a movement towards a form that is a quality of the thing seen. Inasmuch as it is bright in actuality, the medium is in potentiality to this form; the medium is an unbounded transparent (color is a quality of a bounded transparent, as will be said below),[3] and what is unbounded is related to what is bounded as potentiality to actuality, for form is a boundary of matter.

Now because of the different nature *(ratio)* of the transparent in a transparent medium, the medium receives the form of a color in a mode that is different from the mode in which it exists in the colored body, where there is a bounded transparent, as will be said below; for actualities are in receivers according to the mode of the latter.[4] Thus color is in a colored body as a quality complete in its natural being, but it is in the medium incompletely, according to an intentional being. Otherwise something black and something white could not be seen through the same medium. For whiteness and blackness cannot simultaneously be in the same thing as forms complete in their natural being, but with respect to the above-mentioned incomplete being they do exist in the same thing: for this mode of being, because of its imperfection, approaches the mode by which something exists in something else in potentiality, and opposites are simultaneously in potentiality in the same thing.

❖o❖

438b5 Then, when he says *It is reasonable*, in keeping with what was said he gives the cause of the necessity of assigning sight to water, which he showed above only by signs.

He says that, because what causes vision is the alteration of a medium made bright by the body seen, *it is reasonable that what is inside* the pupil, which is the organ of sight, *be made of water: for water is* one of the *transparent* things. But the external medium is a transparent thing that has been illuminated, and nothing can be seen without this illumination: so the light must *also* be *inside* the eye. And because there can be light only in what is transparent, there must also be something *transparent* inside the eye. It is not the heavenly body, because this does not enter into the composition of the human body: and so *it is necessarily water,* which is easier to preserve and thicker than *air,* as was said.[5]

438b8 Then, when he says *For the soul,* he makes clear why light within is required for seeing.

If the power of sight were on the outer surface of the eye, the light of the external transparent, through which the alteration by the color reaches the outer surface of the pupil, would alone suffice for seeing. But *the soul, or the sensitive part of soul, is not* on the outer surface *of the eye, but inside.*

It should be noted that he significantly adds "or sensitive part of soul." Since the soul is the form both of the whole body and of its individual parts, it is necessarily in the whole body and in each of its parts, because a form is necessarily in that of which it is the form.[6] Now the sensitive part of the soul is called the sensitive "power," being the principle of sensitive operation; and the principle of an operation of soul that is exercised by means of the body must be in a determinate part of the body. Thus the principle of sight is within, near the brain, where two nerves coming from the eyes meet.

Therefore, inside *the eye* there must be something *transparent, receptive of light*, so that there is uniform alteration from the thing seen all the way to the principle of sight.

438b11 Then, when he says *This is also clear,* he makes clear what he said by means of a sign, namely something that happens in *some* who are *wounded* around *the temples* in battle: when *the passages* that connect the pupil to the principle of sight are *cut off, a darkening* suddenly occurs through loss of sight, as if *a lamp* were *extinguished. The pupil* is like *a torch* lit up by an external light; thus, when the passages connecting the pupils to the principle of sight are *cut off,* the light of this torch cannot reach all the way to the principle of sight, and so sight is darkened.

438b16 Then, when he says *If, then, what happens in these cases,* having eliminated false opinions of others, he proceeds to the principal proposal.

First with respect to the organs of the non-necessary senses. Second with respect to the organs of the necessary senses, where he says *But the tactile part* (438b30).

On the first point he does two things. First he coordinates sense-organs with elements. Second he clarifies what he said, where he says *For what smelling is in actuality* (438b21).

On the first point it must be considered that it was not in keeping with the thought of Aristotle to assign the sense-organs to elements, as is clear in the book *On the Soul.*[7] But because other philosophers did assign the sense-organs to the four elements, therefore, condescending to them, as it were, in this matter, he says that, presupposing what was *said* about sight, *if one must, following* what others say, *assign each of the sensitive parts*—that is, sense-organs—*to one of the elements,* as others do, *one should think that eyesight* is to be assigned to *water, what is perceptive of sounds* to *air, and smelling* to *fire.*

❖○❖

But this seems to be contrary to what was said in *On the Soul:* "The pupil is of water, hearing of air, and smell is of either of these; but fire either belongs to none or is common to all."[8]

In response to this it must be said that what the sense of smell is can be taken in two ways: in one way according to potentiality, and thus the organ itself of smell is made either of air or of water, as is said in *On the Soul* III;[9] in another way according to actuality, and thus what is said here is true, as he himself will prove. Thus it is significant that he did not say that the "sense of smell" is made of fire, as he did say that "the part perceptive of sounds" is made of air and "eyesight" is made of fire. Rather he says that "smelling" is made of fire. For "sense of smell" refers to the potentiality, but "smelling" to the actuality.

438b21 Then, when he says *For what smelling is in actuality,* he proves what he has said about the organ of smell.

On this point he does three things. First he shows that the act of smelling in actuality is related to fire. Second he concludes to what should be the quality and place of the organ of smell, which is the act of smelling in potentiality, where he says *For this reason* (438b25). Third he shows a resemblance of the organ of smell to the organ of sight, where he says *And the generation of the eye* (438b27).

Accordingly he first says that *the olfactory part*—that is, the organ that has power to smell—must be *in potentiality what* actual *smelling is in actuality.* He clarifies this as follows: *a sensible object makes a sense-power act*—that is, be in actuality, or again, operate. But the sensitive part must be in potentiality the sensible object: otherwise it would not be affected by it. Hence it remains that the sensitive part is *in potentiality* what sensing is in actuality.

Now it is clear that *odor is smoky evaporation.* Not that "smoky evaporation" is the very essence of odor, for this was disproved in *On the Soul* II on the grounds that odor spreads farther than does smoky evaporation.[10] Rather this is said because smoky evaporation is a cause of odor being perceived. *But smoky evaporation* comes *from fire,* or whatever is hot. Therefore the sense of smell is brought to actuality by heat, which is in fire as in its principle. This is why flowers have stronger odor in hot times and places.

438b25 Then, when he says *For this reason,* he concludes from the foregoing that the organ of smell should be in a place near the brain.

For the organ of smell is, in potentiality, odor in actuality; odor in actuality exists by heat or fire; therefore the organ of smell must be hot in potentiality. But *the potentially hot is the matter of what is cold,* because the matter of contraries is the same, and it cannot be in potentiality to one of them without being in actuality under the other, either perfectly or, when it is under the form of an intermediate, imperfectly. So the substance of the organ of smell must be something that is cold and moist in actuality, and this is especially the case around the brain. Hence the organ of *smell is around the brain.*

438b27 Then, when he says *And the generation of the eye,* he shows a point of agreement between the organ of smell and the organ of sight.

He says that *the generation of the eye also has the same mode,* inasmuch as it *stems from the brain.* It does so because *the brain is the coldest and moistest of all parts of the body,* and so it has the nature of water, which is naturally cold and moist. Thus the brain fits both with the organ of smell, which should be hot in potentiality, and with the organ of sight, which should be made of water.

But then it seems that Plato fittingly assigned sight to fire, as Aristotle here assigns smell to fire.

To this it must be said that the organ of smell is made of water inasmuch as water is potentially hot, heat being a feature of fire. But the organ of sight is made of water inasmuch as water is transparent, and consequently luminous in potentiality.

But because fire is also luminous in actuality, as well as hot, someone might then say that sight is fittingly assigned to fire.

To this it must be said that, just as Aristotle assigned smell to fire, so nothing prevents sight from being assigned to fire—not according to the proper qualities of fire, which are heat and dryness, but according as fire is luminous in actuality.

The other philosophers seem to have focused on this, basing their argument on the shining that appears when the eye is moved. Aristotle disproved their opinion in this regard not because they held that sight in actuality is fire, which in a way would be true, inasmuch as sight in actuality does not occur without light, as the act of smelling in actuality does not occur without heat; rather, he did so because they held that the organ of sight is luminous in actuality, holding as they did that sight occurs not by a taking in, but by an extromission.

438b30 Then, when he says *But the tactile part,* he makes a determination about the organs of the necessary senses.

First he shows the element to which they are to be assigned. Second he shows the place where they are situated, where he says *And so the sensitive part* (439a1).

Accordingly he first says that the organ of touch is assigned to *earth,* and similarly the organ of taste, which is *a kind of touch,* as was said in *On the Soul* II.[11]

Now this is not to be taken to mean that the organ of touch or taste is simply made of earth, for we do not perceive by means of hair, which contains even more earth. It is rather that, as is said in *On the Soul* III, earth is mixed into the organs of these senses to the greatest degree.[12]

With respect to the organ of touch, the reason, as is said in *On the Soul* II, is this.[13] In order for the organ of touch to be in potentiality to contrary tangible qualities, it has to have a composition that is intermediate. Therefore, it has to have the greatest amount of earth, which has less active power than do the other elements.

With respect to the organ of taste, the reason is clear. The organ of smell has to contain water in order to be in potentiality the hot thing without which there is no smelling in actuality. Similarly, the organ of taste has to contain earth in order to be in potentiality the moist thing without which there is no tasting in actuality.

439a1 Then, when he says *And so the sensitive part,* he shows where the organ of *taste and touch* is based.

He says that it is *near the heart,* and he gives the reason, namely that *the heart is opposite the brain* with respect to position and quality. As the brain is the coolest part of the body, the heart is *the warmest of* all *the parts* of the body. For this reason they are placed in opposition to one another in order for the heart's heat to be moderated by the brain's coolness.

This is why those who have heads that are small in proportion to their other parts are impetuous, as if the heat from the heart were not being pushed back down enough by the brain. Conversely, those who have unusually big heads are very slow and dull, as if the heat from the heart were being impeded by the size of the brain.

Since the organ of touch is made of earth, it must be in the body's warmest place as in its principle, so that by the heart's heat the coolness of the earth can be brought to a moderate temperature. This does not prevent an animal from perceiving by means of touch through the whole of its body, because as other senses perceive through an external medium, touch and taste perceive through an internal medium, namely flesh. And just as the principle of sight is not on the surface of the eye, but within, the principle of touch is also within, near the heart, a sign of which is that the most painful wounds are those around the heart.

But it cannot be said that there are two sensitive principles in an animal, one near the brain, where the visual, olfactory, auditory principle is established, and one near the heart, where the tactile and gustatory principle is established. The sensitive principle is primarily in the heart, which is also where the source of heat is located in the body of an animal, because nothing is sensitive without heat, as is said in *On the Soul*.[14] The sensitive power flows from the heart to the brain, and from there it proceeds to the organs of three senses, sight, hearing, and smell. But touch and taste are relayed to the heart itself through a medium united to the body, as was said.

439a4 Finally, by way of an epilogue, he says *let it be determined in this way about the sensitive parts of the body*—that is, as was done above.

CHAPTER 5

439A6–B14

439a6 *Concerning sensible objects, in relation to each sensitive part—I mean, for instance, color and sound and odor and taste and touch—it was said in a general way in the discussions On the soul what their action is; and what it is to operate in relation to each sensitive part. But it is necessary to say what each of them is; that is, it must be considered what color is, what sound is, what odor is, what flavor is, and similarly also concerning touch. And first concerning color.*

439a12 *Each, then, is spoken of in two ways: on one hand in actuality, on the other in potentiality. Accordingly, what color in actuality is, and sound, how they are the same as or other than the sense-powers in actuality, namely seeing and hearing, has been said in the discussions On the soul. But let us now say what each of them is that it should cause sensing and actuality.*

439a18 *Accordingly, as was said about light in those discussions, it is the color of the transparent accidentally. For when something lit up exists in the transparent, the presence is light, and the privation darkness.*

439a21 *But what we call the transparent is not a property of air or water or any of the bodies mentioned, but is a common nature and power. It is not separate, but it is present in these and in other bodies, in some to a greater extent, in some to a lesser.*

439a25 *Therefore, as there is necessarily a limit of bodies, so there also is of this. Now the nature of light is in the unlimited transparent. But it is obvious that there will be a limit of the transparent that is in bodies, and that this is color is clear from what happens: for color is on the limit or is the limit. Hence the Pythagoreans called color an "epiphany"; for it is on the limit of a body, but it is not the limit of the body.*

439a33 *Now one must think that it is the same nature that is colored from without and intrinsically. Air and water appear as colored things, for the dawn is such a thing. But in this case, because it is in something indeterminate, neither the air nor the sea has the same color to those who approach close up and from afar. But in bodies, unless something containing makes a change, there is a determinate fantasia of color. Therefore it is clear that both in the former and in the* *latter it is the same thing that is receptive of color. Therefore the transparent, according as it exists in bodies—and it exists in all of them, to a greater or lesser extent—is what causes colors to be participated in. But because color is on the limit, it will be a limit of this.*

439b11 *Therefore color will be the limit of the transparent in a determinate body.*

439b12 *And in transparent things such as water and any other such thing, and in whatever seems to have a color of its own—in all these it is likewise at the limit.*

Commentary

439a6 After The Philosopher has applied the consideration about sense-powers of animals to sense-organs, here he applies it to sensible objects themselves.

First he states his intention. Second he carries out his proposal, where he says *Accordingly, as was said about light* (439a18).

On the first point he does two things. First he proposes his intention. Second he clarifies what he said, where he says *Each, then, is spoken of in two ways* (439a12).

Accordingly he first speaks of proper *sensible objects,* those perceived in relation to *each sensitive part,* that is, each individual sense-organ, which he says to distinguish them from common sensibles. The proper sensibles are *color, sound, and odor,* which are sensed through sight, hearing, and smell; *and taste and touch*—that is, the objects of these senses. He says that *it was said in On the soul in a general way* both how these act on a sense-power and the nature of the sense-power's operation *in relation to each* organ affected by the above-mentioned sensible objects. For it was said in *On the Soul* II that a sense-power is a sensible object in potentiality, and that sensible objects make a sense-power be in actuality.[1] But now *it must be considered what each* sensible object *is* in itself, *that is, what color is, what sound is, what odor is, what flavor is, and similarly concerning touch*—that is, the objects of touch. But *first color,* which is the object of sight, must be discussed, because sight is the most spiritual of the senses.

It is not to be understood by this that he intends to make a determination about all these sensible objects in this book, but rather that consideration of them all is necessary to the proposed intention. But objects of touch are either properties of elements, namely hot, cold, moisture, and dryness, about which a determination was made in the book *On Generation and Corruption*,[2] or they are properties of individual bodies, such as hardness and softness, and so on, about which a determination was made in the book the *Meteorologica*.[3] So what is left now is to make a determination about three things, namely color, odor, and flavor. For a determination about sound was made in the book *On the Soul*, because the account of the production of sound is the same as the account of the alteration of the auditory organ by sound, and the way in which sense-organs are altered by sensible objects belongs to the consideration made in the book *On the Soul*.[4]

439a12 Then, when he says *Each, then, is spoken of in two ways*, he explains what was said, namely that it must be considered what color is, what flavor is, etc.

For *each* of these exists in two ways: in one way inasmuch as it is sensed *in actuality, and* in another way inasmuch as it is sensible *in potentiality. What* each of them *is* according to actuality—that is, according as *color*, flavor, or any other sensible object, is *in actuality* perceived by sense—has *been said in On the soul*. That is, it was said *how* each of them is *the same as or other than* a sense-power *in actuality*, such as *seeing* or *hearing:* for the visible in actuality is the same as seeing in actuality, but the visible in potentiality is not the same as sight in potentiality. Accordingly what each of the sensible objects is in actuality was said in *On the Soul*, where a determination was made about the sense-powers in actuality.[5] *But what each* thing that is of such a nature as to cause the sense-power to be in *actuality* is in itself must be said *now*, in the present book.

439a18 Then, when he says *Accordingly, as was said about light*, he makes a determination about sensible objects in the order already established: first color; second flavor, where he says *Odor and flavor must be discussed* (Chapter 8, 440b28); and third odor, where he says *Odors must be understood in the same way* (Chapter 11, 442b27).

The first part is divided into two parts. In the first he shows what color in general is. In the second he makes a determination about differences among colors, where he says *Accordingly, what causes light* (Chapter 6, 439b14).

On the first point he does two things. First he presents the principles of color. Second he investigates the definition of color on the basis of these principles, where he says *Therefore, as there is necessarily a limit of bodies* (439a25).

Now there are two principles of color: one is formal, namely light; the other is material, namely the transparent. Accordingly he first touches on the formal principle, light; and second on the material principle, the transparent, where he says *But what we call the transparent* (439a21).

Accordingly he first says that, *as was said in* the book *On the Soul, light is the color of the transparent.* He says this according to an analogy *(proportio):* as color is the form and actuality of a colored body, so light is the form and actuality of the transparent. But they are different inasmuch as a colored body has the cause of its color in itself, but a transparent body has its light only from something else. This is why he says that light is the color of the transparent *accidentally,* that is, through something else, and not that light is the actuality of the transparent as such. He shows that light is the actuality of the transparent through something else in the following way. *When* a body that is *lit up*—that is, bright in actuality—is present to *the transparent, light* is caused in the transparent by *the presence* of that body, and *darkness* by its *privation.* But it is not so with color, because the color remains in a colored body whatever is present to or absent from it, although it may not be in actuality visible without light.

439a21 Then, when he says *But what we call the transparent,* he makes a determination about the transparent.

He says that *what* is called *the transparent is not a property of* either *air or water or any* such body—for instance glass and other transparent bodies—*but is a common "nature"* found in many bodies—that is, a natural property found in many things—one that he also calls a *"power" (virtus)* inasmuch as it is a principle of vision. Now Plato held that, just as what is common is separate in intelligibility *(ratio),* so it is also separate in existence *(esse).* Therefore, in order to eliminate this position, he adds that the nature of the transparent *is not* a *separate* nature, *but is in these* sensible *bodies*—namely air and water—*and* also *others, in some to a greater extent, and in some to a lesser.*

❖o❖

To make this clear, it must be known that, as the Philosopher says in *On the Soul* II, the visible is not color alone, but also something else, which is apprehended by reason but unnamed.[6] Accordingly in the genus of the visible, taken in general, there is something that stands as actuality and something that stands as potentiality. What is in this genus as actuality is not a proper quality of any of the elements, but rather light itself, which exists first in the heavenly body, from which it is derived to lower bodies. What is in this genus as potentiality is what is properly receptive of light, which is arranged in an order of three levels.

The first level is reached when what is receptive of light is totally filled with it, being, as it were, perfectly brought to actuality, so that it cannot receive any further quality or form of this kind. Of all bodies this is most true of the sun, which is why the body of the sun cannot be a medium in sight that receives and transmits a visible form. And the property of shining, descending in a certain order, reaches fire, and then, beyond that, certain bodies that, because of the smallness of their light, can shine only at night, as was said above.[7]

The second level belongs to what does not of itself have light in actuality, but is receptive of light through the whole of itself. Such bodies are properly called "perspicuous" or "transparent," or also "diaphanous," for "phenomenon" in Greek means the same as "visible." This property of being transparent is found to the greatest degree in heavenly bodies, except for the bodies of the stars, which conceal what is behind them. Second, it is in fire, that is, fire in its proper sphere, because of its fineness. Third it is in air, fourth in water, and fifth even in certain bodies made of earth, because of an abundance of air or water that is also in them.

The third and lowest level belongs to earth, which is farthest away from the heavenly body, and is by nature receptive of light to the least degree, namely, only on its surface. For its external parts, because of their thickness, overshadow the internal ones so that light cannot reach the latter.

Now although it is only in the case of bodies of the intermediate level that one properly speaks of the "transparent" or "diaphanous" according to the proper meaning of the term, nevertheless, generally speaking, that can be called "transparent" which is receptive of light in any way whatsoever, and it is in this sense that the Philosopher seems to be speaking here of "the transparent."[8]

439a25 Then, when he says *Therefore, as there is necessarily a limit of bodies,* he investigates the definition of color.

First he investigates its genus. Second he investigates its difference, where he says *Now one must think that it is the same nature* (439a33). Third he concludes to the definition, where he says *Therefore color will be* (439b11).

Now it must be considered that one should always put the subject in the definition of an accident, as is said in *Metaphysics* VII,[9] although this is done in different ways.

For if an accident is defined in the abstract, the subject is put in place of the difference and what pertains to the essence of the accident is put in place of the genus, as when it is said that "Snubness is curvedness of nose."

But when an accident is defined in the concrete, conversely the subject is put in place of the genus, as when it is said that "A snub is a nose that is curved."

Accordingly, because here color is to be defined in the abstract, Aristotle first begins by investigating, in place of a genus, what color itself essentially is.

He concludes from what was said that, since the transparent is not a separate nature, but one existing in bodies, *it is necessary that, just as there is a limit of bodies* in which this nature is found if the bodies are finite, *so also* there must be a limit of the transparent itself, which signifies a quality of such bodies. And the argument is the same for all qualities of bodies that are accidentally quantities as a result of the quantities of the bodies, and hence are accidentally limited as a result of the limits of the bodies.

Accordingly it must be considered that, just as some bodies (for instance, those that consist of earth) are said to be "limited" because they are limited by limits of their own, and others are said to be "unlimited" because they are limited not by limits of their own, but by the limits of other things, so it is in the case of the transparent. One kind is "unlimited" of itself because it has in itself nothing determinate by which it may be seen, but another is "limited" because it does have something in itself by which it may be seen with respect to its own limit.

Accordingly, *the unlimited transparent* is receptive of *light,* the *nature* of which is such as to be received not only at a limit, but throughout a whole. *But it is* clear *that there* is *a limit of this transparent that,* as was said, is a quality existing *in bodies.* And *that this is color is clear from what happens. For* colored bodies are seen only at their limits, from which it is evident that *color* either *is the limit* of a body *or is on the limit* of a body. And *hence* it is that *the Pythagoreans called color an "epiphany"*—that is, an "appearance on"—because what appears on the surface of bodies is color. But it is *not* true that color *is the limit of a body,* as the Pythagoreans held, because thus it would be a surface or line or point. But *it is on the limit of a body,* just as the nature of the transparent is on bodies.

439a33 Then, when he says *Now one must think that it is the same nature,* he investigates what is put in the definition of color as the difference, namely its subject, which is the transparent.

He says that *one must think that it is the same nature that* is receptive of color in bodies that are *colored from without*—that is, not by their own color but by something outside them—and in those that are colored *intrinsically* by their own color. Those that are colored from without are transparent, for instance *air and water;* he makes this clear with the color that appears at *dawn* through the shining of the sun's rays on certain bodies.

However, he does provide a difference between bodies that are colored from without and those colored of themselves. In those that are colored from without, *because* they do not have of themselves a determinate color, *the color* does not seem to be the *same* from close up and from afar, as is clear in the case of *the air* and the water of *the sea,* which from *afar* appear to be of another color than they do from *close up;* for because their color is seen by a reflection, its appearance necessarily varies with variation of the location of those looking at it because of the different angles of reflection. *But in bodies* that of themselves have a determinate color, *there is a determinate "fantasia"*—that is, appearance—*of color,* and it does not vary with the different locations of those looking at it, except perhaps accidentally, for instance when a *containing* body causes a *change* of appearance; or when one color is seen through another, as when what is contained in a vessel of red glass seems red; or again by the kind of reflection of light such as appears in the pigeon's neck.

Therefore, because color, which is seen in both kinds of body, does not differ with respect to the proper subject of color, but only with respect to the cause of its appearance, which is either intrinsic or extrinsic, *it is clear* that in both cases *it is the same thing that is receptive of color.* And because *the transparent* is what is receptive of color in what is colored from without, the transparent is clearly also what causes intrinsically colored things to participate in color. Indeed, the transparent is found in bodies according to more and less, as was said: bodies that have more air or water have more of the transparent, and those that have an overabundance of earth have less.

Therefore if we unite the two things said—that color is on the limit of a body, and that bodies participate in color with respect to the transparent—it follows that color is the limit of the transparent.

439b11 Then, when he says *Therefore color will be,* he concludes to the definition of color.

He does so first in the case of what is colored of itself, intrinsically. Second in the case of what is colored from without, where he says *And in transparent things* (439b12).

Accordingly he concludes that *color* is *the limit of the transparent.* He adds *in a determinate body,* because such bodies are those that are of themselves colored, and what is per se should be put in the definition of a thing.

Now his saying that color is the limit of the transparent is not opposed to what he said above, that color is not a limit. For he said that with reference to the limit of a body, but here he is speaking of the limit of the transparent, which he calls a quality of a body, like hot and white. Thus color is not in the category of quantity—like surface, which is the limit of a body—but in the category of quality. The transparent is also in the category of quality, because a limit and that of which it is the limit belong to one category. And just as bodies have surface in their interior in potentiality but not actuality, so they are also colored in their interior in potentiality but not actuality, and this potentiality is brought to actuality when division of the body occurs. For what is interior does not in actuality have the power to move sight, a power that belongs per se to color.

439b12 Then, when he says *And in transparent things,* he clarifies the nature *(ratio)* of color in the case of unlimited *transparent things* such as *water,* or any *other* thing of this kind that has a color: *in all* these there is color only *with respect to the limit.*

CHAPTER 6

439B14–440A15

439b14 *Accordingly, what causes light in the air may be present in the transparent. But it may also not be present in it; instead, its privation may be. Thus, just as in that case the one is light and the other darkness, so white and black are caused in bodies.*

439b18 *But we must speak about the other colors, dividing the number of ways they might come to be. It can happen that, if white and black are placed beside one another, each of them invisible because of their smallness, what is made up of both thus becomes visible. It is seen neither as white nor as black. But because it necessarily has some color, and neither of these is possible, it necessarily is mixed, and is another species of color. Thus one can admit of more colors than white and black.*

439b27 *But many are in a proportion, for they can be put together in the proportion of three to two, and of three to four, and according to other numbers. But some are together in no proportion at all, but in an incommensurable more and less.*

439b30 *So it must be the same as in harmonies: the most well-proportioned colors are those based on numbers, as in the case of harmonies, and these seem to be the most pleasant of colors, for instance scarlet and purple. But such are few, due to the same cause harmonies are also few. And the other colors are those not based on numbers.*

440a3 *Or, all colors are ordered on the basis of numbers, but some are disordered when they are not pure, and they become such because they are not based on number. This is one way for the generation of colors.*

440a7 *Another one is that they appear through one another, in the way that painters sometimes place one color over another, more manifest one, as they do when they wish to make something appear to be in water or in air. And in this way the sun of itself appears white, but through fog and smoke it appears purple.*

440a12 *And there will also be many colors in the same way as described above: there will be a proportion of those on the surface to those in the depth; but some are not in any proportion at all.*

Commentary

439b14 After the Philosopher has shown what color is, here he proceeds to distinguish the species of colors.

First with respect to extreme colors; second with respect to intermediate colors, where he says *But we must speak about the other colors* (439b18).

Now the differences by which species are distinguished should divide a genus per se, not accidentally, as is clear in *Metaphysics* VII.[1] Therefore, he concludes to the variety of species of color from the very nature of color, which he explained through the definition given above.

It is established from the foregoing that the subject of color is the transparent at its limit in limited bodies. But the proper actuality of the transparent as such is light, the presence of which in the unlimited transparent, for instance air, causes light, but the absence of which causes darkness. Therefore, *what causes light in the air* may be present on the limit of the transparent belonging to limited *bodies,* where it will cause the color *white;* and the color *black* will be caused by its absence.

This is not to be understood as if there were no light in the color black, for thus black would not be contrary to white, since it would not participate in the same nature; rather, it would be a pure privation, like darkness. Black is said to be caused by absence of light because it of all colors has the least light, as white has the most; for contraries are things that stand farthest apart in the same genus, as is said in *Metaphysics* X.[2]

439b18 Then, when he says *But we must speak about the other colors,* he proceeds to distinguish intermediate colors.

This is divided into two parts. In the first he presents certain ways for the generation and distinction of intermediate colors not according to their existence, but according to their appearance. Second he gives the true generation of intermediate colors according to their nature, where he says *But there is mixture of bodies not only* (Chapter 7, 440a31).

On the first point he does two things. First he presents two ways for the generation and distinction of intermediate colors according to appearance. Second he compares those ways to one another, where he says *But to say, like the Ancients* (Chapter 7, 440a15).

The first part is divided into two according to the two ways he presents; the second part begins where he says *Another one is that they appear* (440a7).

On the first point he does two things. First he presents the generation of intermediate colors. Second, where he says *But many are in a proportion* (439b27), he gives their distinction.

Accordingly he first says that since the extreme colors have been discussed, *we must speak about the other colors*—that is, the intermediate ones—distinguishing *the number of ways they might* be generated.

Let it be supposed, then, that there is something invisible because of its smallness. Thus *it can happen that if* two small bodies, *invisible because of their smallness, are placed* next to *one another*, one of them being *black* and the other *white*, what is composed of *both* can be seen, because of the greater quantity. Now everything that is seen in bodies of this kind is seen according to some color. But the whole is *seen neither as white nor as black*, because both what is white in it and what is black have been assumed to be invisible because of their smallness. Hence it is *necessarily* seen as a *color mixed* from both, as it were, so that thus there is *another species of color* besides white and black. From this it is clear that *one can admit of more colors than black and white*.

439b27 Then, when he says *But many are in a proportion*, he gives the distinction of intermediate colors.

First he assigns the cause of distinction of intermediate colors to various proportions of black and white. Second he gives the cause why some intermediate colors are pleasant and some not, where he says *So it must be the same as in harmonies* (439b30).

✣o✣

On the first point it must be considered that, as the Philosopher teaches in *Metaphysics* X, the notion *(ratio)* of measure is found first in numbers, and second in continuous quantities.[3] From the latter it is transferred even to qualities, insofar as among them one quality can be more than another, whether by way of intension, as one thing is said to be "whiter" than something else, or by way of extension, as whiteness on a bigger surface is said to be "bigger."

Now because proportion is a relation of quantities to one another, wherever one speaks of quantity in any sense, one can also speak of proportion.

First in the case of numbers, which are all commensurable with one another, for they all share in the first measure that is unity. And there are various proportions of numbers according as various numbers are related to one another: the proportion of three to two, which is called "sesquialteral," is different from that of four to three, which is called "sesquitertial."

But because continuous quantities cannot be resolved into something indivisible as numbers are into unity, not all continuous quantities are necessarily commensurable with one another; rather, one can find some in which one is more than another but they have no one common measure. However, whatever continuous quantities are proportioned to one another according to the proportion of number to number do have one common measure: for instance, if one is three cubits long and another four, both are measured by the cubit.

In this way too, there can be more and less among qualities either according to a numerical proportion or according to an incommensurable difference.

And that is what he says: that there can be *many* intermediate colors in various proportions. *For* it can happen that white is juxtaposed to black in the proportion of *two* to *three,* or of *three to four,* or of any *other numbers;* or again, *in no* numerical *proportion, but* only *in an incommensurable more and less.*

439b30 Then, when he says *So it must be the same as in harmonies,* he shows why some colors are pleasant and some not.

He gives two reasons for this. He gives the second where he says *Or, all colors are ordered on the basis of numbers* (440a3).

Accordingly he first says that, given that intermediate colors are distinguished according to various proportions of white and black, *it must be the same* with intermediate colors as it is with *harmonies,* which are caused according to a proportion between a low and a high tone. For just as *in the case of harmonies,* the most well proportioned and pleasant are those based on numbers, as the octave is in the proportion of two to one, and the fifth in the proportion of three to two; so also in the case of *colors,* those based on numerical proportion are *the most well-proportioned.* And *these* also *seem to be most pleasant,* for example *scarlet and purple,* that is, red and dark red. And just as pleasant *harmonies* are *few,* so also *such* colors *are few*. But *other colors,* those that are not pleasant, are *not* established in numerical proportion.

440a3 Then, when he says *Or, all colors are ordered on the basis of numbers,* he gives another reason why some colors are pleasant and some not.

He says that *all* species of *colors* can be said to be *ordered* according to *numbers.* And he can make this change because now there will be a different species of color not merely if there is difference according to more and less, but only when there is more and less according to a numerical proportion. If this is supposed, it will follow that these same colors *are disordered when they are not "pure,"* that is, if there is more white than black according to one proportion in one part, but according to another numerical proportion in another part, and this confusedly and without order. And so, *because* there will *not* be the same numerical proportion throughout the whole, it will follow that these colors will be disordered and unpleasant.

Finally he concludes that *this is one way of generation of intermediate colors.*

440a7 Then, when he says *Another one is that they appear through one another,* he presents the second way of generation of intermediate colors.

First he explains the generation of intermediate colors; second their distinction, where he says *And there will also be many colors* (440a12).

Accordingly he first says that, besides the above-mentioned way, there is one other way of generation of intermediate colors according to appearance: by one of the colors appearing through another so that from two colors there results an appearance of an intermediate color. And he gives two examples.

The first is taken from artificial things. *Painters sometimes place one color over another,* in such a way that the *more manifest*—that is, the stronger and more lively—color is placed underneath: otherwise, if the weaker one were placed underneath, it would not appear at all. And they do this in particular *when they wish to make something appear* in their picture as if it were *in air or in water,* for instance when they paint fish swimming in the sea: for then they put over the stronger color of the fish some weaker color as the color of the water.

The other example is taken from natural things. *The sun of itself appears white* because of the brightness of light, but when it is seen by us through a medium of *fog*, or *smoke* released from dry bodies, then it seems *purple*—that is, ruddy. Thus it is clear that what is in itself one color, when it is seen through another color, causes the appearance of a third color: for smoke in itself is not red, but rather black.

440a12 Then, when he says *And there will also be many colors*, he gives the explanation of the distinction of colors according to this way.

He says that intermediate *colors* are multiplied, in this way of generating them, *in the same way as* they are in the above-mentioned way, namely according to different proportions: one can take *a proportion of* the color placed underneath—which he describes as *"in the depth"*—to the color placed above—which he describes as *"on the surface."* However, *some* colors placed above and below one another *are not in a proportion*—that is, a numerical one—and so unpleasant colors are caused, as was also said above.

CHAPTER 7

440A15–B28

440a15 *But to say, like the Ancients, that color is an emanation, and is seen due to such a cause, is incoherent. For in any case it was necessary for them to make sensing occur through contact. Therefore it is better to say at once that sensing occurs by the medium of sensing being moved by the sensible object, than by contact and emanations.*

440a20 *Accordingly, in the position that bodies are juxtaposed, just as it is necessary to assume an invisible magnitude, so it is also necessary to assume a length of time imperceptible to sense, so that the movements escape notice as they arrive, and it is thought that they are one thing because they appear simultaneously. But in the latter case there is no such necessity: rather, the color that is on the surface, being immobile, and moved by the one placed under it, will cause a movement that is dissimilar, and so something else will appear, and it will be neither white nor black.*

440a26 *Therefore if it cannot be that any magnitude is invisible, but any one is visible from some distance, this latter case, too, will be a mixture of colors. But also in the former way, nothing stands in the way of a common color appearing to those who are at a distance. For that there is no magnitude that is invisible is to be considered in what comes after.*

440a31 *But there is mixture of bodies not only in the way that some think there is: by minimal parts being juxtaposed, but being unapparent to us because of the sense-power. There is also that of a whole being wholly mixed with a whole, as was said of all bodies in the discussions of mixture in general. For in the former way only those things can be mixed that can be divided into smallest parts, like men, horses, or seeds: men can be divided to a man, and horses to a horse. And so, by juxtaposition of these there is mixed together a multitude that consists simultaneously of both. But we do not say that one man is mixed with one horse. But whatever is not divided into a smallest part cannot be mixed in this way, but by being mixed from the whole, and such things are by nature mixed most thoroughly. How it is possible for this to occur was said before in the discussions on mixture.*

440b13 *But at the same time it is clear what necessity there is, when these are* mixed, for colors also to be mixed. And this—not overlay, nor juxtaposition—is the principal cause of there being many colors,: for it is not just from a distance, and not close up, that one of the mixed colors appears, but from anywhere.

440b18 And there will be many colors because what is mixed together can be mixed in many proportions, some on the basis of numbers, but some according to difference alone. And the other things that were said about colors placed beside one another, and about overlay, can similarly be said of mixtures also. But the cause of species of colors, and those of flavors and of sounds, being limited and not infinite, must be considered later.

440b26 What color is, then, and the cause of there being many colors, has been said. But about sound and voice something was said before in the discussions On the soul.

Commentary

440a15 Having presented two ways of generation of intermediate colors, here he compares the ways mentioned to one another.

On this point he does three things. First he eliminates a position from which one of the ways mentioned followed. Second he compares the ways mentioned to one another, where he says *Accordingly, in the position that bodies are juxtaposed* (440a20). Third he shows how far each of the ways mentioned can be maintained, where he says *Therefore if it cannot be that any magnitude is invisible* (440a26).

Accordingly he first says that *the Ancients* held that *color is* nothing but *an emanation* from bodies that are seen. For as was said above, Democritus and also Empedocles held that vision occurs from such a *cause* as this, namely emanation of "idols" from bodies that are seen. And because everything is seen by means of its own color, they believed that color is nothing but this emanation. But *to say* this *is* completely *incoherent*. For they could not hold that these bodies emanating from bodies seen enter inside the eye, because thus its substance would be destroyed. Hence *in any case* they had to hold that vision occurs *through contact* of the released bodies on the eye itself, which by this contact is altered to a state of seeing. Hence if such alteration suffices to cause vision, *it is better to say that* vision *occurs by the medium being* immediately, from the beginning, *moved by the sensible object, than* to say that vision occurs through *contact* and emanation: for nature provides for herself by means of as few things as possible.

✤o✤

But there are also other considerations that show the abovementioned position to be false.

First because if vision occurred by contact, the sense of sight would not be distinct from touch, which is clearly false, for sight is not apprehensive of the contraries of touch.

Second because bodies seen through continuous emanation would be diminished, and finally completely used up; or if their quantity were preserved by other emanations coming to them, <. . .>.

Third because since these bodies emanating from things seen would be extremely fine, they would be driven by the winds, and so direct vision would not occur.

Fourth because sight would not need light for seeing, since vision would occur through contact of the visible.

And many other such inconsistencies follow, which, because they are obvious, the Philosopher passed over.

✤o✤

440a20 Then when he says *Accordingly, in the position that bodies are juxtaposed,* he compares the two ways mentioned to one another.

Here it must be considered that the first way of generation of intermediate colors was given by those who held that color is an emanation; and so, after Aristotle shows the falsity of the position in itself, he concludes to an inconsistency that follows for them in this way of explaining the generation of colors.

He says that in holding that intermediate colors are generated by the extreme colors being *juxtaposed, it is necessary* for them to say not only that there is a *magnitude* that is *invisible,* but *also* that there is a *length of time* that is *imperceptible,* to maintain their proposal. For because they held that vision occurs through local motion of emanating bodies, and because nothing is moved any distance by local motion except in time, they must assign some time in which the emanation from the thing seen to the eye occurs, and they must posit a greater time to the extent that there is greater distance. Now it is clear that there is not the same distance to the eye for all the infinitesimal bodies juxtaposed, and thus there must be different lengths of time in which *the movements* from them reach the eye. Therefore the whole composed of such bodies will not be seen as *one thing,* as was held above, unless the time in which one movement precedes another *escapes notice*, in which case it is necessary to posit an imperceptible length of time in this way of explaining the generation of colors.

But *in the latter case*—that is, in the second way—*there is no necessity* for an imperceptible length of time to be posited, because it is not held that vision occurs through emanation by local movement. But although the *color* placed *on the surface* remains *immobile* with respect to place, it is nevertheless changed by way of alteration by the color underneath, so that it affects sight in a way *dissimilar* to that in which either the color placed on top or the one placed underneath would of itself. Hence another, intermediate color *will appear, and it will be neither white nor black.*

Now it must be considered that, even if we set aside the generation of intermediate colors that they posit, it follows for those who hold that sight occurs through emanation and contact that there is a length of time that is imperceptible. For they must say that any whole body is not seen all at once, but only through a succession of time, since they hold that sight occurs by contact, and it is not possible for a whole large body or its emanation to be touched all at once by the pupil, because of its smallness. And so it follows that there is an imperceptible length of time, since in the case of some things, it does seem to us that we see the whole of them all at once.

But it must be considered that a body that presents itself to sight can be considered in two ways.

In one way according as it is one whole in actuality, and its individual parts existing in it are in a way in potentiality: thus vision is directed to the whole all at once, as a unit, but not determinately to any part of it.

In the other way, a body that presents itself to sight can be considered according as a part of it is taken as determinate in itself, and distinct, as it were, from other parts. And thus sight is not directed to the whole all at once, but to one part after another. And this time by which the sight of the whole is measured is not simply imperceptible, since the soul, in sensing before and after in movement, senses time, as is clear from *Physics* IV.[1] But this time is more perceptible to the extent that the sense-power is sharper, and greater attentiveness is applied.

440a26 Then, when he says *Therefore if it cannot be that any magnitude is invisible,* he shows how the two ways of generation of colors can be maintained, and how far they extend, namely to appearance.

He concludes from what was said above that, *if it cannot be that any magnitude is invisible, but any* magnitude *is visible from some distance,* it indeed follows that there will be *a mixture of colors,* that is, by layered colors. And *also in the former way*—that is, by placing of colors next to one another—*nothing* prevents *a common color* from *appearing* from a certain distance from which neither of the simple colors can be seen because of the smallness of the bodies. But *that* no *magnitude is* simply *invisible* because of smallness he says *is to be* made clear *in what* follows.

440a31 Then, when he says *But there is mixture of bodies not only,* he presents the way of the generation of intermediate colors that is according to existence, not just appearance.

First he determines the generation of intermediate colors; second he gives the reason for their distinction according to this way of generation, where he says *And there will be many colors* (440b18).

But because this way of the generation of intermediate colors is understood in relation to mixture of bodies, first he prefaces something about mixture of bodies, and second he adds something about mixture of colors, where he says *But at the same time it is clear* (440b13).

Accordingly he first says that *mixture of bodies* with one another does *not* occur *only in the way that some* thought—namely by some *infinitesimals* being *juxtaposed* with others, all of them being *unapparent to* our senses because of their smallness. Rather, some bodies can be totally mixed into one another, in such a way that whole is mixed with whole, *as was said in* the book *On Generation,*[2] where there was treatment of *mixture* of bodies *in general.*

But it is true that some things *are mixed in the former way*—that is, by juxtaposition of minimal parts—namely whatever can be divided down *to smallest parts,* as a multitude of *men* is divided down *to* one *man* as its one smallest part, and a multitude of *horses* down *to* one *horse,* and a multitude of seeds down to one seed, i.e. one grain of wheat or some such thing. Hence it can certainly be said that *a multitude* of such things is *mixed* by the smallest parts being juxtaposed, for instance if men are confusedly mixed with horses or seeds of wheat with seeds of barley. However, the mixture of such things will not be total, for individual parts of the multitudes will remain unmixed, because *one man* will *not* be *mixed with one horse,* nor any other such thing with any other.

But whatever is not divided into a smallest part—that is, bodies that are continuous and have similar parts, such as wine and water—*is not mixed in* the above-mentioned *way*—that is, by juxtaposition of smallest parts—because one cannot take a smallest part in them. Rather, it happens by a whole *being mixed* with a *whole* in such a way that no part remains unmixed. And *such things are by nature most thoroughly*—and most truly—*mixed. How this* can *occur was* determined in the book *On Generation.*[3]

440b13 Then, after mixture of bodies, he touches on mixture of colors, when he says *But at the same time it is clear.*

He says that from what was determined above it is clear *what necessity there is* that when bodies *are mixed, colors* are *mixed.* For it was said above that the transparent, according as it exists in bodies, makes colors be participated, and that the transparent is found in bodies in different ways, namely according to more and less, as is also likewise brightness. And so when bodies, in which there are brightness and the transparent, are mixed, a mixture of colors necessarily occurs, *and this is the principal cause* of there being *many colors* besides white and black. The principal cause is *not overlay*—that is, one color being placed over another—*nor* is it *juxtaposition*—that is, infinitesimal colored bodies being placed next to one another—because an intermediate *color* besides white and black *appears not just from afar* and *not close up, but from* any distance. Thus it is clear that this is the way of the generation of intermediate colors according to their existence, but that the other two ways pertain only to their appearance.

440b18 Then, when he says *And there will be many colors,* he gives the cause of the distinction of intermediate colors according to the way of generation just described.

He says that *many* intermediate *colors* are generated *because* bodies *can be mixed together in many proportions,* and consequently so can colors themselves: *some* according to determinate *numbers, but some according to* incommensurable *difference alone. And* all *the other things* must *similarly be said* here about mixture *that were said* above in the other two ways, namely juxtaposition of colors and imposition of one color over another.

There is one thing that remains to be determined *later*, namely why *species of colors, flavors, and sounds are* finite *and not infinite*.[4]

440b26 Finally, by way of epilogue, he concludes that it *has* now *been said what color is and the cause of there being many colors*. He excuses himself from a determination of *sound and voice* because a determination was already made *about* these *in* the book *On the soul*. For the account of their generation is the same as that of the alteration by which they alter the sense-power, which pertains to the consideration of the book *On the Soul*.[5]

CHAPTER 8

440B28–441A29

440b28 *Odor and flavor must be discussed, for they are almost the same affection. But the two of them are not in the same things.*

440b30 *But the genus of flavors is more evident to us than that of odor. The cause of this is that we have a sense of smell that is worse than that of other animals and than the senses that are in us, but a surer sense of touch than do the other animals. But taste is a kind of touch.*

441a3 *The nature of water, then, tends to be flavor. Therefore, according to what Empedocles says, water necessarily has in itself the kinds of flavors, imperceptible because of the smallness. Or, such matter is present in it like a "panspermia" of flavors, and all of them are made of water, different ones from different parts. Or, water does not contain the difference, but the cause is something acting; as some might say, it is heat and the sun.*

441a10 *Now to say what Empedocles did is a very obvious falsehood. For we see that heat changes flavors when fruits are placed in the sun, or on a fire, in such a way that these flavors are not caused by a "drawing in" from water, but by a change and a drying in the fruit itself. And when they are laid out for a time, they are changed from sweet to harsh, bitter, and everything else. And when they are cooked they are changed to every kind of flavor, so to speak.*

441a18 *Likewise it is also impossible for water to be the matter of a "panspermia." For we see different flavors caused from the same thing, and from the same food. It remains, then that the water is changed in being affected by something.*

441a21 *It is clear, then, that it does not get this power we call flavor only from the power of heat. For water is the finest of all moistures, finer even than oil itself. Oil spreads out farther than water because of its stickiness; water is easily broken up, which is why it is harder to hold water in the hand than oil. When water—water alone—is heated, it does not show thickening. Therefore it is clear that there is another cause. For all flavors have more density. But heat is a co-cause.*

Commentary

440b28 After the Philosopher has determined about color, here he next determines about flavor.

First he says what his intention is about. Second he carries out the proposal, where he says *The nature of water* (441a3).

Accordingly he first says that after color *odor and flavor must be discussed.*

On this point he gives the cause of two things.

The first is why these should be treated in conjunction, namely because of their association, for the two are *almost the same affection.* He calls each of them an "affection" because both are in the third species of quality, which is "affection" or "passible quality." He says that flavor and odor are "almost the same" affection because both are caused by mixture of moistness and dryness following an alteration caused by heat. However, *the two of them are not* altogether *in the same things,* because odor is more a result of dryness, and so is more principally in evaporation of smoke, but flavor is more a result of moistness.

440b30 Second, where he says *But the genus of flavors,* he gives the cause why flavor must be discussed before odor. For it would seem that odor should be discussed immediately after color, because odor like color is perceived through an external medium, but flavor is not.

But the order of learning requires that one proceed from the more to the less evident, *and the genus of flavors is more evident to us than that of* odors. Hence flavors must be treated first.

Flavor is more evident to us because it is perceived by us with a surer sense. For *we have a sense of smell that is worse* both in comparison to *other animals* and in comparison to other *senses that are in us.*

The reason for this is that, as was said above, the sense of smell is brought to complete actuality by heat of fire. Now the organ of smell is near the brain, which is cooler and moister than all other parts of the body, as was established above, and the human being of all animals has the largest brain in relation to the size of his body, as is said in the book *On Parts of Animals.*[1] Therefore the human being is necessarily deficient in the sense of smell.

But the human being has *a surer sense of touch than do the other animals,* for the following reason. Since an animal's body is constituted out of objects of touch—namely heat and cold, moistness and dryness, and other such things that follow from these—it was impossible for the organ of touch to be divested of every tangible quality in the way that the pupil is without any color: rather, the organ of touch had to be in potentiality to tangible qualities in the way that an intermediate is in potentiality to the extremes, as is said in *On the Soul* II.[2] And so the sense of touch is necessarily surer to the extent that the body's complexion is more well-tempered, being brought, as it were, to an intermediate state. This must be most true in the human being, in order for his body to be proportioned to the noblest form, and so the human being of all animals has the surest touch, and consequently the surest *taste,* which is *a kind of touch.* A sign of this is that the human being is less able to withstand extremes of cold and heat than are other animals. And even among human beings, one is more mentally capable than others to the extent that he has a better sense of touch, which is evident in those who have soft flesh, as was said in *On the Soul* II.[3]

441a3 Then, when he says *The nature of water,* he carries out the proposal.

First he makes a determination about flavor according to the truth; second he eliminates the false positions of some on the nature of flavor, where he says *Democritus and most students of nature* (Ch.10, 442a29).

The first part is divided into two. In the first he determines what the nature of flavor is. In the second he determines the species of flavors, where he says *As colors come from mixture* (Ch.10, 442a12).

On the first point he does two things. First he eliminates some opinions about the generation of flavors. Second he determines the truth, where he says *However many flavors* (Ch.9, 441a30).

On the first point he does two things. First he presents three opinions about the generation of flavors. Second he disproves them, where he says *Now to say what Empedocles did* (441a10).

In determining the nature or generation of flavor he starts with water, which seems to be the subject of flavor.

He says that *the* very *nature of water* of itself *tends to be*—that is, has a natural aptitude to be—flavorless,[4] and if water does have some flavor, this is from admixture of something earthen. Yet although water is of itself flavorless, it is the root and principle of all flavors, and how this is possible was explained in three ways.

Empedocles said that all *flavors* are *in water itself* in actuality, but are *imperceptible because of the smallness* of the parts they are rooted in.

The second opinion was that of Democritus and Anaxagoras, as Alexander says in the commentary.[5] It was that flavors are not in water in actuality, but that there is in water a *matter* of flavors *like a "panspermia"*—that is, a universal seed—in such a way that *all* flavors *are made of water, different* flavors *from different parts* of water; for they held that the principles of bodies are indivisible parts. But no indivisible part is flavored in actuality: rather, a flavored body must be something composite. And so they held that these parts are not flavors in actuality, but the "seeds" of flavors, in such a way that different indivisible bodies are seeds of different flavors, as well as of different natures.

The third opinion is of those who say that *the difference* among flavors is due not to *water* itself, but to an agent that alters water in different ways, such as *the sun* or some other *hot* thing.

441a10 Then, when he says *Now to say what Empedocles did*, he disproves the opinions mentioned in order.

First, the opinion of Empedocles. He says that the statement of *Empedocles is* an *obvious falsehood*. For if the difference among flavors were present in actuality in the small parts of water, it would have to be that a change of flavor could occur only by different parts of water being drawn into the body of which the flavor is changed. But this is not always what happens: if *fruits* picked from a tree are exposed to *the sun*, or again, cooked at *a fire*, it is clear that their flavor is *changed by* the action of *heat, not* by some *"drawing in" from water.* The latter might be said about fruits that change flavor while hanging on a tree by drawing different moistures from the earth. But in fruits cut from a tree we see a change of flavor that is caused by the fruits themselves *changing* when there is a dissolution of the moisture in them through drying. Thus, *when they are laid out for a* certain *time* in the sun, they change *from sweet* to *bitter,* or the reverse, or to any other *flavors,* according to different amounts of cooking.

441a18 Second, when he says *Likewise it is also impossible* (441a18), he disproves the second opinion, that of Democritus and Anaxagoras.

He says that *it is also impossible for water to be the matter* of flavors in the sense that it contains the "seeds" of them all in such a way that its different parts would be the seeds of the different flavors, because *we see* that one and *the same* body changes to different *flavors.* For just as the same *food* taken by an animal or plant is converted into different parts of the animal or plant, so it is also converted into the different flavors appropriate to the different parts; for example, in one and the same plant there are different flavors in the root, the seed, and the fruit. And different plants fed the same nourishment have different flavors. This is a clear indication that different flavors are not caused by different parts of water. *It remains, then, that* they are caused by the fact that *water changes* from one flavor to another according as it is somehow *affected by something* that alters it.

441a21 Third, where he says *It is clear, then* (441a21), he disproves the third opinion, that of those who say that flavors are caused only by alteration of water by heat.

He says that *it is clear that* water does *not get* the quality of *a flavor only from the power of heat* that alters it. *For water is the finest of all moistures*— that is, of all bodies that are perceptibly moist; he does not say "of all moist things" because air, which is moist, is finer than water.

Now there might be a doubt about oil, because it floats on water and spreads out farther than water does. And so, to remove the doubt, he adds that water is *finer even than oil itself.* The fact that oil floats on water is because of its component of air, which is also why wood floats on water. The fact that *oil* spreads out *farther than water* is *because of* its slipperiness and *stickiness; water* is very easily divided, and so one part of it does not follow after another, as happens with oil. And because water is finer and more easily divided than oil, *it is* more difficult *to hold water in the hand than oil,* for the whole of it more easily slides out of the hand.

If *water* is pure and has nothing mixed with it, then, because of its fineness, it is *not thickened* by a hot agent as are other things, in which there are earthen parts that remain when the fine moisture evaporates. Therefore, it clearly follows *that* one must posit *another cause* of the generation of flavors than alteration of water by heat, because *all flavors* are found in bodies with some density. This does not exclude *heat* as a cause that changes water to a certain flavor; but it is not the whole cause, for something else is required. Hence it is *a co-cause* rather than a cause.

CHAPTER 9

441A30–442A11

441a30 *However many flavors show up in fruits, these exist also in earth.*

441b1 *Therefore many of the ancient students of nature say that water is of the same kind as whatever earth it passes through. This is most evident in salty water, for salt is a kind of earth. And that which is filtered through ash, which is bitter, produces a bitter flavor. There are also many springs, some bitter, some sharp-tasting, and others with every other kind of flavor.*

441b7 *And so it is reasonable that the genus of flavors is produced especially in growing things.*

441b8 *For the moist is naturally affected by its contrary, as are other things, and the contrary is the dry. Therefore it is also affected in some way by fire, for the nature of fire is dry. And heat is proper to fire and dryness to earth, as was said in the discussion of elements.*

441b12 *As fire, then, and as earth, they by nature neither act nor are affected at all; nor is this the case with anything else. Rather, they act and are acted on inasmuch as there is contrariety in each of them.*

441b15 *Accordingly, just as those who soak colors and flavors in moisture make the water be of the same kind, nature does likewise with the dry and earthen: by filtering the moist through what is dry and earthen, and by changing it through heat, it makes the moist be of a certain quality.*

441b19 *And this is flavor: an affection caused in moistness by the dryness just mentioned, an affection capable of changing the sense of taste in potentiality to actuality.*

441b21 *For it brings the sensitive part which already exists in potentiality to this. For sensing is not like learning,[1] but contemplation.*

441b23 *Now we must take it that flavors are affections or privations not of every kind of dryness, but only the kind that nourishes, because it is neither dryness without moistness nor moistness without dryness. For food for animals is not one simple thing, but something mixed. Neither is food for plants: it is something mixed.*

441b27 *Of the sensible qualities of the food provided to animals, the objects of touch are what produce growth and diminution: for the cause of these is the heat and cold that is provided, for these produce growth and diminution. But what is provided nourishes according as it is an object of taste: for everything is nourished by sweetness, whether it is simple or mixed.*

442a3 We must determine about these points in the discussion of generation, but touch on them now as far as is necessary. Heat augments, and it prepares nourishment, because it draws out what is light, but leaves what is bitter and salty because of its weight. Thus what the external heat does in external bodies is what the heat in the nature of animals and plants does. Therefore they are nourished by sweetness.

442a8 But other flavors, like spicy and sharp, are mixed into food for seasoning. And they are for opposing, because sweetness is excessively nourishing, and floating.

Commentary

441a30 After the Philosopher has eliminated opinions of others on the cause of the origin of flavors, here he gives the true cause according to his own opinion.

On this point he does three things. First he gives the cause of the generation of flavors. Second he defines flavor, where he says *And this is flavor* (441b19). Third he clarifies something he said, where he says *Now we must take it that flavors are affections* (441b23).

On the first point he does three things. First he shows that flavors pertain to earth, and not only, as the Ancients held, water. Second he shows that water is changed with respect to flavors by dryness of earth, where he says *For the moist is naturally affected* (441b8). Third he concludes to the cause of generation of flavors, where he says *Accordingly, just as those who soak colors* (441b15).

On the first point he does two things. First he proposes what he intends. Second he clarifies the proposal, where he says *Therefore many of the ancient students of nature* (441b1).

Accordingly he first says that all *flavors* that *show up in fruits* of plants, in which flavors are clearly differentiated, are *also* present *in earth*. Not that pure earth has flavor, for it has no moisture: but with a small admixture of moisture, together with an alteration caused by heat, it does acquire a flavor.

441b1 Then, when he says *Therefore many of the ancient students of nature,* he clarifies what he said by means of two signs.

The first is taken from a saying on which *many of the ancient* natural philosophers agree, namely those who *say that water is of the same kind* of flavor *as* the *earth it passes through. This is most evident in salty water:* not that of the sea itself, for that has another cause, as was shown in the book *The Meteorology;*[2] rather, this is evident because the waters of certain springs are salty, having passed through earth that is similar. This should not seem surprising, because *salt is a kind of earth,* as are alum and sulphur; thus some mountains are made of salt. The point is also clear in the case of waters *filtered through ash,* which have a *bitter flavor,* as does the ash through which they are filtered. And *there are also springs* of different flavors because of the different kinds of earth through which they pass.

It should be considered that Aristotle does not introduce this point to show the universal cause of the generation of flavors, because it only clarifies the cause of flavors in water. Rather, he introduces all this as a sign to show that flavors pertain to earth, and not only to water.

441b7 He presents the second sign where he says *And so it is reasonable.*

He says that because flavors pertain to earth, *it is reasonable that the genus of flavors* is most evident and most various in what grows directly out of the earth, because of the affinity of such things with earth.

441b8 Then, when he says *For the moist is naturally affected,* he proves that moisture of water is changed with respect to flavors by earth.

First he proves the proposition. Second he eliminates an obstacle, where he says *As fire, then* (441b12).

Accordingly he first says that *the moist is naturally affected by its contrary,* just as all *other things* are also affected by their contraries, as was proved in *On Generation* I.[3] But what is *contrary* to the moist is *the dry.* Hence the moist is naturally affected by the dry. And because not only earth is *dry,* but also *fire,* the moist *is also affected by fire.*

Now although two of the four elemental qualities belong to each individual element—fire is hot and dry, air is hot and moist, water is cold and moist, earth is cold and dry—each individual quality is in one individual element principally, as proper to that element.

Heat is proper to fire, for because fire is the noblest of the elements and the one closest to the heavenly body, what belongs to it properly and of itself is heat, which is the most active quality. Dryness belongs to fire because of the extremity of the heat: the moistness is as it were consumed.

Heat belongs to air secondarily because of the latter's affinity with fire. What belongs to air of itself is moistness, which is the nobler of the passive qualities. The heat as it were dissolves the moistness, but does not completely consume it, because of air's greater distance from the first cause of heat, the heavenly body.

What properly and of itself belongs to water is cold, which is the second active quality, being as it were privatively related to heat. What belongs secondarily to water is moistness, in keeping with the nearness of water to air.

Cold belongs to earth secondarily, because of earth's nearness to water, as it were. *Dryness* belongs properly and of itself to earth: because of earth's very great distance from the source of heat, as it were, it is not dissolved into moistness, but remains at the extreme of density.

These points were determined in the book on *elements*—that is, in *On Generation* II.[4]

Hence the moist is by nature most affected by dryness of earth.

441b12 Then, when he says *As fire, then,* he eliminates an obstacle.

It does not follow that the moist is more affected by a greater dryness unless it is affected by dryness as dryness. But someone might deny this by saying that the moist is most affected by fire as fire.

So to eliminate this, he says that fire, *as fire, by nature neither acts nor is affected at all;* nor is this the case with any other body. He proves this as follows. Things by nature *act* and *are affected* by one another, according as they have *contrariety,* as was shown in *On Generation* I. But nothing is contrary to fire inasmuch as it is fire, or to earth inasmuch as it is earth, or to any substance. Hence it remains that these bodies do not act and are not affected inasmuch as they are fire or earth or any such thing, but inasmuch as they are hot and cold, moist and dry.

Difficulties

I

But against this there seems to be a difficulty: if it belongs to fire of itself to be hot and dry, then, if fire acts inasmuch as it is hot, it seems to follow that it acts inasmuch as it is fire.

On this point it must be known that some thought that heat is the substantial form of fire, and according to this position, fire will have a contrary according to its substantial form, and consequently will be active according to it. But because "fire" signifies not the form alone, but the composite of matter and form, it is said in the text that fire is not active and that there is nothing contrary to it. This is how Alexander solves the difficulty in the commentary.[5]

But this cannot stand, because the same thing cannot be in the genus of substance and that of accident, according to the Philosopher's remark in *Physics* I: what truly is does not become an accident of anything.[6] But substantial form is reduced to the genus of substance. Hence it cannot be that heat is the substantial form of fire, since it is an accident of other things.

Again, substantial form is perceived not by sense but by intellect, for "what something is" is the proper object of intellect, as is said in *On the Soul* III.[7] Hence, since heat is something sensible per se, it cannot be the substantial form of a body.

Therefore it must be said that heat per se is present in fire not as its substantial form, but as its proper accident. And because natural action belongs to a contrary that causes alteration, fire acts according to its heat, to which there is something contrary, and not according to its substantial form, which has no contrariety.

This is unless "contrariety" is taken in a wide sense with respect to the difference between perfect and imperfect in the same genus. In this sense contrariety is also found in numbers according as a smaller number stands as something imperfect, and a part, in relation to a larger one. The substantial forms of things are like numbers, as is said in *Metaphysics* VIII.[8] And in this sense there is also contrariety between the differences of any genus, as is said in *Metaphysics* X, for thus animate and inanimate, and sensible and insensible, are contraries.[9]

II

But there still might be a difficulty. For if the principle of action in the elements is not substantial, but accidental, form, then, since nothing acts beyond its own nature, it does not seem that matter is changed by the natural action of the elements with respect to substantial form, but only with respect to accidental form.

For this reason some held that all substantial forms are from a super-natural cause, and that a natural agent merely disposes to a form by altering.[10] This reduces to an opinion of the Platonists, who held that separate forms are the cause of generation and that all action is from an incorporeal power. On the other hand the Stoics, as Alexander says, held that bodies act of themselves, that is, inasmuch as they are bodies.[11] But Aristotle here holds the middle way, which is that bodies act according to their qualities.

And so it must be said that each thing acts according as it is a being *(ens)* in actuality, as is clear from *On Generation* I.[12] But just as the being *(esse)* of elemental qualities is derived from their essential principles, so, necessarily, power of acting also belongs to such qualities from the power of the substantial forms. But everything that acts by the power of something else produces something like that in the power of which it acts: for instance a saw makes a house by the power of the house that is in the soul; and natural heat generates animate flesh by a power of soul. And it is also in this way that matter is changed by the action of elemental qualities with respect to substantial form.

441b15 Then, when he says *Accordingly, just as those who soak colors,* he concludes from the foregoing to the generation of flavors.

He says that just as *those who soak colors and flavors*—that is, colored and flavored bodies—in *moisture* of water *make the water be of the same kind* of color and flavor, so, conversely, when moistness of water is filtered through dryness of earth, and at the same time there is a change caused by *heat* digesting the moistness, and making a kind of mass of moistness with dryness, then the moistness of water becomes qualified by a flavored quality.

441b19 Then, when he says *And this is flavor,* he introduces a definition of flavor on the basis of the foregoing.

He says that *flavor is* nothing but *an affection caused in moistness* of water *by the dryness mentioned*—that is, dryness of earth—with addition of heat; an affection that, by *changing the sense of taste in potentiality,* brings it *to actuality.* This last part is added to differentiate odor from other affections that are caused by moistness and dryness through action of heat, but that alter not taste, but other senses.

441b21 Then, when he says *For it brings the sensitive part,* he clarifies the definition of flavor just stated with respect to its last part. For the first part is clear from the foregoing; but he said that flavor alters the sense of taste "in potentiality."

To clarify this he adds that flavor, like any sensible object, *brings to actuality the sensitive part,* which previously was *in potentiality to* the sensible object, because *sensing,* which follows from the action of a sensible object on a sense-power, *is not like learning, but contemplation.* That is, it is unlike what learning is, because a habit of science is newly produced in one who learns, but a sense-power is not newly produced by the action of the sensible object in one who senses: rather, the sense-power is made operative in actuality, which is like what happens in one who contemplates in actuality.

441b23 Then, when he says *Now we must take it that flavors are affections,* he clarifies something he said above, namely that flavor is not only in moistness or in dryness.

On this point he does three things. First he shows that flavor is based on the moist and the dry together. Second he proves something he presupposed, where he says *Of the sensible qualities* (441b27). Third he clarifies the proof, where he says *We must determine* (442a3).

Accordingly he first says that *flavors are affections*—with respect to sweet—*or privations*—with respect to bitter, which is related to sweet, as black is to white, that is, as something imperfect and a privation—*not of* just any *dryness, but of* nourishing dryness—that is, the dryness by which animals or plants can be nourished. From this we can take it *that neither dryness without moistness nor moistness without dryness* pertains to flavor, because the *food* by which *animals* are nourished *is not* what is just moist or dry, *but something mixed* from these. For we are nourished by the same things out of which we are composed, as was said in *On Generation* II.[13] And the argument is the same in the case of *plants.*

441b27 Then, when he says *Of the sensible qualities,* he proves something he presupposed, namely that flavor is an affection or privation in nourishment.

Here it must be considered that the food that is provided to animals serves them for two purposes, namely growth, by which they are brought to perfect size, and nourishment, by which their substance is preserved. Food also serves them for generation, but this no longer pertains to the individual, but the species.

Accordingly he says that *the food provided to animals,* being *sensible* objects inasmuch as they are *objects of touch,* cause *growth and diminution,* because *heat and cold* cause growth and diminution: heat properly causes growth, for it belongs to heat to expand and spread out, moving, as it were, towards a circumference; cold causes diminution, because it belongs to cold to constrict, moving, as it were, towards a center. Hence animals grow in youth and shrink in old age. The remark in *On the Soul* II that food causes growth inasmuch as it is quantitative does not contradict this, because quantity would not suffice for growth if there were not heat to convert and digest it.[14]

But the food *provided nourishes* inasmuch as it is *an object of taste.* He proves this as follows: *everything is nourished by sweetness,* which is perceived by taste, *whether* by *simple* sweetness *or* by sweetness *mixed* with other flavors. And the remark of *On the Soul* II that touch is "the sense of food" does not contradict this, because there he places "moisture"—that is, flavor—among the objects of touch, and in the same place he says that flavor is "the pleasurable in food" inasmuch as it indicates suitability of food.[15]

442a3 Then, when he says *We must determine,* he confirms the foregoing proof.

First inasmuch as he said that everything is nourished by sweetness. Second inasmuch as he said something about admixture of other flavors, where he says *But other flavors* (442a8).

Accordingly he first says that *we must determine* what pertains to growth and nourishment *in the discussion of generation.* He said something about this in the book *On Generation* in general,[16] but still more has to be said about it in the book *On the Generation of Animals,* to which the consideration of food of animals pertains.[17] *But now, as far as* pertains to the present proposal, one point must be touched on, namely that natural *heat* actively *augments* by an expansion, *and prepares nourishment* by digesting, inasmuch as it *draws out what is light* and sweet and *leaves what is salty and bitter because of* its heaviness, which is why all feces of animals are quite bitter or salty. He illustrates this by something similar in the universe as a whole. What natural *heat* does in *animals and plants,* the sun's *heat does in external bodies:* it draws out the fine moistness and leaves what is earthen and dense. Hence rainwater is sweet, although the sea, from which most evaporation occurs, is salty. From this he concludes that all things are *nourished by sweetness*, which is drawn out by natural heat.

442a8 Then when he says *But other flavors*, he gives the cause of the admixture of other flavors into food.

He says that *other flavors are mixed* in sweet *food*, which alone nourishes, *for seasoning*, as is evident with the *spicy and sharp* flavor, so that they may restrain the *sweetness* from *nourishing excessively*. For sweetness is extremely filling, *and floating*, for it is easily drawn out by heat because of its lightness.

CHAPTER 10

442A12–B26

442a12 *As colors come from mixture of white and black, so flavors from sweet and bitter.*

442a13 *And these are also according to proportions, for each is more or less, whether according to numbers in the mixture and the change, or indeterminately. But the ones that cause pleasure are only those mixed numerically.*

442a17 *The sweet flavor is rich-tasting; bitter and salty are almost the same; pungent, harsh, astringent, and sharp are in the middle.*

442a19 *The species of moistures and of colors are almost equal. If one posits seven species of each, then, as it is reasonable for gray to be a kind of black, it follows that yellow belongs to white as oily does to sweet. And in the middle between black and white are punic, alurgon, green, and cyanum. And the others are mixed from these.*

442a25 *As black is privation of white in the transparent, so bitter and salty are of sweet in the nourishing moist. Therefore the ash of all burnt things is bitter, for the potable has been evaporated from them.*

442a29 *Democritus and most students of nature—whichever ones speak about the senses—do something very inconsistent: they make all sensible objects, objects of touch. If this is so, it is clear also that each of the other senses is a kind of touch. But it is not difficult to discern that this is impossible.*

442b4 *Moreover, they treat the common objects of all the senses as if they were proper. Size and shape, rough and smooth, and the sharp and dull that are in masses, are common objects of the senses—if not of all of them, then of sight and touch. Therefore they are deceived about these, but they are not deceived about the proper objects; for instance, sight is not deceived about color or hearing about sounds.*

442b10 *Some reduce the proper objects to these, as Democritus does. Of white and black, he says that one is "rough," the other "smooth." And he reduces flavors to shapes.*

442b13 *But to know the common objects belongs either to no sense, or above* *all to sight. If it were above all to taste, then, since it belongs to the surest sense to discern what is smallest in any genus, taste would have to be best at perceiving the other common objects, and best at discerning shapes.*

442b17 *Moreover, all sensible objects have contrariety, for example of white to black in color, and of bitter to sweet in flavors. But shape is not thought to be contrary to shape. For to which of the polygons is the circumference contrary?*

442b21 *Moreover, since there are infinite shapes, there would necessarily be infinite flavors. Why then does this one cause a sensation but not that one?*

442b23 *Something, then, has been said about flavor and the object of taste. Other affections of flavors have their proper consideration in the philosophy about plants.*

Commentary

442a12 After the Philosopher has determined the generation of flavor, here he distinguishes species of flavors.

On this point he does three things. First he shows the generation of intermediate flavors in general. Second he shows how intermediate flavors are diversified, where he says *And these are also according to proportions* (442a13). Third he shows how sweet and bitter are related to one another, where he says *As black is privation of white* (442a25).

Accordingly he first says that as intermediate *colors* are generated from *mixture of white and black, so* intermediate *flavors* are generated from mixture of *sweet and bitter,* whether from these in themselves or from mixture of the causes of sweet and bitter.

Heat causes the sweet flavor by thoroughly digesting the moisture. The cause of bitterness is privation of this completely digested moisture. Other flavors are caused according as the moisture is in an intermediate state because it is neither wholly consumed nor wholly undigested.

Flavor more immediately follows from moisture than from heat. Therefore, one should consider the intermediate and extremes not in relation to heat, but in relation to moisture affected in a way by dryness and heat, for the nature of flavor principally consists in this. Otherwise, if the intermediate and extremes in flavor were taken in relation to heat, sweet and bitter would not be extremes, but sweet would be intermediate. For intense heat that consumes the cold, but does not digest <the moisture>, causes bitterness; heat that, because of the dominance of cold, entirely fails to digest <the moisture> causes the pungent or the sour flavor; and a moderate heat sufficient to digest <the moisture> causes sweetness.

442a13 Then, when he says *And these are also according to proportions,* he treats of the distinction of intermediate flavors.

First with respect to the difference between pleasant and unpleasant; second with respect to terms, where he says *The sweet flavor is rich-tasting* (442a17); third with respect to number, in a comparison with colors, where he says *The species of moistures* (442a19).

Accordingly he first says that intermediate flavors vary *according to* different *proportions* of the mixture, that is, inasmuch as *each* of them either *more or less* approaches sweetness or bitterness. This happens in two ways, as described in the case of colors:[1] in one way *according to* a numerical proportion observed in *the mixture* described, and in the alteration of the moisture by the heat; in another way according to an indeterminate difference without numerical proportion. And *only* those flavors are pleasing to taste that are *mixed* according to a numerical proportion.

442a17 Then, when he says *The sweet flavor is rich-tasting,* he distinguishes intermediate flavors by name.

He says that the *rich-tasting* flavor is almost the same as the *sweet,* for both indicate digestion of the moisture by the heat. However, the heat evidently dominates the moisture more in the sweet flavor. Thus the rich-tasting flavor is closer to a watery or insipid flavor, because of an abundance of the moisture in it.

Likewise the *bitter* flavor *and* the *salty are almost the same,* for both evidence an extreme heat that consumes the moisture. However, there seems to be greater consumption of moisture in the bitter than in the salty: in the salty the moisture infused into the body seems to be consumed; but in the bitter the moisture binding together the substance of the body seems to be not just consumed, but dissolved, whether in whole or in part. Hence the remains of dissolved and burnt bodies are bitter.

In the middle are the pungent flavor, i.e. the flavor with "bite"; *the harsh,* i.e. vinegary flavor; *the astringent; and the sharp.*

The pungent and the vinegary consist in moisture that, because of the weakness of the heat, is undigested. For this reason unripened fruits have either a vinegar flavor, like sour plums, or a pungent flavor, like sour pears. But the pungent seems to have more earth, which is why earth has an almost pungent flavor. The vinegary seems to have more cold.

The astringent flavor seems also to have much earth: it is close to the pungent, but it has more heat, for it more closely approaches digestion <of the moisture>. Hence some dried fruits *(digesta),* for example myrtle-berries, have an astringent flavor.

The sharp flavor indicates an excess of heat that does not consume, but thoroughly digests, the moisture.

442a19 Then, when he says *The species of moistures,* he distinguishes intermediate flavors with respect to number by means of a comparison with colors.

He says that *the species of "moistures"*—that is, flavors—*are almost equal* in number to the species *of colors. Seven species* of flavors are to be enumerated, in such a way that the rich-tasting flavor is not distinguished from the sweet, but the salty is distinguished from the bitter. Thus, if to the other four are added these three flavors, there will be seven flavors.

Likewise it is *reasonable* to say, on the side of colors, that *gray* is related to *black* as salty is to bitter; and that *yellow* is related to *white as* rich-tasting is to *sweet.*

In the middle will be these colors: *"punic,"* i.e. red; *"alurgon,"* i.e. citron; *green; and "cyanum"* or blue, i.e. the color of the sky. These are arranged such that green and blue more closely approach black, while red and citron more closely approach white.

There are also very many *other* species of colors and flavors by mixture of the species mentioned with one another.

442a25 Then, when he says *As black is privation of white,* he compares bitter to sweet.

He says that as *black is the privation of white in the transparent, so bitter* or *salty* is the privation *of sweet in nourishing moisture.* For one of two contraries always stands as a privation, as is clear from *Metaphysics* X.[2] Because bitter is the privation of sweet, *the ash of all burnt things is bitter,* because of evaporation of the nourishing moistness, which he calls *"the potable."*

442a29 Then, when he says *Democritus and most students of nature,* he eliminates false opinions of others about the nature of flavors.

First with reference to all sensible objects in general. Second with reference to flavors in particular, where he says *Some reduce the proper objects* (442b10).

On the first point he does two things. He disproves the opinion of the Ancients, first inasmuch as they reduced all sensible objects to tangible qualities; second inasmuch as they reduced proper sensible objects to common sensibles, where he says *Moreover, they treat the common objects* (442b4).

Accordingly he first says that *Democritus and most* natural philosophers—*whichever ones* got involved in speaking *about the senses—do something very inconsistent,* because they say that *all sensible objects* are *objects of touch. If this* were true, it would follow that any sense-power would be *touch,* since powers are distinguished according to objects. But it is easy to see that this is false, because other senses perceive through an external medium, and touch does not.

442b4 Then, when he says *Moreover, they treat the common objects,* he criticizes the Ancients for treating *the common* sensible *objects as if they were proper.* They reduced colors, flavors, and other sensible objects to size and shape. *Size and shape; rough and smooth* according as they pertain to shape; *and* likewise *sharp and dull,* which pertain to features of shapes that have angles—these *are common objects of the senses.* Although *not* all of them are perceived by *all* senses, all are perceived at least by *touch and sight,* and so they are not proper sensibles, because thus they would be perceived by only one sense.

He speaks of the sharp and the dull *"in masses" (in glebis),* or, according to another reading, *"in bulks" (in molibus).*[3] He means the sharp and the dull "in bodies," and he says this in order to distinguish them from what is called "sharp" in the case of voices, and in the case of flavors.

He shows that the foregoing are common sensibles by means of a sign: the senses *are deceived* about the kinds of things mentioned, but *are not deceived about the proper* sensibles; *for instance, sight is not deceived about color or hearing about sounds.*

442b10 Then, when he says *Some reduce the proper objects,* he eliminates the opinions on a specific point.

First he relates them. Second he disproves them, where he says *But to know the common objects* (442b13).

Accordingly he first says that *some reduce the proper* sensible *objects to these* common ones. For example, *Democritus* said that *black* is *rough,* thinking that the darkness of black is caused by higher parts in the roughness hiding the other parts; and he said that *white* is *smooth,* thinking that the brightness of white comes from the smoothness being completely illuminated because its parts lie level. *And he* reduced *flavors to shapes,* because he found "sharp and dull" in flavors as well as in shapes, being deceived by an equivocation.

442b13 Then, when he says *But to know the common objects,* he disproves the abovementioned opinion about flavors by three arguments.

The first is that *no sense* apprehends shapes as its proper objects, and if they were the proper objects of a sense, they would pertain *above all to sight.* But if flavors were shapes, it would follow that taste above all would know them. *If* this is true, then, since any sense is surer inasmuch as it can better *discern* even *what is smallest in any genus,* it would follow that *taste,* as *the surest sense,* would be *best* at sensing the *common* sensibles, *and best at discerning shapes,* which is obviously false, because sight is more powerful in this regard.

442b17 He presents the second argument where he says *Moreover, all sensible objects.*

It is this. *All sensible objects have contrariety,* because alteration occurs with respect to them, as was proved in *Physics* VII.[4] *For example, in color* the contraries are *black* and *white, in flavors sweet* and *bitter,* and the same is clear in other cases.

There seems to be an exception in the case of light, which of itself does not have contrariety: for it exists as a proper quality of the highest body, which is without contrariety; and darkness is opposed to it as a privation, not a contrary. However, light does have contrariety according as it is participated in colors.

But shape does *not* seem *to be contrary to shape, for* it is impossible to determine *to which of the polygons*—that is, figures with several angles—*the circumference*—that is, the circle, which has no angles—*is contrary.* For contraries stand farthest apart, but no shape can be instanced such that another shape with more angles cannot be found. Therefore flavors are not shapes.

442b21 He presents the third argument where he says *Moreover, since there are infinite shapes.*

It is this. *Shapes* are *infinite,* as are also numbers, for they are multiplied according to the number of angles and lines, as is clear in the triangle and the square. Therefore, if flavors were shapes, it would follow that there are *infinite* species of *flavors*. This is clearly false, because there is no reason *why* one flavor would be perceived and *not* another. But the sense-power does not discern an infinite number of flavors. Therefore flavors are not shapes.

442b23 Finally, adding an epilogue, he concludes that *something has been said about flavor and the object of taste,* but *other* properties *of flavors have their proper consideration in* the book *On Plants.* However, Aristotle did not write this book, but Theophrastus, as Alexander says at this point in the commentary.[5]

CHAPTER 11

442B27–443B16

442b27 *Odors must be understood in the same way. For what dryness causes in moistness, enchymous moistness causes in another genus, namely air, and water as well.*

442b29 *We now call what is common in these the transparent. But this is an object of smell not according as it is transparent, but according as it is capable of being soaked or cleansed by enchymous dryness.*

443a2 *The odorous is not only in air, but also in water. This is clear in the case of fish and testacea, for they seem to smell. And air does not exist in water, for it floats to the top when it is in water. And these animals do not breathe.*

443a6 *Accordingly, if one holds that water and air are both moist, odor will be the nature of enchymous dryness in moisture, and the odorous is what is such.*

443a8 *That this affection is caused by the enchymous is clear both from what has and from what does not have odor. For the elements, namely fire, air, earth, water, are odorless, because both the dry and the moist ones are achymous unless a mixture is made. This is why the sea has odor, for it has moisture and dryness. And salt is more odorous than niter (the fact that oil flows out of these is revealing), but niter has more earth.*

Moreover, a stone is odorless, for it is achymous. But woods are odorous, for they are enchymous, and those that are watery are less odorous.

Moreover, among metals, gold is odorless, for it is achymous. Brass and iron are odorous, but when the moisture is burned out of them, their slag is made odorless. Silver and tin are more odorous than some, but less than others, for they are watery.

443a21 *Now it seems to some that odor is a smoky evaporation, and that this is common to earth and air. They all speak of odor on this basis. Thus Heraclitus says that if all beings became smoke, the nostrils would discern them. They all introduce some such cause of odor, some presenting it as an "exhalation," some as an "evaporation," and some as both of these. Vapor is a kind of moisture, but smoky exhalation, as was said, is something common to air and earth. Water is produced from the former, but a kind of earth from the latter.*

443a29 *But odor seems to be neither of these, for vapor belongs to water, but smoky evaporation cannot occur in water. For animals in water also smell, as was said above.*

443b1 *Moreover, they use the term "evaporation" as they do the term "emanations." Therefore, if the latter is not correct, neither is the former.*

443b3 *Therefore it is not hard to see that moisture—both that in wind and that in water—can receive and be affected in some way by enchymous dryness. For air too is by nature moist.*

443b6 *Moreover, if this produces in what is moist and in air something like dryness that has been soaked, it is clear that odors must be analogous to moistures.*

443b8 *And in some cases they are so, for odors are also "sour" and "sweet" and "harsh" and "pungent" and "rich." And one might say that what is putrid is analogous to what is bitter: as the latter is difficult to drink, what is putrid is dysanapneustic. It is clear, then, that what flavor is in water, odor is in air and water.*

443b14 *For this reason cold and cohesion make flavors dull and drive out odors: for cold and cohesion remove the heat that moves and generates them.*

Commentary

442b27 After the Philosopher has made a determination about flavors, here he begins to make a determination about odors.

This is divided into two parts. In the first he makes the determination about odors. In the second he compares the sense of smell to the other senses, where he says *The senses exist in an odd number* (Chapter 13, 445a4).

On the first point he does two things. First he determines the generation and the nature of odor. Second he determines the species of odor, where he says *There are two species of the odorous* (Chapter 12, 443b17).

On the first point he does two things. First he shows what is passive in the generation of odors. Second he shows what is active in it, where he says *That this affection is caused by the enchymous* (443a8).

On the first point he does three things. First he presents his intention. Second, he explains something he said, where he says *We now call what is common* (442b29). Third he proves it, where he says *The odorous is not only in air* (443a2).

Accordingly he first says that the generation of *odors must be understood in the same way* as that of flavors: that is, there is something passive and something active. What was said about flavors was that the *moistness* of water is affected by the *dryness* of earth, and thus is brought by the action of heat to the condition of being flavored. But what is active in the generation of odor is *enchymous moistness*. It is called "enchymous" from "en," which means "in," and "chymous," which means "moisture": for the moisture exists as, so to speak, drunk in by and incorporated into something dry. This, then, is what is active in odor. What is passive is *another genus* that includes *air and water*.

442b29 Then when he says *We now call what is common,* he explains what this genus is that is common to air and water and is receptive of odor.

He says that *what is common* to the two is called *the transparent*. However, the transparent *as transparent is* receptive *not* of odor, but of color, as was established above:[1] *but* it is receptive of odor *according as it is capable of being soaked or cleansed by enchymous dryness,* that is, according as it is receptive of enchymous dryness. He calls this reception a "soaking" or a "cleansing" inasmuch as a thing is naturally washed or cleansed by the moisture it receives.

443a2 Then when he says *The odorous is not only in air,* he proves something he presupposed, namely that not only air but also water is receptive of odor.

First he introduces a proof of this. Second he concludes to what is properly receptive of odor, where he says *Accordingly, if one holds that water and air* (443a6).

Accordingly he first says that odor is received *not only in air, but also in water.* This is clearly shown by the fact that *fish and testacea*—that is, hard-shelled animals that live in water—*seem to smell* from the fact that they are attracted from a distance by odor to food they cannot see. From this it is clear, by two arguments, that water is receptive of odor.

First, these animals live not in air but water. And he proves that there is no air under water, where fish of this kind live, by the fact that *air floats to the top* of water even if it is put underwater. This is evident in the case of an inflated bag, which, if submerged by force, will float to the surface of the water.

Second, even granting that there is air under water, nevertheless such animals *do not breathe* air. Therefore, if only air were receptive of odor, they would not perceive odor.

443a6 Then, when he says *Accordingly, if one holds that water and air,* he concludes to what is properly receptive of odor.

He says that because *air and water,* which are receptive of odor, *are moist,* it follows that *odor* is nothing but the *"nature"*—that is, the form—impressed by *enchymous dryness* on the *moisture* that is air and water. *And the odorous is what is such:* that is, moisture with a "nature" impressed on it by enchymous dryness.

443a8 Then, when he says *That this affection is caused by the enchymous,* he proves that the enchymous causes odor.

He proves this in three ways: first by what has and what does not have odor; second, where he says *Now it seems to some* (443a21), by different opinions some have held about odor; third, where he says *Moreover, if this produces* (443b6), by the affinity of odor with flavor.

Accordingly he first says that it *is clear, both from what has and from what does not have odor, that this affection* that is odor is impressed *by the enchymous*—that is, by moistness instilled in and absorbed by dryness, as was said above.[2]

First, because all *the elements,* namely *fire, air, water,* and *earth,* lack odor. For whether they are *moist* or *dry,* they *are achymous*—that is, without moisture absorbed by dryness—for those that are moist have moistness without dryness, and those that are dry have dryness without moistness. This is the case *unless a mixture* of elements *is made.* Thus *the sea has* an *odor,* because *dryness* of earth has been mixed into *moisture* of water in it, as is clear from its salty flavor: for *salt* has even *more* odor *than* does *niter.* And that these two—salt and niter—do have something of the enchymous, is clear from the *oil* that is brought *out of* them by means of a certain technique, which shows that there is in them an oily moisture absorbed by dryness. *But niter* has less of this moisture than does salt, and so is less odorous.

Second, he shows the same thing in the case of stones and woods. He says that a solid and hard *stone* lacks odor because, due to its great component of earth, it does not have the odor-causing moisture mentioned. *But woods* do have odor because they do have something of the moisture mentioned, as is clear from the fact that they are inflammable because of an oiliness that exists in them. Hence woods that have a more *watery* and less oily moisture—one that is not absorbed, as it were, by dryness—are less odorous. This is clearly the case with poplar wood. But fir and pine woods are very odorous because of the oiliness of their moisture.

Third, he shows the same thing in the case of *metals,* among which *gold is* completely *odorless,* because it lacks the moisture mentioned; this is due to its large component of earth, which is indicated by its very great weight: for it is heavier than other metals. *Brass and iron are odorous,* because the moisture in them is digested and drunk in by the dryness, but not wholly overcome by it, as it is in the case of gold; hence *their slag* is less odorous because of the burning off of *the moisture* in them. *Silver and tin are more odorous than* gold, *but less than* brass and iron: for they have a moisture that is more *watery* and less absorbed by dryness than do brass and iron; however, because their moisture is in a way absorbed by dryness, they are not completely odorless like gold.

443a21 Then, when he says *Now it seems to some,* he shows that the enchymous is what is active in odor through opinions of others.

On this point he does three things. First he presents the opinions of the others. Second he eliminates them, where he says *But odor seems to be neither of these* (443a29). Third he concludes to his proposal, where he says *Therefore it is not hard to see* (443b3).

Accordingly he first says that *it seems to some that odor is a smoky evaporation,* smoke being *common to air and earth,* i.e. an intermediary between them, as it were, because it is something dissolved from dryness of earth that does not achieve the fineness of air. *All* of the Ancients *speak of odor* in a way close to this position. Hence *Heraclitus says that if all beings* were dissolved into *smoke, the nostrils,* in perceiving odor, *would discern* all beings, as if to say that all beings would be odors. For Heraclitus thought that vapor is a principle of things. But not all philosophers held that odor is smoke; some held that it is just something like it. Therefore, in order to show this diversity, he adds that *some* assigned *"exhalation"* to *odor, some "evaporation," and some both.* And he shows the difference between these two: evaporation is nothing but dissolved *moisture* of water, but exhalation or smoke *is something common to air and earth,* since it is something dissolved from dryness of earth, *as was said.*[3] A sign of this difference is that when vapor is condensed, *water is* generated from it, but when exhalation of smoke is condensed, something earthen is generated from it.

443a29 Then, when he says *But odor seems to be neither of these,* he eliminates the above-mentioned positions by two arguments.

The first is that *vapor* pertains to *water,* which is not odorous without an admixture of dryness, as was said above.[4] But smoke *cannot occur in water,* although odor does occur in it, as was shown above by the fact that some animals can smell in water. Therefore odor is neither smoke nor vapor.

443b1 Then, when he says *Moreover, they use the term "evaporation,"* he presents the second argument.

It is this. The argument that odor should be called an *"evaporation"* is similar to the argument that colors should be called *"emanations."* But, as was shown above, *the latter is not a correct* description of colors;[5] *therefore, neither is the former* a correct description of odors. For in both cases it would follow that sensing occurs through contact, whether of the odors or of the colors, and that bodies seen and smelled are diminished and finally completely dissolved by the emanation or dissolution. And this is unreasonable, especially since a thing can be seen and smelled from such a distance that there is no way that something dissolved from the body could be carried that far. Rather, perception of both color and odor occurs at such distance through a spiritual alteration of the medium.

443b3 Then, when he says *Therefore it is not hard to see,* he concludes to the proposal, namely that, because odor is neither vapor nor smoke, it is clear that *moisture in "wind"*—that is, air—*and water* is *affected by enchymous dryness,* and thus odor occurs and is perceived. *For* moisture is present not only in water, but also in *air.*

443b6 Then, when he says *Moreover, if this produces,* he shows that the enchymous is what is active in odor by the affinity of odor with flavor.

On this point he does three things.

First he presents the proposal. He says that *if* the enchymous causes odor in the moisture of water *and air,* in the way that the *dryness* of earth *soaked* by the moisture of water causes flavors, *it is clear that odors must be analogous to* flavors.

443b8 Second, where he says *And in some cases,* he clarifies the proposal by co-coordinating odors with flavors.

He says that *in some cases* this coordination is evident. *For odors* are called *"sour" and "sweet" and "harsh"*—that is, astringent—*and "pungent" and "rich,"* just like flavors. But we do not call odors "bitter": rather, *putrid* odors correspond analogously to *bitter* flavors, for just as bitter flavors are swallowed with difficulty, so *what is putrid is "dysanapneustic"*—that is, difficult to inhale. Hence *it is clear* from this affinity of odor with flavor that *flavor* occurs *in water* in the way that *odor* occurs *in air and water.*

443b14 Third, where he says *For this reason,* he proves the above-mentioned affinity through impediments to flavor and odor.

Flavors are made *dull, and odors* are driven out, by *cold and* freezing, inasmuch as *the heat that generates and moves* odors and flavors is removed by cold and freezing, as is clear from what was said.[6]

CHAPTER 12

443B17–444B7

443b17 *There are two species of the odorous. For it is not the case that, as some say, there are no species of the odorous; there are. But the ways in which there are and are not must be determined.*

443b19 *One kind of odor is ordered according to flavors, as was said. These contain the pleasant and unpleasant accidentally. For because odor is an affection of nourishment, these odors are pleasant to those that have an appetite. But to those that are full and not in need, neither the odors nor the food that has the odors is pleasant. Therefore, as we said, these contain the pleasant and unpleasant accidentally, and for this reason they are common objects for all animals.*

443b26 *But some odors, such as those of flowers, are pleasant of themselves.*

443b28 *For they do not follow from food with respect to more and less. And they do not contribute anything to desire, but rather the contrary. For what Thracius said in criticism of Euripides is true: "When you cook lentils, you don't pour on ointment."*

443b31 *And those who do mix such virtues into drinks do violence to pleasure by the practice until it becomes pleasant to two senses, in the way that one thing is pleasant to one.*

444a3 *This species of the odorous, then, is proper to the human being. But the kind that is ordered according to flavors is also an object for other animals, as was said above. And because the latter contains the pleasant accidentally, its species are divided according to flavors. But the former is not, because its very nature is, of itself, pleasant or unpleasant.*

444a8 *Now the cause of this kind of odor being proper to the human being is the coolness around his brain. For the brain is cool by nature. And the blood around it in narrow veins is fine and pure, but easily cooled. For this reason, fumes from food, when cooled because of the coolness of this region, cause rheumatic illnesses in human beings. This kind of odor is produced as an aid to health, for it has no other function than this, and this it clearly has.*

444a16 *The odor that is pleasant because of food, dry or moist, is often un-*

healthy. But that which is pleasant because of odor that is of itself odorous, what-
ever it may be, is always useful, so to speak.

444a19 *For this reason it is done by breathing—not in all animals, but in*
human beings and those that have blood, such as quadrupeds and those partici-
pate more in the nature of air.

444a22 *When odors rise to the brain because of the lightness of the heat in*
them, this area is healthier. For odor by nature has the power of heat. Nature
uses breathing for two things: actively as an aid to the chest, and adventitiously
for odor. For in breathing one causes movement through the nostrils as through a
passageway. This genus of odor is proper to the nature of the human being be-
cause he has a bigger and moister brain in proportion to his size than do the oth-
er animals. And for this reason the human being, alone among the animals so to
speak, senses and enjoys the odors of flowers and such things: for their heat and
movement are commensurate with the hyperbole in this area of coolness and
moistness.

444b2 *To the other animals that have lungs nature gave sensation of the oth-*
er kind of odor by means of breathing, so as not to make two sensitive parts. For
this is sufficient. Just as it is by breathing that human beings have sensation of
both kinds of the odorous, in the same way these animals have sensation of just
one kind.

Commentary

443b17 After the Philosopher has determined the generation and nature of odor, here he determines the species of odors.

On this point he does two things. First he determines the various
species of odor. Second he determines the modes of smelling, where he
says *For this reason* (444a19).

On the first point he does three things. First he proposes that there
are species of odor. Second he determines the species of odor by correspondence with species of flavor, where he says *One kind of odor*
(443b19). Third he determines the species belonging to odor of itself,
where he says *But some odors* (443b26).

Accordingly he first says that *there are two species of the odorous,* one by
correspondence with flavors, the other pertaining to odor in itself. For
what *some say,* that *the odorous* does not have species, is false, for it does.
But we have to determine *the ways in which* it does and does *not* have
species.

It is possible to determine species of odors by agreement with species of flavors, as was said above.[1] But the species of odor in itself are determined only by reference to the different kinds of odorous things, as when we say that the odors of roses, violets, and other such things are different. It is in these odors that the pleasant and the unpleasant are discerned.

443b19 Then, when he says *One kind of odor,* he determines about the species of odors that follow from the species of flavors.

He says that among odorous things, *one kind is ordered according to* the species of flavor, *as was said* above, *and* so *the pleasant and unpleasant* are in them *accidentally,* that is, not inasmuch as they have odor, but inasmuch as their odor indicates nourishment. For odor *is* an *affection of nourishment,* as flavor also is: for an animal discerns appropriate nourishment from a distance by means of odor, as it discerns appropriate nourishment taken in by means of flavor. And so these *odors* are not *pleasant* to animals *that are full and not in need* of food, just as neither is *food that has* these *odors pleasant* to them; but it is *pleasant to* animals *that have an appetite* for food—that is, ones that are thirsty or hungry—just as food or drink is also desirable to them. Hence it is clear that this kind of odorous contains *the pleasant and unpleasant accidentally*—that is, because of nourishment—*as* was *said.*[2] And because nourishment is common to all animals, *all animals* perceive these odors. But the "all" must be understood with reference to animals that have forward movement, and have to seek food from a distance by means of odor; in the case of immobile animals, taste and touch suffice for discerning suitability of food.

443b26 Then, when he says *But some odors,* he determines the per se species of odor.

First he presents these species of odor. Second he shows which animals perceive them, where he says *This species of the odorous* (444a3).

On the first point he does three things. First he presents what he intends. Second he proves the proposal, where he says *For they do not follow* (443b28). Third he eliminates an objection to the contrary, where he says *And those who do mix* (443b31).

Accordingly he first says that *some odors are pleasant* of their very selves, that is, not in relation to food, and this is said to be the case with the odors *of flowers.*

443b28 Then, when he says *For they do not follow*, he proves that such odors are of themselves pleasant.

This is because they are not related to *food* as a consequence of it, that is, such that animals with an appetite for food take *more* pleasure in these odors, and animals that are full *less* pleasure. Also, such odors *do not contribute anything to desire* for food in the way that the odors discussed above provoke an appetite for food. *Rather the contrary* occurs: food is made unpleasant by being mixed with things that have this kind of odor, because often what smells good inasmuch as it has this kind of odor, nevertheless has a bad taste. To confirm this he introduces a saying of a certain comic poet named *Thracius* or Stratides, who, in criticism of another poet—namely *Euripides*, who devised very fastidiously prepared dishes—said: *"When you cook lentils, you don't pour on ointment"*—that is, sweet-smelling perfume; as if to say: "You shouldn't add anything sweet-smelling to your relish."

443b31 Then, when he says *And those who do mix*, he eliminates an objection that could be made because of the custom of some who do mix such things into food.

He answers by saying that *those who do mix "virtues"*—that is, odorous things—of this kind with food and drink *do violence to* natural *pleasure by* their custom in order to reach a point where one and the same thing is *pleasant to two senses*, namely taste and smell, whereas by nature *one thing is* pleasant *to one* sense.

444a3 Then when he says *This species of the odorous*, he shows by what animals such objects of smell are perceived.

On this point he does three things. First he presents what he intends. Second he gives a cause of what was said, where he says *Now the cause of this kind of odor* (444a8). Third he excludes an objection, where he says *The odor that is pleasant* (444a16).

Accordingly he first says that *this species of the odorous* that of itself pleases or displeases *is proper to the human being*, for the human being alone discerns such objects of smell and is pleased or displeased by them; hence, to this extent, the sense of smell is richer in the human being than in other animals. But odor that is coordinated with flavor *is also an object for other animals*, which have a more acute sense than does the human being for discerning such odors; and to this extent, as he said above, we have a worse sense of smell than do other animals. And because those odors that are coordinated with flavors *contain the pleasant accidentally*—that is, in relation to food—their *species* are distinguished *according to* species of *flavors,* which is *not* the case with these odors that of their own *nature* contain the *unpleasant or pleasant:* rather, species of this kind of odor can be distinguished only with reference to odorous things, as was said.[3]

444a8 Then, when he says *Now the cause of this kind of odor,* he gives the cause of what was said.

He says that *odor* that is of itself pleasant is an object *proper to the human being* for moderating the *coolness* of his *brain.* For the human being has a larger brain, in relation to the size of his body, than do other animals. But *the brain is by* its *nature cool, and the blood* contained in fine *veins around* the brain is *easily cooled.* Because of this, vapors dissolved from *food,* rising upwards and being *cooled because of* the coolness of *the region,* sometimes become thick, which causes *rheumatic illnesses in human beings.* And so *this kind of odor* was given to human beings as *an aid to health,* to counter the excessive coolness of the brain. And if such odors sometimes cause headache, this is because they are not applied as they should be, but rather overheat the brain and cause too much evaporation. But if they are applied in the right way they contribute to health. And *this clearly* appears from their effect, although no other usefulness of such odor is apparent: for perception of such odors hardly serves intellect at all for investigating natures of things, whereas sight and hearing serve it very much, as was shown above.[4]

444a16 Then, when he says *The odor that is pleasant,* he eliminates an objection. For someone might say that the other kind of object of smell, which is coordinated with flavor, would suffice for the remedy for health mentioned.

He answers that the kind of odor *that is pleasant* because of *food often* rather causes headache, because of either excessive moistness or excessive dryness. *But* the kind of odor *that is in itself* pleasant *is always useful* for health of its own nature. He adds *"so to speak"* because of the improper use.

444a19 Then, when he says *For this reason,* he concludes from what was said above to the appropriate modes of smelling.

First in the human being and other breathing animals; second in non-breathing animals, where he says *It is clear that the ones that do not breathe* (Ch.13, 444b7).

On the first point he does three things. First he presents what he intends. Second he gives the cause proposed with reference to human beings where he says *When odors rise to the brain* (444a22); and third with reference to other animals where he says *To the other animals* (444b2).

Accordingly he first says that because odor is useful for moderating coolness of the brain, smelling *is done by breathing—not in all* animals, *but in human beings and those that have blood, such as quadrupeds* and birds, the latter of which also *participate more in the nature of air,* as their movement shows.

444a22 Then, when he says *When odors rise to the brain,* he shows the cause why odor is perceived by breathing with reference to human beings.

He says that *odors rise to the brain* because *the heat* of fire that releases odors gives them a *lightness* so that they move towards higher regions, and from this there follows a condition of health in the *area* of the brain. *For odor* has *power* to heat because of the heat of fire by which it is caused and released. Hence *nature uses breathing for two things: actively—* that is, principally—*as an aid to the chest*—that is, the breast; in other words, for cooling the heart's heat—but *adventitiously*—that is, secondarily—for perceiving *odor. For* when the human being breathes, he moves air *through the nostrils* by drawing it in, and so causes odors to go to the organ of smell. The reason why *this genus of sensible objects is proper to* human *nature* is *because* the human being *has a bigger brain* in proportion to his *size, and* a *moister* one, *than do the other animals.* And the reason why *the human being alone among the animals senses and* takes pleasure in *the odors of flowers and* other *such things* is that the *heat* of such odors *and* their *movement* towards the brain reduce *the "hyperbole"*—that is, the excess—of the brain's *coolness and moistness* to the right measure. He added *"so to speak"* because other animals do flee bad odors inasmuch as they are destructive.

444b2 Then, when he says *To the other animals,* he gives the cause of smelling by breathing with reference to other animals.

He says that *nature gave to animals with lungs,* which are the only ones that breathe, *sensation of the other kind of odor*—that is, the one related to food—*by means of breathing so as not to make two* organs, one an organ of breathing and the other an organ of smelling. For the organ of breathing *is sufficient* also for smelling: just as for *the human being* it suffices for the two kinds of *the odorous,* so for other animals it suffices for the *one* alone.

CHAPTER 13

444B7–445B2

444b7 *It is clear that the ones that do not breathe have sensation of the odorous. For both fish and the whole class of insects keenly sense from a distance because of the nutritive species of odor, although they are very far from their proper food. So do bees in relation to honey; and the genus of small ants some call "hexapods"; and, among marine animals, the purple-fish. And many other such animals acutely sense their food because of odor.*

444b15 *But what they sense it with is not so clear. Therefore someone might raise the difficulty what it is they sense odor with, since smelling takes place in all animals that do breathe in one and the same way: for this is what seems to happen in all animals that do breathe, but none of these animals breathe, and yet they do sense. Unless there is some other sense besides the five? But this is impossible: for the odorous is the object of the sense of smell, and the odorous is what they sense.*

444b21 *But perhaps not in the same way. In the ones that breathe, the breath removes something that lies over as a covering, which is why they do not sense when they are not breathing. But in the ones that do not breathe this is absent. It is similar with the eyes. Some animals have eyelids, and when these are not opened they cannot see at all. But animals that have hard eyes do not have these, and so they do not need anything to open them; rather, they see immediately by the faculty in them.*

444b28 *Likewise, none of the other animals disdains what is of itself foul with respect to odor, unless something happens to be injurious, and they are injured by such things in the same way. Just as human beings suffer cold in the head from coal-smoke, and are often injured by it, and are injured by the power of sulfur, so other animals also avoid these because of the affection. But they do not care about the foulness itself in itself—although many growing things have foul odors—but only whether it affects the taste or the food.*

445a4 *The senses exist in an odd number, and an odd number has a middle. The sense for smelling seems to be a middle between the tactile senses, touch and taste, and those that sense through something else, sight and hearing. Thus the* *odorous is an affection of nourishment; the objects of the former senses are in the same genus. But it is also in the genus of the visible and the audible; thus things are smelled both in air and in water. So the odorous is something common to both; it is both in the genus of the tangible, and in that of the transparent and the audible. Therefore odorous enchymous dryness in moistness and fluidity is reasonably compared to a tincture and a wash. Let this much be said, then, about how we should speak of species of the odorous, and how we should not.*

445a16 What some Pythagoreans say is not reasonable: they say that some animals are nourished by odors.

445a17 For, first, we see that food must be composite, for what is nourished is also non-simple. This is also why a superfluity of food is produced, whether inside, or, in the case of plants, outside. Moreover, water alone is not going to nourish by itself, for what is going to build up has to be something bodily. Moreover, it is much less reasonable that air should become bodily.

445a23 In addition to this, we see that all animals have a place that is able to receive food, from which, after the food enters, the body receives it. But the part for the odorous is in the head, and odor enters with the breath, and so goes to the place for breathing. It is clear, then, that the odorous as such does not contribute to nourishment.

445a29 But it is clear that it does contribute to health, both from observation and from what has been said. Thus the odorous is to health what flavor, in the nourishing part, is to nourishment.

445b1 Let this be the determination, then, with respect to each sensitive part.

Commentary

444b7 After the Philosopher has shown that men and certain other animals smell by breathing, here he inquires into the way non-breathing animals smell.

On this point he does two things. First he shows what is clear in such animals; second what is unclear, where he says *But what they sense it with* (444b15).

Accordingly he first says that *it is clear that* animals *that do not breathe* sense *the odorous,* because, as we see, *fish and the whole class of insects*—that is, partitioned animals such as ants, bees, and the like—*acutely sense* their nourishment *from a distance,* when they are too distant *from their proper food* to be able to perceive it by their own sense of sight. Hence it is clear that they perceive it *because of the nutritive species of odor*—that is, inasmuch as they perceive the kind of odor that is analogous to flavor and indicates quality of nourishment. He gives the example of *bees,* which are moved from a distance to seek *honey;* and that of *small* six-legged *ants,* which are also moved from a distance to seek their food; and that of certain other animals called *purple-fish* because of their color. Likewise *many* non-breathing *animals* are found that *acutely sense their food* from a distance *because of odor.*

444b15 Then, when he says *But what they sense it with,* he shows what the difficulty is with such animals.

On this point he does three things. First he raises the difficulty. Second he solves it, where he says *But perhaps not in the same way* (444b21). Third he clarifies the solution by means of a comparison, where he says *Likewise, none of the other animals* (444b28).

Accordingly he first says that although it is clear that the above-mentioned animals perceive odor, *what they sense it with is not so clear.* The reason for the difficulty is that *all* breathing animals sense odor *in one and the same way,* namely by breathing: for it is clear from experience that *this seems to happen* in all breathing animals. But in the case of the above-mentioned animals, it is clear that they do not *breathe,* and that *yet they do sense* the odorous.

However, one might give a reason for this difference by saying that such animals sense the odorous by *some other sense besides the five senses* to which names have been given. This answer might seem probable for the following reason. To sense is to be affected by something, and so a different mode of sensing is as it were a different mode of being affected that indicates a difference of passive power. It is like the way in which a different mode of acting signifies a difference of active power; as we see, the stronger heat is, the more vehement is the action of heating. Likewise, then, on the side of what is passive, what is affected in a different mode seems to have a different passive power, and thus what senses in a different mode seem to have a different sense-power.

But it is *impossible* for them to sense the odorous in a different mode, because where there is the same sensible object there is the same sense-power, for powers are distinguished according to objects. But it is the same sensible object that both kinds of animal *sense,* namely *the odorous.* Hence it cannot be that the sense-powers are different.

444b21 Then, when he says *But perhaps not in the same way,* he solves the difficulty presented as follows: the two kinds of animal perceive the same object of smell, and with the same sense-power, *but not in the same way.*

For it must be considered that the mode of sensing can be varied in two ways.

One is per se: this is according to the different relationships of sensible objects to sense-powers, and such variation in mode of sensing makes for different senses. For example, one sense, such as touch, perceives an object united to it, but another, such as sight, perceives a remote object.

But there is another variation in mode of sensing that is accidental: this does not make for different sense-powers; rather, it is understood with respect to removal of an impediment. It is this kind of variation in mode of sensing that is under discussion.

For *in* animals *that breathe, something that lies over* the organ of smell *as a covering* is removed by the breathing, and so *when they are not breathing* they are prevented from smelling because of this covering. But animals *that do not breathe* lack such a covering, and so they do not need to breathe in order to smell.

Likewise we see that *some animals have eyelids,* and if these are not opened such animals *cannot see.* Nature gave such eyelids to animals that need a more acute sense of sight in order to preserve their eyes, which are soft. Hence animals *that have hard eyes*—animals that, as it were, do not need an acute sense of sight—*do not have* such eyelids, *and so do not need* any movement of opening the eyelids in order to see. *Rather* the eye has *the faculty* for seeing *immediately,* without the removal of anything.

444b28 Then, when he says *Likewise, none of the other animals,* he clarifies the above-mentioned solution through another comparison involving the sense of smell, in which there is another variation among animals that does not make for difference of sense-power.

None of the other animals besides the human being is pained by what has *foul odor of itself*—that is, not in relation to nourishment. He said this above,[1] but there might be a difficulty on the point, because some animals seem to avoid foul odors of this kind; and so he has returned to the point to remove this difficulty.

He says that the other animals do not avoid odors that are of them-selves foul except accidentally, that is, inasmuch as a foul odor of this kind *happens to be injurious.* For since odor is caused by heat, moisture, and dryness, as was said above,[2] it sometimes happens that a foul odor comes from a great disorder in the qualities mentioned, and so, in re-ceiving the odor, the medium is simultaneously altered to an extremely harmful condition that destroys the bodies of the other animals as well as that of the human being. The other animals sense this alteration by touch, and so flee such foul things. He gives the example of *human be-ings suffering cold in the head from coal-smoke,* because of its disorder, some-times to the point of destruction; and it is the same with *sulfur.* Hence *animals avoid* these destructive things *because of the affection* of destruction they perceive. *But they do not care about the foulness itself* of the odor con-sidered *in itself—although many things* that grow from the earth *have foul odors—but only* according as the foulness of the odor represents some-thing concerning *taste,* or concerning the suitability of their proper nour-ishment.

445a4 Then when he says *The senses exist in an odd number,* he com-pares the sense of smell to other senses.

First he determines the truth. Second he eliminates an error, where he says *What some Pythagoreans say* (445a16).

On the first point it must be considered that, following the custom of the Pythagoreans, the Philosopher here uses a property of number in order to draw a comparison among the senses.

An odd number cannot be divided into two halves like an even one: rather there remains something undivided in the *middle* between two equal parts, as in a group of five there remains an intermediate unit be-tween two groups of two. Now *the senses* are set up *in an odd number,* that is, a group of five. Two of them are *tactile,* because they do not perceive their objects, which are united to them, through external media, and these are *touch and taste.* Two of them, namely *sight and hearing, perceive* their remote objects *through something else,* that is, external media. But smell is in the middle between the two groups of two, and so it also has something in common with both groups.

It has something in common with touch and taste, which are the senses of nourishment, as is said in *On the Soul* II,[3] inasmuch as *the odor-*

ous is an affection of nourishment, according as odor is analogous to flavor, and thus objects of touch and taste *are in the same genus* with objects of taste.

The genus *of the visible and the audible* is the same as that of the odorous inasmuch as both are apprehended through external media; hence animals smell through *air and water,* just as they also see and hear through them.

Thus it is clear that *the odorous is something common to both* genera of sensible objects. For *it is in the genus of the tangible* according as it is an affection of nourishment and thus comes together in the same genus with the tangible and tastable qualities. Likewise, it is in the genus of *the transparent and the audible*—that is, it is perceived through the transparent medium through which a thing is seen as well as heard, namely air and water, although it is perceived through these not inasmuch they are transparent, but inasmuch as they are receptive of enchymous dryness, as was said above.[4] And so some *reasonably* compare it to two things: the being of *odorous enchymous dryness in moistness* of water *and fluidity*—that is, fluidity of air—is, because of its ready diffusion, like *a tincture*—which refers to alteration of a medium by color—*and* like *a wash*—which refers to flavors—for odor has something in common with both.

After this, as an epilogue, he concludes that it has been said *how we should* distinguish *species of the odorous, and how we should not,* namely inasmuch as odors are taken in themselves.

445a16 Then when he says *What some Pythagoreans say,* he eliminates an error.

On this point he does three things. First he relates the erroneous opinion. Second he disproves it, where he says *For, first, we see that food* (445a17). Third he responds to a tacit objection, where he says *But it is clear* (445a29).

Accordingly he first says that *what some Pythagoreans* said—*that some animals are nourished by odors*—is not reasonable. According to them, smell would not be intermediate among the senses, as was said,[5] but would have to be completely included with the senses of nourishment. They were moved to say this because they saw that human beings and other animals are fortified by odors.

445a17 Then, when he says *For, first, we see that food,* he disproves the above-mentioned opinion by two arguments.

The *first* is *that food must be composed* of more than one element. For simple elements do not nourish, because animals that are *nourished* by them are composed of the four elements, and a thing is nourished by the same things by which it exists, as was said in *On Generation* II.[6] He concludes that a sign of this is that a *superfluity* is produced from *food: whether* within, as is evident in animals, in the bodies of which are places assigned for the gathering of superfluities; *or outside, in the case of plants,* the superfluities of which are immediately expelled outward, as is clear in the case of gums of trees and other such things. If an animal or plant were nourished by one simple element, no superfluity would occur, since in a simple element there is uniformity of parts. And although no one element is suitable for nutrition, because of its simplicity, *water* in addition has a special impediment because of which it cannot *nourish alone,* without the admixture of something earthen, which is why farmers add manure to nourish plants with water mixed with something: nourishment *builds up* and generates something in the substance of what is nourished, and so *it has to be something bodily* and solid, which is not true of water. Hence water alone cannot nourish, and *much less* can *air.* And hence it remains that neither can odor nourish: for it is clear that odor, since it is a quality, cannot of itself build up a substance by nourishing it, except perhaps by reason of what is receptive of it, namely air or water. Even if odor were evaporation, or exhalation of smoke, as the Ancients said, the argument would still stand, because both of these pertain to the nature of air, as was said above.

445a23 Then, when he says *In addition to this, we see,* he presents the second argument.

He says that *all animals have a place* in which *food* is first received—that is, the stomach—*from which* it is drawn off into individual parts of *the body.* If we consider *the odorous* itself, it is clear (since most animals smell by breathing) that it is perceived by an organ near the brain, as was said above. But the air inbreathed, with which odor is drawn in, *goes to the place for breathing,* that is, the lung. Now it is clear that neither the brain nor the lung is the place in animals that first receives food. Hence *it is clear* that odor does not nourish. But it does fortify because of alteration by heat, moistness, and dryness, and because of pleasure; just as bad odor is destructive, as was said above.

445a29 Then, when he says *But it is clear,* he responds to a tacit objection. For one might object: if odor does not nourish, it is utterly useless.

He answers that, although it does not nourish, nevertheless *it does contribute to health,* as is *clear from observation, and from what has been said* above. Hence he concludes that, as *flavor* is ordered to nutrition, so odor is ordered to *health.*

445b1 Finally, by way of epilogue, he concludes that sensible objects have been discussed *with respect to each* organ of sense.

CHAPTER 14

445B3–446A20

445b3 *But someone will raise an objection: if every body is infinitely divisible, are sensible affections also? For instance, color and flavor and odor and sound, and heaviness and coldness, and hot and light, and hard and soft.*

445b6 *But this is impossible. For each of these is something that activates a sense-power. For all are named from the fact that they are able to move a sense-power. Necessarily, then, sense is infinitely divisible, and every magnitude is sensible. For it is impossible to see something that is white but not a quantity.*

445b11 *For if this is not so, then there can be a body that has no color, or heaviness, or other such affection, and so is not sensible at all: for these are the sensible objects. Therefore, there will be something sensible composed of what is not sensible. But it necessarily is, for it is not composed of mathematical objects.*

445b15 *Moreover, what will we assign them to other than intellect, or how will we know them? But they are not intelligible, for intellect does not understand what is outside except with sensation.*

445b17 *But if this is so, it seems to support those who make indivisible magnitudes: thus the discussion is resolved. But this is impossible, as was said before in the discussions of motion.*

445b20 *With the resolution of this, it will at the same time also be made clear why the species of color and flavor and sounds and other sensible objects are limited. For what is inside the extremes is necessarily determinate, and extremes are contraries. But every kind of sensible object has contrariety, for instance black and white in color, sweet and bitter in flavor. And so in all the others there are extremes that are contraries.*

445b27 *A continuum, then, is divisible into an infinite number of unequal parts, but into a finite number of equal ones. And what is not of itself continuous is divisible into finite species.*

445b29 *We must speak of the affections as "species," although they exist in a continuity and in these parts. Therefore, we must take it that what is in potentiality and what is in actuality are different. For this reason a tenth of a thousandth of a grain of millet escapes the notice of sight, although sight goes over it.*

And the sound in a diesis escapes notice, although all of the singing, which is continuous, is heard. The distance between the extremes escapes notice. It is similar with the extremely small in other sensible objects. They themselves are visible in potentiality, but not in actuality when they are not separated. Thus a one-foot length exists in potentiality in something two feet long, and exists in actuality when it is divided off.

446a7 *But it is reasonable that separated parts of such extremely small size are dissolved into the surroundings, like a tiny amount of flavor poured into the sea.*

446a10 *But there is no extremity of the sense-power to correspond to that of the sensible object itself, even if it is separated. The extreme smallness is in potentiality to a surer sense-power. And a separated sensible object of such a size will not be sensed in actuality. Still, it will be a sensible object, for there is already the power, and it will be in actuality when a sense-power comes to it. Thus it has been said that some magnitudes and affections escape notice; and for what cause; and the way in which they are sensible objects, and the way in which they are not.*

446a16 *But since there are quantities existing within so as to be sensible in actuality, and not only as in the whole, but also separately, they—colors and flavors and sounds—are necessarily finite according to some number.*

Commentary

445b3 After the Philosopher has determined about sense-organs and sensible objects, here he determines some questions about the sense-power and sensible objects.

First he raises a question about sensible objects themselves. Second he raises another about alteration of the sense-power by a sensible object, where he says *But someone will raise an objection* (Ch.15, 446a20). Third he raises a third about the sense-power itself, where he says *But there is also another such objection* (Ch.16, 447a12).

On the first point he does three things. First he raises the question. Second he introduces arguments about it, where he says *But this is impossible* (445b6). Third he solves it, where he says *With the resolution of this* (445b20).

Accordingly he first says that *every body is infinitely divisible:* for this is of the nature of a continuum, as is clear in the book the *Physics.*[1] But sensible qualities—which are called *affections,* as is said in the *Categories*[2]—are in a body as in their subject. Therefore there is a question someone can raise in *objection:* whether *sensible* qualities themselves, such as *color and flavor* and so on, are infinitely divisible *also.*

445b6 Then, when he says *But this is impossible,* he raises objections concerning the question posed.

First he raises objections to show that sensible qualities are not infinitely divisible. Second he raises objections on the other side, where he says *For if this is not so* (445b11). Third he eliminates a false solution, where he says *But if this is so* (445b17).

Accordingly he first says that it seems *impossible* for sensible qualities to be divided infinitely, because each of the above-mentioned sensible qualities naturally acts on a sense-power. For the proper nature of each of them consists in this: it is *able to move a sense-power;* for example, it belongs to the nature of color to be able to move the sense of sight. If, then, the above-mentioned qualities are infinitely divisible, the consequence will be that *sense*—that is, the act of sensing itself—*is infinitely divisible.* Now an instance of being moved is infinitely divisible according to division of the magnitude through which a thing is moved; and so it would follow that, as something moved goes through every part of the magnitude, so one who senses would sense any magnitude, however small, *and* so *every magnitude* would be *sensible.*

But he adds a reason why he does not conclude that even points are perceptible to sense: because it *is impossible to see something white that is not a quantity;* and the argument is the same with respect to other sensible objects. The reason for this is that a sense-power is a power in a magnitude, since it is the actuality of a bodily organ, and so it can be affected only by what has magnitude: for what is active must be proportioned to what is passive.

There remains the problem that every magnitude is perceptible; how this is to be understood will be made clear below.[3]

Hence it can be concluded that sensible qualities are not infinitely divisible.

445b11 Then, when he says *For if this is not so,* he raises objections on the opposite side with two arguments.

The first is this. If sensible qualities are not infinitely divisible, *then there can be a* minimal *body* that transcends division of sensible qualities and has no sensible quality, i.e. neither *color* nor *heaviness* nor any *other* such quality. And so such a body will not be *sensible*, because only the qualities mentioned are *sensible objects*. *Therefore*, since these tiny bodies are parts of a whole body that is sensible, it will follow that a *sensible body* is *composed of what is not sensible*. But a sensible body *is necessarily* composed of what is sensible, for it cannot be said that a sensible body is *composed of mathematical* bodies, in which quantity is considered without sensible qualities. Therefore it remains that sensible qualities must be infinitely divisible.

445b15 He presents the second argument where he says *Moreover, what will we assign them to.*

His argument proceeds from the point that the soul by nature knows all things, whether by sense or intellect, as was established in *On the Soul* III.[4]

Accordingly, if the above-mentioned minimal bodies that transcend division of sensible qualities are not sensible because they lack sensible qualities, they can be assigned only to *intellect* as the power that knows them. *But* it cannot be said that they are *intelligible: for intellect* understands none of the things *outside* the soul *except with sensation* of them— that is, by simultaneously sensing them. If, therefore, these minimal bodies are not sensed, they will not be able to be understood.

He says this to eliminate an opinion of Plato, who held that the forms understood exist outside the soul. But according to Aristotle the things understood are the very natures of things in singulars, which, inasmuch as they are in singulars, fall under the apprehension of the sense-power. But the intellect apprehends these natures in an absolute way and assigns to them certain intelligible intentions, namely that of being a genus or species. These intentions exist only in the intellect, not outside it: hence only the intellect knows them.

445b17 Then, when he says *But if this is so*, he eliminates a false response.

One might argue as follows. A problem follows from positing the infinite divisibility of magnitude, whatever may be said about sensible qualities, whether that they are infinitely divisible or not. This, then, *seems to support* the opinion of *those who* posit *indivisible magnitudes*, because the difficulty *is solved* in this way: for if a body is not infinitely divisible, then, since sensible quality is not infinitely divisible, it will not follow that there are bodies that cannot be sensed. *But this* opinion that some magnitudes are indivisible *is impossible,* as is evident from what was said *in the discussions of motion,* that is, in *Physics* VI.[5]

445b20 Then, when he says *With the resolution of this,* he solves the question he raised above about division of sensible qualities.

And first he treats their formal division, that is, of genus into species. Second their quantitative division, where he says *A continuum, then* (445b27).

Accordingly he first says that, together with *the solution* of the above-mentioned difficulties, *at the same time* it will have to be *made clear why the species of color and flavor and other* such things are finite: for he promised above that this would be determined.[6]

He gives the following reason for this. If it is possible to reach the *furthest* point starting from either extreme, what is in the middle is *necessarily* finite, as was proved in *Posterior Analytics* I.[7] Now it is clear that in any genus of *sensible* objects there is *a contrariety* that is the greatest distance, and so the contraries must be the extremes, *for instance black and white in color, sweet and bitter in flavor, and* likewise *in the others.* Hence it remains that intermediate species are finite.

445b27 Then, when he says *A continuum, then,* he solves the question raised earlier about quantitative division of sensible qualities.

First he makes some presuppositions. Second he proceeds to solve the question where he says *We must speak of the affections* (445b29).

On the first point he makes two presuppositions.

The first is that *a continuum is* in a way *divisible into an infinite number of parts,* and in another way *into a finite number.* For if a division into *equal* parts is made, it will not be able to proceed to infinity as long as the continuum is finite, because if one repeatedly removes something the size of a palm from anything finite, it will be completely taken away. But if a division into *unequal* parts is made, it will proceed to infinity: for instance, if a whole is divided in half, and again the half in half, which is a quarter of the whole, the division will proceed to infinity.

The second supposition is that *what is continuous not of itself,* but accidentally, for example color and other such things, is of itself formally divided *into finite species,* as was said a little before.[8]

445b29 Then, when he says *We must speak of the affections,* he proceeds to solve the principal question, which was about division of sensible qualities.

Because he had taken his argument on this question from what appears in sensation, first he inquires about division to infinity with respect to the act of sensing itself. Second he concludes to his proposal with respect to sensible things themselves, where he says *But since there are quantities* (446a16).

On the first point he does two things. First he inquires whether sensing proceeds to infinity with respect to parts existing in a whole. Second, whether it does so with respect to separated parts, where he says *But it is reasonable* (446a7).

Accordingly he first says that because *we must speak of the affections*—that is, the sensible qualities—*as "species"* and forms that are not, considered in themselves, infinite, as was said; and nevertheless *they exist in* a continuum as their subject, by division of which they are accidentally divided; it follows that, as in a continuum there is something in actuality—namely a separated part—and something else in potentiality—namely a part existing in the continuum unseparated—so also in these qualities that are divisible accidentally a separated part exists in actuality, and hence can be sensed in actuality, but a part not divided off exists in potentiality, and so is not sensed in actuality. And thus, *although sight goes over a grain of millet,* nevertheless some tiny part of the latter—say *a tenth of a thousandth—escapes the notice of sight.* Likewise, *although a* whole *continuous singing is heard,* nevertheless some small part of the singing—such as *a diesis,* which is the smallest unit in melody, being a distance between a tone and a semitone—*escapes* the *notice* of hearing. For this kind of intermediate *distance between the extremes escapes notice.* And so in the case of *other sensible objects* what is *extremely small* altogether escapes the notice of the sense-power. For it is *visible in potentiality, but not in actuality,* except when it is separated. Similarly we see in magnitudes that a one-foot line *exists in potentiality in* a *two-foot* line, but *exists in actuality* when it is *divided* from the whole.

It is clear from the foregoing that what some mathematicians say is false: that nothing is seen whole all at once, but rather sight runs over the parts of a visible object as if seeing were a continuum, like being moved. They are mistaken in this, because the parts of a continuum are visible not in actuality, but only in potentiality. Hence sight takes a visible whole as an indivisible unit belonging to a genus of its own—unless it takes parts that are not divided off as if they were, as when it looks at each, one by one. Nevertheless, even this does not reach as far as every minimal part, because then sensing would be infinitely divisible, which was dismissed above as inconsistent.

446a7 Then, when he says *But it is reasonable,* he shows that not even parts separated off are infinitely perceptible by sense.

First from the point of view of the parts themselves. Second from the point of view of the sense-power itself, where he says *But there is no extremity* (446a10).

Accordingly he first says that if *extremely small parts* are *separated* from a whole, it seems *reasonable,* because of the smallness of their power of self-preservation, that they cannot continue to last; for bodily power is divided according to division of magnitude, as is clear from *Physics* VII.[9] And so those separated minimal parts are immediately converted into the surrounding body, for instance air or water, as is clear in the case of flavored drink *poured into the sea.*

From this it is clear why a mathematical body—in which only the nature of quantity, which has nothing to oppose infinite division, is considered—is infinitely divisible. But a natural body, which is considered under a whole form, cannot be infinitely divided, because once it is reduced to its smallest part, it is immediately, because of the weakness of its power, changed into something else. Hence one can find a smallest part of flesh, as is said in *Physics* I.[10] But a natural body is not, as was said in objection, composed out of mathematical ones.

446a10 Then, when he says *But there is no extremity,* he shows the proposal from the point of view of the sense-power itself.

For evidence on this point it must be known that the more excellent a sensitive power is, the more it can perceive a smaller alteration of the organ by a sensible object. But it is clear that the smaller a sensible object is, the smaller the alteration it causes of the organ, and so the more excellent power of sense it needs in order to be sensed in actuality. But it is clear that sensitive power cannot be increased infinitely, any more than can other natural powers.

Hence even if sensible bodies were infinitely divisible, nevertheless there would not always be *extremity of the sense-power* in superiority of power *to correspond to* the extremity *of the sensible object* in smallness—*not even* if the extreme smallness of the sensible object continued to last when *separated.* For the extreme smallness of the sensible object *exists in potentiality,* to be perceived by *a surer* and more perfect sense-power, and if the latter is not present, it will not be able to *be sensed in actuality. Still, it will be a sensible object* in itself, *for already,* by being separated, *it* has active *power* to alter a sense, *and when* a sense *comes to it,* it will be perceived *in actuality.* Therefore it is clear that what he said above is true, that no magnitude is invisible—that is, in itself, although a magnitude may be invisible because of imperfection of sight.

Therefore he concludes that *it has been said that some magnitudes and* affective qualities *escape* the *notice* of the sense-power; *and for what cause; and the way in which they are sensible objects, and the way in which they are not.*

446a16 Then, when he says *But since there are quantities,* he concludes from the foregoing that *since* some parts of sensible bodies have quantity in this way—*so as to be sensible in actuality* not only when existing in a whole, but also when divided off—parts of this kind *are necessarily finite according to some number,* whether in the case of *colors* or *flavors* or *sounds.* And thus, according as they are perceptible in actuality, they are not infinitely divisible.

CHAPTER 15

446A20–447A11

446a20 *But someone will raise an objection: do either the sensible objects or the movements caused by the sensible objects—however sensation occurs—first reach a midpoint when they act? Odor and sound seem to do this: for one who is closer senses odor earlier, and sound arrives after the striking. Is it the same, then, in the case of a visible object and light?*

446a26 *Empedocles says that light from the sun in this way arrives at a midpoint before arriving at the sense of sight or the earth.*

446a28 *It might be thought reasonable that this is what happens. For what is moved is moved from something to something, and so there is necessarily a time in which it is moved from one to the other. But every length of time is divisible. Thus there was a time when the ray was not seen, but was still being brought in the medium.*

446b2 *Everything simultaneously hears and has heard, and in general senses and has sensed. There is no generation of sensations; they have no coming into being. Nevertheless sound is not already at the sense of hearing when the blow is struck. The reconfiguration of letters when they are carried through a medium makes this clear: people apparently have not heard what was said, because the air carried is reconfigured in being carried. It is thus in the case of color and light: for it is not the case that this sees and that is seen if they are related in just any way. This is how it is with things that are equal: neither has to be in a particular place, since when things are made equal, it makes no difference if they are either near to or far from one another.*

446b13 *On the other hand, it is reasonable for this to happen in the case of sound and odor. For air and water are indeed in a way continua, but the movements of both are divisible. For this reason too, it is the same thing that the first person and the last person hears and smells, but in a way it is not. But there seems to some to be an objection also about this. For some say that it is impossible for each person, by means of what is different, to hear and see and smell the same thing. For it is not possible for many who stand apart from one another to hear and smell the same thing, that is, for it to be cut off from itself. On the other hand, all sense the original mover—for example the quince, or incense, or fire—which is numerically one and the same. What is individual is numerically different, but specifically the same. Therefore many simultaneously see and smell and hear.*

446b25 *But these things are not bodies, but an affection and a movement. For otherwise this would not happen. Nor are they independent of body.*

446b27 *But the account of light is different, for there is light through some one single being, but there is not a movement.*

446b28 *In general, alteration and transfer are not alike. For it is reasonable that transfers should first reach a midpoint; and sound seems to be a movement of transfer. But what is altered is not like this.*

447a1 *For it can happen that a whole is altered all at once, not half of it first, for example when a whole body of water is solidified all at once.*

447a3 *Nevertheless, if what is heated or solidified is large, what is contiguous is affected by the contiguous. But the first is necessarily altered, all at once and instantaneously, by the very thing that is acting. And tasting would be like odor if we existed in moisture, and sensed it from a distance before touching it.*

447a8 *But it is reasonable, where the sensitive part has a medium, that not all of it be affected all at once, except in the case of light, because of what was said above, and, for the same reason, in the case of seeing: for light causes seeing.*

Commentary

446a20 After the Philosopher has followed up the first question, which concerns sensible things themselves, here he proceeds to the second question, which concerns the alteration of the sense-power by sensible objects.

On this point he does three things. First he raises the question. Second he argues it, where he says *Empedocles says* (446a26). Third he solves it, where he says *On the other hand* (446b13).

On the first point it must be considered that, as was established above, some held that a sense-power is changed by sensible things by way of an emanation, so that it is the sensible things themselves—that is, the emanations from them—that reach the sense-power. But Aristotle himself held that the sensible things change the medium by way of a certain alteration, so that it is the changes of this kind that reach the sense-power.

Therefore there is a question, *however sensation occurs:* whether *the sensible objects* themselves—according to the opinion of others—or alterations *caused by the sensible objects*—according to Aristotle's own opinion—*first reach a midpoint* before reaching the sense-power. There is no difficulty about this in the case of hearing and smell, for it is clear that *one senses odor earlier* from nearby, and similarly that *sound* reaches hearing *after the striking* of the blow that causes sound occurs, as one who sees the blow from a distance can clearly perceive. And it is clear that this question has no place in the case of taste and touch, because they do not perceive through an external medium. Hence the difficulty seems to be about sight alone, that is, whether *a visible object and* the *light* that causes seeing first reach a midpoint before reaching the sense-power or any terminus.

446a26 Then, when he says *Empedocles says,* he raises an objection concerning the question asked.

First he argues on the false side of the question. Second he eliminates a false solution where he says *Everything simultaneously hears* (446b2).

He argues in response to the question first by the authority of *Empedocles,* who said that *light* proceeding *from the sun* first reaches *a midpoint before* reaching *the sense of sight* that sees the light, *or the earth* that is seen by means of the light, and beyond which the sun's ray does not proceed.

He touched on this question in *On the Soul* II, but disproved the opinion as follows: in such a great distance as there is from the rising sun to ourselves, it is impossible for a temporal succession to escape our notice.[1]

446a28 Second, where he says *It might be thought reasonable,* he argues the same point by reason.

He says that it seems *reasonable for this to happen*—that is, for the visible object or light to first reach a midpoint before reaching the sense of sight. For there seems to be some movement of the visible object itself, or of the light, in coming to the sense of sight. But everything that *is moved is moved from something to something,* in such a way that before, it is at the terminus from which it is moved, and after, it is at the terminus to which it is moved: otherwise, if it were simultaneously at both termini, it would not be moved from one to the other. But before and after in movement are counted by time. Therefore *there is necessarily* some *time in which* the visible object, or the light, *is moved from* the visible or illuminating body *to* the sense of sight. *But every length of time is divisible,* as was proved in *Physics* VI.[2] Therefore if we take the midpoint of the time in question, at that point *the ray* of light, or the visible object itself, has not yet reached the sense of sight, but is *still* being moved through *the medium,* because the magnitude through which something is moved must be divided according to division of time, as was proved in *Physics* VI.[3]

446b2 Then, when he says *Everything simultaneously hears,* he eliminates an inadequate response.

Someone could think that sensible objects do not first reach a midpoint before reaching the sense-power because sense perceives a sensible object all at once, without successiveness. Thus, in hearing, hearing does not come before having been heard in the way that, in what is successive, being moved does come before having been moved: rather, when someone *is hearing,* he *simultaneously* already *has heard,* because the whole act of hearing is completed in an instant. And this is universally true of every sense, that is, that it simultaneously *senses and has sensed* something. This is so because *there is no generation of sensations; they have no coming into being.*

We say that there is a "generation" of things that have a being *(esse)* which is reached by a successive or gradual movement: whether the terminus of the successive movement is the very form of the things, as when a white thing is said to be generated because a thing reaches whiteness through successive alteration; or whether the terminus of the successive movement is a disposition to their form, as fire and water are said to be generated because dispositions to their forms—that is, elemental qualities—are acquired through successive alteration.

But those things begin to be without being generated or coming into being that are not—either of themselves or with respect to any preceding dispositions in them—caused through successive movement. For example, "to the right" is caused in a thing not by any successive movement pre-existing in it, but by something else having been made "to the left" of it. Likewise, air begins to be illuminated not by any movement pre-existing in it, but at the presence of an illuminating body. And likewise, a sense-power begins to sense not by any movement pre-existing in it, but at the requisite placing of a sensible object before it.

Thus one simultaneously senses and already has sensed. Nevertheless it is not for this reason necessary that sensible objects, or movements of sensible objects, reach a sense-power without succession. For it is clear that one simultaneously is hearing and has heard, *and nevertheless sound* does *not* reach *hearing* immediately *when the blow* that causes the sound *is struck.*

This is made *clear* by the *reconfiguration of letters* that occurs when someone's speech is heard from a distance, indicating that the sound of the voice formed into letters is being *carried* successively through the *medium.* It is for this reason that those who hear the sound *apparently have not* by hearing distinguished the letters pronounced: *because the air* moved in the medium *is reconfigured,* as if losing the impression made by the one who first caused the sound. This sometimes happens because of some other alteration in the air, for example when, because many are speaking, it is impossible to make out what one of them is saying, for the movements impede one another. But sometimes it happens because of distance: for as the action of heating is weakened in what is farther away, so also does the alteration of the air by the one who first produces the sound, and as a result the sound of the speech may reach those who are near the speaker perfectly, with the requisite articulation of letters, but reach those who are farther away with some confusion.

446b9 The case of *color and light,* then, seems to be similar, for color and light also cannot be seen by being positioned *in just any way:* rather, a determinate distance is required. For just as utterances are heard by those at a distance without distinction of the letters, so also bodies are seen by those at a distance without distinction of the arrangement of individual parts. The relation between the sense of sight and the visible object is not like the relation of equality: for no determinate location is required in order for things to be *equal;* rather, however their location varies, they always remain equal in the same way, and *it makes no difference* whether they are *near or far.* Therefore it seems that just as the reconfiguration of letters makes it clear that sound reaches the sense of hearing by succession, although once it has reached hearing, it is heard all at once; so the incomplete vision of remote visible objects seems to indicate that color and light reach the sense of sight by succession, although they are seen all at once.

446b13 Then, when he says *On the other hand,* he presents the true solution, showing the difference between sight and the other two senses that perceive through external media, namely hearing and smell.

This is divided into two parts. First he gives the difference of sight from hearing and smell. Second he concludes to his proposal, where he says *But it is reasonable* (447a8).

The first part is divided into two according to the two differences he gives. The second begins where he says *In general, alteration and transfer* (446b28).

Accordingly he first says that *it is reasonable for this to happen in the case of sound and odor,* namely that they reach the sense-power by succession. He gives as the reason for this the fact that *air and water,* which are the media by which these objects are brought to the sense-power, *are indeed,* in their substance, *continua,* and yet *movements* distinct from one another can take place in them.

This can happen because of the easy divisibility of air and water, which, as the Philosopher shows in *Physics* VII, is evident in the movement of throwing something, where there are many movements, many movers, and many things moved.[4] For one part of the air is moved by another, and thus there are different movements succeeding one another, because a part of the air that has been moved still remains a mover after it ceases to be moved. Thus the movements of the parts of the air are not all simultaneous; rather they succeed one another, as is shown in *Physics* VIII.[5]

This is also evident in the case of sound, which is caused by a striking of air, but not in such a way that the whole of the air in between is moved by what strikes it in one movement. Rather, there are many movements succeeding one another, for one part, having been moved first, then moves another. Thus in a way *it is the same thing that the first person hears*—the one who is close to the striking that causes the sound—and that *the last person* hears—the one who is at a distance. *But in a way it is not* the same thing.

446b17 According to some, *there seems to be* a difficulty on this point: *some say that,* since different people sense by means of different organs, *it is impossible* that they sense *the same thing.* Now this is true if it refers to what proximately moves the sense-power, because the senses of different people are immediately altered by the different parts of the medium that are close to them, and so what one senses is *"cut off,"* and distinct from, what another senses. But if what is understood is what *first* moves the medium, then *all sense one and the same* thing. For instance everyone, whether near or far, hears the sound of the one blow; likewise, every-one smells the one odorous body, *for example the quince, or the incense* burning in *fire. What* reaches each one individually one *is numerically dif-ferent, but* is *specifically the same,* because all these alterations are caused by the same form, the form of what first activates them. Hence *many si-multaneously see and smell and hear* the same sensible object by the differ-ent alterations that reach them.

446b25 *But these things* that reach the senses of each individual *are not bodies* emanating from a sensible body, as some held: rather, every indi-vidual one of them is *a movement and an affection* of a medium that has been altered by the action of a sensible object. For if they were different bodies that reached different individuals by emanation, then *this*—that is, everyone sensing the same thing—*would not happen,* but each would perceive only the body that reached him. And although they are not bodies, nevertheless they are not *independent of body,* or of the medium that is as it were affected and moved, or of the sensible object that is as it were what first moves and acts.

446b27 It is clear, then, from what has been said that sound reaches the sense of hearing through many successive movements of parts. And it is similar in the case of odor, except that alteration by odor occurs through alteration of a medium, but alteration by sound through local movement. *But the account of light is different. For light* does not reach the sense of sight through many movements succeeding one another in dif-ferent parts of the medium, but *through one single being (esse)*—that is, by the whole medium being moved, as one moveable thing, in one move-ment, by an illuminating body. In this case *there is not one movement* suc-ceeding another, as there was said to be in the case of odor and sound.

The reason for this difference is that what is received in something as in its proper and natural subject can remain in it and be a principle of action, but what is received in something only as an adventitious quali-ty can neither remain in it nor be a principle of action.

Now because substantial forms are the principles of qualities and of all accidents, that quality is received in a subject according to its proper and natural being which disposes the subject to the natural form of which it is receptive. For instance, water, by reason of its matter, is re-ceptive of the substantial form of fire, which is the principle of heat; and so heat is received in water as disposing it to the form of fire, and when fire is removed, the water still remains hot and capable of heating. Likewise odor is received in air and water, and sound in air, both according to their proper and natural being, and according as air and water are altered by enchymous dryness, or air by the striking of a body. Thus, when the striking ceases, sound remains in the air; and when the odor-causing body is removed, odor is still perceived in the air. The reason is that the part of the air that has been changed so as to take on a sound or odor can likewise change another part, and thus different movements are produced that succeed one another.

But the transparent is not receptive of the substantial form of the illuminating body, for instance the sun, which is the first "root" of light, and neither is it disposed by reception of light to any substantial form. Hence light is received in the transparent as an adventitious quality that neither remains when the illuminating body is absent, nor is able to be a principle of action on something else. Hence one part of the air is not illuminated by another, but the whole of the air is illuminated by what first illuminates it, however far the power of the illuminating body is able to reach. Thus, there is one thing illuminated, and one illumination of the whole medium.

446b28 Then, when he says *In general, alteration and transfer,* he shows the second difference.

He says that, to speak generally about *alteration and "transfer"*—that is, change of place—the two *are not alike. It is reasonable that* changes of place *should first reach* the *midpoint* of the magnitude over which the movement takes place before reaching the terminus, since in change of place there is movement from one extreme of a magnitude to its other extreme. Hence, the moveable thing must reach the midpoint of the magnitude at the midpoint of the time. Thus the argument introduced above has a place in the case of change of place. *And sound* is a consequence of local *movement* inasmuch as the air is disturbed by the striking that causes the sound all the way to the power of hearing. It is reasonable, then, that sound should reach a midpoint before reaching the sense of hearing.

But in the case of what is *altered,* it is *not like this.* For the termini of alteration are not extremes of a magnitude, and so the time of the alteration is not necessarily, of itself, commensurate with a magnitude in such a way that at the midpoint of the time, the movement would reach the midpoint of the magnitude, whether the midpoint of the magnitude over which the movement occurs (for this cannot be given in alteration, which is not a movement in a quantity or a "where," but in a quality), or the midpoint of a magnitude that is itself moved.

447a1 *For it* can sometimes *happen that* the *whole* of a body *is altered all at once, not half* of it *first,* as we see that *a whole body of water* may be frozen *all at once.*

In local movement, the time is commensurable with the magnitude over which the movement passes, and is divided according to division of the magnitude, as is proved in *Physics* VI.[6] Likewise, in alteration, the time is commensurable with the distance between the termini, and so, other things being equal, more time is required for something cold than for something tepid to be made hot. Thus if there are some extremes between which one cannot take a midpoint, transition from one extreme to the other must occur without intermediary. Now a contradiction is an opposition that of itself has no intermediary, as is said in *Posterior Analytics* I.[7] And, with the supposition of the receptivity of a subject, the account of privation is the same, for privation is nothing but negation in a subject. Hence all alterations of which the termini are being and non-being, or privation and form, are instantaneous and cannot be successive, for in successive alterations the succession is noted by means of determinate intermediaries with respect to the distance of one contrary from the other.

447a3 Within this distance, the whole magnitude of the body over which the power of the first cause of the alteration immediately extends is considered as one single subject that instantaneously, all at once, begins to be moved. But if there is a body that is capable of being altered, but is so large that the power of the first cause of the alteration cannot reach it as a whole, but only part of it, it will follow that after the first part has been altered, it will subsequently alter another one.

And so he says that *if* it is a *large* body that *is heated* or frozen, *what is contiguous is* necessarily *affected by the contiguous*—that is, a subsequent part is necessarily altered by the immediately preceding one. *But the first part is altered, all at once and instantaneously, by the very thing that* first causes the alteration, because here there is not succession from the point of

view of magnitude, but only from the point of view of contrary qualities, as was said. It is because of this that odor first reaches a midpoint
before reaching the sense-power, even though this occurs by alteration
without local movement. For an odorous body cannot alter the whole
medium all at once; rather, it alters one part, which alters another, and
so the alteration reaches the sense of smell by succession, through several movements, as was said above. And it would be the same in the
case of taste as it is in the case of smell *if we* lived *in* watery *moisture,*
which alone is receptive of flavor, as we now live in air, which is receptive of odor; and if, again, flavor could be sensed by alteration of the
medium from a distance before we touched a flavored body, as is the
case with smell.

✤○✤

Now what is said here seems to be contrary to the argument by
which the Philosopher proves in *Physics* VI that everything that is moved
is divisible, because part of it is at the terminus a quo and part at the terminus ad quem.[8] Thus it can be seen that while something is being
changed from white to black, when one part of it is white, another is
black. Thus it cannot be that the whole is altered all at once, but rather
part after part.

But some say that the intention of the Philosopher there is to show
not that one part of a moveable thing is at the terminus a quo and another at the terminus ad quem, but that the moveable thing is at one
part of the terminus a quo and at another part of the terminus ad quem.
And so in alteration it is necessary not that one part of the moveable
thing be altered before another, but that the whole moveable thing that
is altered, for instance from white to black, have a part of whiteness and
a part of blackness.

But this does not agree with Aristotle's intention, because this would
not directly prove that a moveable thing is divisible, but rather that the
termini of movement are somehow divisible. Nor again does it agree
with the words Aristotle uses, as is clear to anyone who carefully looks
at his text, where the passage clearly refers to the parts of the moveable
thing.

Thus a different explanation has to be given, namely that the demonstration is understood with reference to local movement, which is truly
and of itself continuous. For in *Physics* VI Aristotle treats of movement

under the aspect of the continuous. But movements of growth and alteration, as was said in *Physics* VIII, are not simply continuous.[9] Hence Aristotle's remark is not universally true of all alteration, but only of alteration inasmuch as it gets continuity from a moveable thing in which one part alters another. But a moveable thing that the power of the first cause of the alteration reaches all at once, as a whole, is something indivisible inasmuch as it is altered all at once.

❖o❖

447a8 Then, when he says *But it is reasonable,* he concludes from the foregoing to the principal intention.

He says that *it is reasonable,* in the case of the senses for which there is a medium between the sensible object and the organ of sensing, that the whole medium *be affected* and moved *not all at once,* but by succession, *except in the case of light,* and this *because of what has been said:* first, because illumination does not, as Empedocles held, occur by local movement, as the spread of sound does, but by alteration; second, because in illumination there are not several movements, as there were said to be in the case of odor, but only one. To these points we must add a third: that light has no contrary, but darkness is rather opposed to it as simple privation, and so illumination occurs all at once.

And the same must be said *about* vision, because *light causes seeing,* and hence the medium is altered by visible objects analogously to the way it is altered by light.

CHAPTER 16

447A12–448A1

447a12 *But there is also another such objection raised concerning the senses: whether it can happen that two sense simultaneously at the same indivisible point of time, or not?*

447a14 *If a greater movement always drives off a lesser, which is why people do not sense what is brought under their eyes if they are intensely thinking about something, or are afraid, or are hearing a loud sound. . . . Let this, then, be supposed, and also that one can sense anything better when it exists as simple than when mixed: for example, wine that is unmixed can be better sensed than wine that is mixed; and honey; and color; and a note alone better than one with the octave, because they obscure one another. Now it is things from which some one thing is made that do this.*

447a21 *If, then, a greater drives off a lesser, then, if they are simultaneous, even the former is, necessarily, less able to be sensed than if it were alone. For something is taken away by admixture of the lesser one, if indeed everything that is simple is better able to be sensed. Therefore, if they are equal, but exist as separate, neither will be sensible, for each obscures the other; and it is impossible to sense either as simple. Therefore either there will be no sensation, or there will be a different one out of the two. This seems to be brought about by things mixed together, whatever they may be mixed together into.*

447a29 *From some objects, something else can be made; but from some it cannot, and these are objects that come under different senses. For objects that can be mixed together have extremes that are contraries. But one object cannot be made out of white and high-pitched, except accidentally, but not in the way that a harmony is made out of high-pitched and low-pitched.*

447b3 *Therefore it is not possible to sense them simultaneously. For when their movements exist as equal, they will drive out one another, because one movement is not made out of them. But if they are unequal, it will be the stronger that causes sensation.*

447b6 *Moreover, it is more likely that the soul will simultaneously sense two objects of one sense, such as high-pitched and low-pitched, with the one sense: for* *it is more likely that movements of one sense would occur simultaneously than of two, for instance sight and hearing.*

447b9 *But it is not possible to sense two objects simultaneously with one, if they have not been mixed. For a mixture tends to be one thing. But one sense-power at one moment has one object. And it is itself one at the one moment. Therefore it necessarily senses mixtures all at once, because it senses by means of one sense-power in actuality. For as numerically one in actuality, it has one object; but as specifically so, it is one in potentiality or power.*

Therefore, if it is one sense-power in actuality, it will say that one object. Therefore, they are necessarily mixed together. Therefore, when they are not mixed, there will be two senses in actuality. But, with respect to one power, at one indivisible moment, there is necessarily only one operation, for there is only one use, and one movement, of one thing at one time, and it is one power. Therefore it is not possible to sense simultaneously two objects with one sense-power.

447b21 *But if this is impossible simultaneously in the case of objects that come under the same sense-power if there are two of them, it is obvious that it is still less possible to sense simultaneously objects of two senses, such as white and sweet.*

447b24 *The soul seems to say that something is numerically one by nothing other than this "all at once"; but it seems to say that something is specifically one by the sense that judges, and by the manner. What I mean is this. The same proper one will judge that, say, white and black are different. And one sense, different from that one, but itself the same, will judge that sweet and bitter are different. They judge each of the contraries in a different way, but they judge the corresponding elements in the same way: for instance, as taste judges sweet, sight judges white; and as the latter judges black, the former judges bitter.*

Commentary

447a12 Having solved two questions, here the Philosopher follows up the third, which is from the point of view of the sense-power itself.

On this point he does three things. First he raises the question. Second he argues for the false position where he says *If a greater movement* (447a14). Third he determines the truth where he says *With respect to the objection* (Ch.18, 448b17).

Accordingly he first says that *concerning the senses* themselves *there is another such objection raised,* namely *whether it can happen that two* senses *sense simultaneously* and *at the same indivisible point of time,* for instance that while sight sees a color hearing simultaneously hears a voice.

447a14 Then, when he says *If a greater movement,* he argues for the false position, attempting to show that two senses cannot sense simultaneously.

First he presents arguments to show this. Second he eliminates a false solution by which this position was maintained, where he says *Some of those who discuss symphoniae* (Ch.17, 448a19).

On the first point he presents three arguments. The first is based on alterations caused by sensible objects. The second is based on the sense-power itself; it starts where he says *Moreover, it is more likely* (447b6). The third is based on contrariety of sensible objects; it starts where he says *Moreover, if movements of contraries are contrary* (Ch.17, 448a1).

He prefaces the first argument with two presuppositions.

The first is that *a greater movement drives* back *a lesser.* Because of this, he says, the result is that often human beings *do not sense what* lies *under their eyes,* because of a more powerful movement. This may be an interior movement, whether of reason, as when *they are intensely thinking about something,* or of appetitive power, as when they are intensely *afraid.* Or it may be an external movement caused by some sensible object, as when they *are hearing a loud sound. This,* then, he says, is to *be supposed* as evidence.

The second presupposition is that *anything* is sensed *better* if it is *simple* than if it is *mixed* with something else, as *wine* has a stronger taste if it is pure than if it is *mixed* with water. The same is true of *honey* with respect to taste; and of *color* with respect to sight. And, with respect to hearing, it is true of one single *note,* which is better sensed if it is *alone* than if it is heard in harmony with another tone such as *the octave,* or in any other harmony. This is so because things mixed together *obscure one another.* But this second presupposition applies only to *things from which one thing* can be *made,* for such things alone are thoroughly mixed together.

447a21 From these two presuppositions he goes further when he adds *If, then, a greater drives off a lesser.*

He says that *if a greater* movement *drives* back *a lesser,* as the first presupposition says, *then,* if both movements *are simultaneous,* even the greater one *is necessarily less able to be sensed than if it were alone,* because *something* of it *is taken away by admixture of the lesser one,* as appears from the second presupposition, namely that what is *simple is better able to be sensed* than what is mixed. It is significant that he has said "if they are simultaneous," because the greater movement is sometimes so strong that it does not allow another movement to occur, and then it is not at all diminished by a lesser movement, because there is none. But if it does not prevail to the extent that it completely prevents the lesser movement from occurring, then, while the two movements exist, the lesser movement necessarily obscures the greater one to some extent. *Therefore, if* the movements are completely *equal, but exist as* different, *neither will be sensible,* because *each* wholly *obscures the other*—unless perhaps from the two movements one movement is made by mixture, but then what is *simple* in them cannot be sensed. And thus it must be *either* that *no sensation* of the equal movements occurs, *or* that there is *a different* sensation composed *from both,* that is, inasmuch as what is sensed is composed out of the two. And this is clearly the case in everything that is *mixed together,* because the mixture is not any of the things that are mixed together, but something else composed out of them. It is clear, then, from the foregoing that if two movements are unequal, the greater obscures the lesser, but if they are equal, either nothing or a mixture is sensed.

447a29 And from these points he proceeds further.

He proposes that there are *some objects* out of which some one thing *can be made, but* there are *some* out of which one thing cannot be made, and such are objects, such as color and odor, sensed by *different senses.* For only those objects *can be mixed together* in which the *extremes* are *contraries,* because mixture occurs by alteration. But objects that are sensed by different senses are not contrary to one another, and hence cannot be mixed together. For example, some *one object* is not made out of a *white* color and a *high-pitched* sound, *except* perhaps *accidentally,* inasmuch as they come together in the same subject; *but not* per se, *in the way that a harmony* is constituted *out of a low-pitched and a high-pitched* tone.

447b3 From this he concludes that it is in no way *possible to sense* objects of different senses *simultaneously,* because if *their movements* are *equal,* they will entirely destroy *one another,* since *one* thing cannot be *made out of them; but if they are unequal,* the greater movement will prevail, and it alone will be sensed.

447b6 Then when he says *Moreover, it is more likely,* he presents the second argument, which is based on the unity and plurality of the senses. He argues by denial of what is more likely.

It seems *more likely that the soul* is able to *sense simultaneously two objects* pertaining to *one sense—such as high-pitched and low-pitched* in sounds—by means of *the one sense,* than that it is able to sense simultaneously different objects pertaining to different senses by means of the two senses. He gives the following reason for this. To the extent that movements are more different, they seem less able to be attributed to the same thing. But two movements by which the soul, by means of different senses, senses different objects belonging to different genera are more different from one another than are two movements by which the soul perceives through one sense different objects belonging to the same genus. Hence *it* seems *more likely that there* could *simultaneously* be in one soul *movements of one sense* in relation to different sensible objects of the same genus, *than* movements *of two* senses, *for instance sight and hearing.*

447b9 Having presented this comparison, he eliminates what seems more likely.

He says that *it is not possible to sense simultaneously,* by means of *one* sense, *two objects,* unless the two have been *mixed* together, and then when they have been mixed together, they are not two objects, because *a mixture* is naturally some *one thing.*

He proves in the following way that one sense cannot simultaneously know several things except to the extent that they become one thing by means of mixture. *One sense-power* can be in actuality *at one moment* with respect to only *one object,* just as the terminus of any one operation or movement can be only something that is one. And a sense-power in actuality must, at one and the same moment, be one and the same sense-power in actuality; for no power simultaneously receives different forms. Thus if a sense-power, for instance sight or hearing, has to sense several things simultaneously, *it necessarily senses* them inasmuch as they have been made one by mixture, *because* the sensitive power senses the two things *by means of one sense-power in actuality*—that is, one sensitive operation. A sense-power in actuality—that is, a sensitive operation—has numerical unity because *it has one* sensible *object. But* it is *specifically* one sense-power in actuality—or one sensitive operation—because it is *one in potentiality or power.* For instance, all seeings of any visible things are specifically the same because of the unity of the power; but the seeing of one thing differs numerically from the seeing of another.

Therefore, if it is one sense-power in actuality, it must *"say"*—that is, judge of—*one object. Therefore,* if there are many objects, they must be *mixed together* into one. *Therefore,* if *they are not mixed,* there must be two *senses in actuality*—that is, two sensitive operations. *But there is necessarily only one operation* of *one power at one* and the same *indivisible moment,* because there can only be *one use, and one movement, of one thing at one time.* Hence, since sensitive operation is nothing but a "use" in which the soul uses a sensitive power, as well as a "movement" of the power itself, inasmuch as the sense is moved by a sensible thing, therefore, since one sense *is one power, it is not possible to sense simultaneously two objects with one sense.*

447b21 Therefore, if objects of one sense cannot be sensed *simultaneously if there are two of them,* it seems clear *that it is still less possible to sense simultaneously objects of* different *senses, such as white and sweet.*

447b24 Next he clarifies this inference.

He says that *the soul seems* to judge *that something is numerically one* in no other way than the thing's being perceived by it *all at once,* for sensitive operation itself is numerically one inasmuch as it is all at once, as was said. But the soul says that something is *specifically one* not because the latter is sensed all at once, but because it is the same *sense* that *judges* of each of two objects, and because it is the same *manner* in which it senses each. To explain what he said, he adds that *the same proper one—* that is, the same proper sense-power—judges of two different objects, namely *white and black.* Likewise, a sense that *itself* is *the same,* judges *sweet and bitter,* for both are apprehended by the same sense, namely taste. But this sense that, while being the same, knows sweet and bitter, is *different from* the one that knows white and black. Nevertheless, one and the same sense knows *each of the contraries in a different way:* for it knows one as a possession and something perfect, and the other as a privation and something imperfect, since all contraries are related in this way. However the way in which both senses know *the corresponding elements—*that is, the principles that analogously correspond to one another—is the same: for *sight* senses *white* the way *taste* senses *sweet,* and taste senses *bitter* as sight senses *black.*

Therefore it is clear that the soul judges that things are specifically different either by a different sense-power, as in the case of white and sweet, or by a different manner of sensing, as in the case of white and black; but it judges that a thing is numerically one by perceiving it all at once. If, then, it is impossible for what is specifically one to be numerically one, it seems to be impossible for the soul to sense simultaneously either things that are known by different senses, or even things that are known by one sense but in different ways, and which seem to be less different from one another than are things known by different senses.

CHAPTER 17

448A1–B16

448a1 *Moreover, if movements of contraries are contrary; and contraries cannot simultaneously be in the same atomon; and there are contraries, for instance sweet and bitter, under one sense-power—then one cannot sense them simultaneously.*

But likewise, clearly, neither can one simultaneously sense objects that are not contraries. For some belong to white and some to black. And likewise in other cases: for instance some flavors belong to sweet and some to bitter.

Nor can one simultaneously sense mixtures simultaneously, for the proportions belong to opposites, for instance the octave and the fifth; unless they are perceived as one, but thus one proportion is made of the extremes, but otherwise not.

For there will be simultaneously many to few, or odd to even, or few to many, or even to odd.

If, then, the so-called "corresponding elements," which are in different genera, stand apart and differ from one another still more than do objects in the same genus (I call sweet and white, for instance, corresponding elements in different genera, and sweet differs specifically from black much more than white does); then one can sense these simultaneously still less than those in one genus. So if not the former, then neither the latter.

448a19 *Some of those who discuss symphoniae say that sounds do not arrive simultaneously, but they seem to, and it escapes notice, since the time is insensible. Is it correct to say this or not? Perhaps someone will say that it is also because of this that one thinks that he simultaneously sees and hears, namely because the intervening lengths of time escape notice.*

448a24 *Or perhaps it is not true that any length of time can be insensible or escape notice: rather, absolutely all of them can be perceived.*

448a26 *For if, when one senses oneself or something else in a continuous length of time, it cannot escape his notice that it is existing; and something is existing in a continuous length of time; and it is so brief as to be completely insensible; it is clear that it will then escape his notice whether he himself is existing, and that he is seeing, and that he is sensing, and whether he is sensing.*

448a30 *Moreover, there will be no length of time (and no thing that one senses) during which it is not the case that it is being sensed in some part of it (or that one sees some part of the thing)—if indeed there is some magnitude of time and of a thing that is insensible because of smallness.*

For if one is seeing and sensing the whole during the same continuous length of time not because one does so in some part of it—then let GB, in which it was not being sensed, be subtracted. Accordingly, one does not sense "during a part of it," or "a part of it," in the way that one sees the whole earth because one sees a part of it, and one walks during a year because one does so during this part of it. Rather, one senses nothing in GB. Therefore, it is because one senses it in a part, namely AG, that one is said to sense the whole of AB, and the whole thing. But the same account also applies to AG: it is always a case of "during a part of it," and "a part of it," and it is impossible to sense the whole of AGB.

448b12 *All things, then, are sensible, but do not appear to be everything that they are: the size of the sun appears from far away to be four cubits. A thing does not appear to be everything that it is: rather, sometimes it is indivisible, but one sees what is not indivisible. The cause of this has been stated in the foregoing.*

448b16 *Therefore it is clear from these remarks that no length of time is insensible.*

Commentary

448a1 Having presented two arguments to show that it is impossible for two senses to sense simultaneously, here he presents a third argument for the same conclusion based on the contrariety of sensible objects.

He says that alterations caused by *contraries are contrary,* for instance heating and cooling. *But contraries cannot simultaneously be in the same "atomon"*—that is, the same indivisible part (contraries can simultaneously be in the same divisible part with respect to different parts of it). *But* it is clear that objects *under one sense-power* are *contraries, for instance sweet and bitter.* Therefore they cannot be sensed *simultaneously.*

The argument is similar in the case of *objects that are not contraries,* that is, intermediate objects, some of which more closely approach one extreme, and some the other. For instance, as was said above about colors and flavors, *some* intermediate colors pertain to *white* and *some to black, and likewise some* intermediate *flavors* pertain *to sweet and some to bitter.*

And the argument is the same in the case of all *mixtures,* for different mixtures have a contrariety between themselves because they are made in different *proportions,* and different proportions have an opposition to one another. This is clear in harmonies: one is called *the octave,* which consists in the double proportion, that of two to one; another is called *the fifth,* which consists in the sesquialteral proportion, that of three to two. Such things, I say, thus mixed together in different proportions, cannot be *simultaneously* sensed, because of the opposition between proportions—*unless,* perhaps, two *are perceived as one,* because *thus one proportion* will be *made* out of two *extremes.*

Next he shows that different proportions are opposed according to the two kinds of opposition found in numbers. One is according to many and few, by which the proportion of double and the proportion of half are opposed: for the proportion of double is one of *many to few,* but the proportion of half is one of *few to many.* The other kind of opposition is according to even and odd, by which the double proportion and the sesquialteral proportion are opposed: for the double proportion is one of two to one, that is, of *even to odd,* but the sesquialteral proportion is of three to two, that is, of *odd to even.*

Thus it is clear that objects falling under the same sense cannot be sensed simultaneously. But objects that correspond to one another as "corresponding elements" existing *in different genera—for instance sweet and white—stand farther apart from one another than* do objects belonging to one *genus.* For objects belonging to one genus, such as white and black, are specifically distinguished only because of the manner of sensing. But objects belonging to different genera can differ *specifically* not only from the point of view of the sense-power, but also from the point of view of manner of sensing: for instance, *sweet differs from black more than white does.* Hence they are *less* able to be sensed *simultaneously,* which is, as it were, to be numerically one, as was established above.[1] Therefore, if objects belonging to one genus cannot, because of their contrariety, be sensed simultaneously, much less can objects belonging to different genera be sensed simultaneously.

448a19 Then when he says *Some of those who discuss symphoniae,* he eliminates a false solution of this question.

First he relates it. Second he disproves it, where he says *Or perhaps it is not true* (448a24).

Accordingly he first says that *some* who treated of *"symphoniae"*—that is, musical harmonies—said that the harmonizing *sounds do not* reach the sense of hearing *simultaneously,* but that they *seem to* reach it simultaneously because the intervening *time* is *insensible* on account of its brevity. There might be doubt about this: *Is it correct to say this or not?* If it is correct, someone who agrees with the arguments presented above will be able to say that, likewise, with respect to the question posed, it is not possible to simultaneously see and hear, although this does seem to the sense-power to happen, *because the intervening lengths of time* between the vision and the hearing *escape* our *notice.*

448a24 Then when he says *Or perhaps it is not true,* he disproves the above-mentioned solution.

On this point he does three things. First he eliminates something that the solution stated presupposes. Second he proves what he has said, where he says *For if, when one senses oneself* (448a26). Third he clarifies what is true in the solution, where he says *All things, then, are sensible* (448b12).

Accordingly he first says that something that the solution stated presupposes *is not true,* namely that there is a *length of time* that is *insensible,* or escapes the notice of the sense-power. For no length of time is like this: *rather, all* lengths of time *can be sensed.*

448a26 Then when he says *For if, when one senses oneself,* he proves what he has said by two arguments.

Concerning the first of these, we must consider that time is not sensed as a permanent thing presented to a sense-power in the way that color or size is presented to sight. Rather, time is sensed because something that is in time is sensed. It follows, then, that if there is some length of time that is insensible, what is in that length of time is insensible.

Accordingly he says that if at some point, *in some continuous length of time,* a human being *senses* that he himself is existing, *it cannot escape his notice that* that length of time *is existing.* Now it is clear that the human being, or the *something else,* is existing in some *continuous length of time.* And however *brief* you say the *insensible* length of time is, *it is clear that it will escape* the human being's *notice* that *he himself is existing* during that time, and it will escape his notice *that he is seeing,* or *sensing,* during that time, which is entirely unreasonable. Therefore it is impossible for a length of time to be insensible.

448a30 He presents the second argument where he says *Moreover, there will be no length of time.*

Concerning this it must first be considered that, as the Philosopher says in *Physics* V, a thing is said to move or be moved in three ways: in one way accidentally, for instance, if we say that the one who is musical is walking; in another way with respect to a part, for instance, if we say that a man is healed because his eye is healed; and in a third way primarily and per se, that is, when a thing is moved or moves not because just one part of it is moved or moves, but because the whole is moved with respect to every one of its parts.[2]

Likewise, a thing can be said to be sensed in three ways: in one way accidentally, as, for instance, what is sweet is seen; in another way with respect to a part, for instance, if we say that a man is seen because just his head is seen; and in a third way primarily and per se, that is, not because just some part of it is seen.

Accordingly he says that *if there is some magnitude*—whether *of time,* or *of a* bodily *thing—that is insensible because of smallness,* what will follow is this: *there will be no length of time and no thing that one senses* (i.e. no thing that is sensed, or that a sense-power senses) *during which* (i.e. during which length of time) *it is not the case* (i.e. during which the time is not being sensed) because it is being sensed *in some part of it.* In other words: there will be no length of time that is sensible "primarily," i.e. that is not said to be sensed because some part of it is being sensed. And with reference to the bodily thing he adds *or because one sees some part of the thing.* In other words: there will be no bodily magnitude that is not sensed because some part of it is sensed, which means that no bodily magnitude is sensible "primarily."

To prove what he has said he adds that *if* someone *sees,* or *senses* by any sense, *during* some *continuous length of time not* by reason of a part of the time or magnitude; and nevertheless some magnitude and length of time are held to be insensible because of smallness; then let there be a magnitude—whether of time or of a bodily thing—namely AGB, and *let* the part of it that is the *GB* be insensible because of smallness. *Accordingly,* it cannot be said of this part that is insensible because of smallness that it is sensed *"in a part of it"*—if it is an insensible length of time—or that *"a part of it"* is sensed—if it is an insensible body—as *the whole earth* is said to be seen by someone *because* a part of the earth is seen, and as someone is said to *walk during a year because* he walks *during* a *part* of the year. Therefore, because *one senses nothing in GB,* it remains that *one is said to sense the whole of AB*—whether it is a time or a body—because the whole of AB is sensed in the part of it that is left, *namely AG.* And *the account* of the magnitude *AG,* which is held to be sensed, is the *same,* because a part of it will be insensible because of smallness. And so anything sensible will *always* be said to be sensed because it is sensed *in a part of it*—if it is a length of time—or because *a part* of it is sensed—if it is a body. *But* it will be *possible to sense* nothing *whole,* such as *AGB.*

But this seems unreasonable. Therefore there is no length of time or body that is insensible because of smallness.

But this argument does not seem to work. For a thing is sensed because it has power to alter a sense. Now it is proved in *Physics* VII that if some whole moves something moveable in some length of time, it need not be the case that a part of the whole moves the moveable thing in any length of time.[3] But although no part of the whole, perhaps, could cause the movement, nevertheless, the whole that causes the movement is said to be the first mover. Likewise, it seems, one could say that a thing can be sensible "primarily" although some parts of it are insensible because of smallness.

In response to this it must be said that there is a difference between speaking of a part existing in a whole and a part separated from a whole. If a part of what primarily causes movement is separated, it may not be able to cause movement. But if, while existing in the whole, it did not cooperate in the power to move of the whole, but completely lacked power to move, it would follow that the whole would be the mover not "primarily," but by reason of the part to which power to move does belong.

Likewise, too, nothing prevents a part taken separately from escaping the notice of a sense-power because of smallness, as was established above, while nevertheless, the part as existing in the whole does fall under the sense-power inasmuch as the sense-power is brought to bear on the whole, with no part left out.

448b12 To address this doubt, next, when he says *All things, then, are sensible,* he shows what is true in the foregoing.

He says that *all things*, whether big or small, *are sensible, but do not appear to be everything that they are*, that is, they do not appear as they are in every way. This is clear in the case of *the sun*, the *size* of which is far greater than that of the earth, and nevertheless, because it is *far away*, it *appears to be four cubits* in size, or even smaller. Likewise, although all things are sensible by their nature, nevertheless an object *does not appear* in actuality *to be everything* that it is: *rather, sometimes it is indivisible, but one sees what is not indivisible*. This can be understood in two ways.

One way is according as "indivisible" refers to some minimal natural body that cannot be further divided without being destroyed, and then absorbed into the surrounding body. Thus the meaning will be that an indivisible body is sensible in itself, although the sense-power cannot see an indivisible object of this kind.

In the other way, "indivisible" can be understood as what is not divided off in actuality, for example a part of a continuum. The sense power does not see this kind of indivisible object in actuality.

What he adds fits either explanation: that *the cause of this has been stated* above, that is, in the determination of the first question. But the second explanation seems to be better, because by means of it the above-mentioned objection is resolved, because any part whatsoever of a continuous magnitude is indeed sensed within the whole inasmuch as it is in the whole in potentiality, although it is not sensed in actuality as separate.

448b16 Finally he concludes that *it is clear from* what has been said *that no length of time is insensible.*

CHAPTER 18

448B17–449B4

448b17 *With respect to the objection stated above, it must be considered whether it is possible or not possible to sense several things simultaneously. By "simultaneously" I mean together in one indivisible moment of time.*

448b20 *First, then, whether it is possible to sense simultaneously by means of a different part of the soul, which is not indivisible, but is indivisible in the way that something continuous is.*

448b22 *Or first, the case of objects sensed by one sense. For instance if sight senses different colors with different parts of itself, it will have several parts specifically the same, for what is sensed belongs to the same genus.*

448b26 *If someone says that, since there are two eyes, nothing prevents it from being like this in the soul as well—it must be said that perhaps out of these some one thing is made, and they have one operation. But in the other case, if some one thing is made out of two, that will be what senses; but if they are separate, it will not be like the other case.*

448b29 *Moreover, there will also be several senses that are the same, as if someone were to speak of sciences that are not different. For there can be neither an operation without its own power, nor a sense-power without the former.*

449a2 *But if it senses this by one indivisible part, it is clear that it also senses the others. For it is more possible for several of these to be sensed simultaneously than ones of different genera. If, then, the soul senses sweet by one part but white by another, out of these either some one thing is made or it is not. But it necessarily is, for the sensitive part is some one part. What one object, then, does it have? For there is no one object made out of these objects. Therefore there is necessarily some one part of the soul by which it senses everything, as was said before, but it senses different genera by means of different parts.*

449a10 *Accordingly, inasmuch as it is indivisible it is one power in actuality able to sense sweet and white. But when it is made divisible, it is different in actuality.*

449a13 *Or again, as it is in things themselves, so also in the soul. For one and numerically the same thing is white, and sweet, and many other things, if* *the affections are not separable from one another. But the being* (esse) *of each is different. Similarly, then, we should posit that also in the soul the power that is able to sense all things—although these differ in being, some in genus and some in species—is one and numerically the same. Hence it will also perceive by means of what is simultaneously one and the same, but not the same in aspect* (ratio).

449a20 *Now it is clear that everything that is sensible is a magnitude, and what is indivisible is not sensible. For there is an infinite distance from which it will not be able to be seen, but that from which it can be seen is finite. And it is similar with the audible and the odorous, and whatever senses without touching the things themselves. And so there is a limit to the distance from which it cannot be seen, and a point from which it can first be seen. And so there is necessarily something indivisible beyond which there is no sensing, but on this side of which there is necessarily sensing. If, then, something indivisible is sensible, when it is placed at the limit that is the last point from which it is not sensible and the first point from which it is sensible, it will simultaneously be visible and invisible. But this is impossible.*

449b1 *Something has been said, then about the sensitive parts, and sensible objects, how they are related, both in general and with respect to each sensitive part. Of what remains, the first to be considered are memory and recollection and sleep.*

Commentary

448b17 After the Philosopher has eliminated a false solution, here he seeks the true one.

On this point he does three things. First he investigates the truth about the aforementioned question. Second he proves something he presupposed in the foregoing, where he says *Now it is clear that everything that is sensible* (449a20). Third he adds an epilogue to what was said in this book, where he says *Something has been said, then* (449b1).

On the first point he does two things. First he proposes what he intends. Second he carries out the proposal, where he says *First, then, whether it is possible to sense simultaneously* (448b20).

Accordingly, on the basis of the fact that what some have said has been eliminated—namely that several things are sensed simultaneously not in a moment of time that is indivisible according to the truth of the matter, but in a length of time that is imperceptible because of brevity—we must consider, *with respect to the objection* raised *above, whether it is or is not possible to sense several things simultaneously,* taking "simultaneously" to mean *in an indivisible moment of time.*

448b20 Then when he says *First, then, whether it is possible to sense simultaneously,* presupposing that an animal does sense different sensible objects simultaneously—for we obviously have experience of this—he investigates how this is possible.

On this point he does three things. First he presents a false way. Second he disproves it, where he says *Or first, the case of objects sensed by one sense* (448b22). Third he presents the true way, where he says *Accordingly, inasmuch as it is indivisible* (449a10).

Accordingly he first says that it must *first* be considered *whether it is possible to simultaneously sense* different sensible objects *by means of a different part of the soul,* the sensitive part of the soul being, as it were, *not indivisible*—that is, not incapable of being divided—although it *is indivisible* in the sense that it is not divided in actuality, being like a *continuous* whole. For if we understand the sensitive part of the soul to be like a continuum, the arguments presented above are dissolved, because nothing will prevent different and contrary things from being in the sensitive power of the soul with respect to its different parts, in the way we see that one body is white in one part and black in another.

448b22 Then when he says *Or first, the case of objects sensed by one sense,* he disproves the way just mentioned.

On this point he does three things. First he shows that it will follow that even one sense, for instance sight, is divisible into several parts. Second he shows that this is impossible, where he says *If someone says* (448b26). Third he shows that it is also not possible with respect to different senses, where he says *But if it senses this by one indivisible part* (449a2).

Accordingly he first says that since one can simultaneously sense several objects *by* the same *sense,* as when *sight* distinguishes between white and black, according to the foregoing argument one will have to say that it senses the different colors by different parts of itself, and so it will follow that the same sense *will have several parts specifically the same.* For it cannot be said that parts of the sense of sight differ specifically, because everything *sensed* by sight *belongs to the same genus,* and there is specific difference among sensitive powers only because of different genera of sensible objects.

448b26 Then when he says *If someone says,* he disproves what was said by two arguments.

The first is that *if someone says that,* just as there are two organs of sight—that is, *two eyes—nothing prevents* there being two senses of sight *in the* sensitive *soul as well,* in response to this *it must be said that out of* the two eyes *some one thing is made, and* that there is *one operation* of both eyes—that is, inasmuch as the seeings of the two eyes concur, by way of certain nerves, at an inner organ of sight that is near the brain, as was said above.[1] But *if,* likewise, in the soul *some one thing is made out of two* powers of sight by the two powers concurring in some one principle, it is to that one principle that the operation of sensing will be attributed. But *if* the two powers of sight are altogether *separate* in the soul because they do not concur in some one principle, the relation of powers of sight in the soul *will not be like* that of eyes in the body, and so the comparison was not suitable for showing what was proposed. Therefore, it does not seem reasonable to say that there are two powers of sight in the soul.

448b29 He presents the second argument where he says *Moreover, there will also be several senses.*

He says that according to the position stated above *there will be several senses that are* specifically *the same,* for instance several senses of sight or several senses of hearing. It would be *as if someone* said that there are, in the same human being, several sciences that are *not* specifically *different,* for instance several grammars or several geometries. It is certainly possible for there to be numerically several grammars or several powers of sight in different human beings, but not in one and the same human beings, just as it is impossible for there to be numerically several whitenesses in one and the same subject. To show that there cannot be several senses specifically the same in the same human being, he adds that sensitive power and operation follow from one another in such a way that *neither* can there be a power *without* its proper and per se operation, *nor an operation without its* proper *power.* But sensitive operation is distinguished according to sensible objects, and so where sensible objects are completely the same, there are not different sensitive powers causing different operations. The habits of the sciences are similar: their acts are distinguished according to their objects.

449a2 Then when he says *But if it senses this by one indivisible part,* he shows that this is impossible for objects of different senses, that is, that it is impossible for them to be sensed by different parts of the soul.

He says that *if* sensible objects belonging to different genera are perceived by some *one* and the same *indivisible part* of the soul, *it is clear that* much more so are *the others,* that is, those belonging to one genus. For it was proved above that *it is more possible for* objects belonging to one genus *to be sensed simultaneously than* objects belonging to *different genera,* and this is especially true with respect to the identity of the one perceiving.

He proves as follows that the soul does perceive sensible objects of different genera by the same indivisible part. *If* the soul *senses sweet* by *one* part of itself and *white* by *another, out of these* two parts *either some one thing* will be made or it will *not.* But one must *necessarily* say that there is some one thing to which all these parts—that is, the different senses—are referred, because *the sensitive part is some one part* of the soul. But it cannot be said that the sensitive part of the soul has some *one* genus of sensible objects—unless, perhaps, it were said that *out of* all objects of particular senses—for instance color, sound, and other such objects—is made *one* sensible *object* that would correspond to the one part of the sensitive part that is common to all proper senses. But this is impossible. *Therefore there is necessarily some one part of the soul by which* an animal *senses everything, but it senses different genera by means of different parts,* for instance color by sight, and sound by hearing, and so on.

Now here it must be considered that wherever there are different ordered powers, a lower power is related to a higher one as an instrument, because the higher moves the lower, and action is attributed to the principal agent acting by means of an instrument, as we say that a builder cuts by means of a saw. It is in this way that the Philosopher says here that the common sense perceives by means of sight, and by means of hearing, and by means of other proper senses, which are different potential parts of the soul, and not, as was claimed above, like different parts of a continuum.

449a10 Then, when he says *Accordingly, inasmuch as it is indivisible,* he shows how the same indivisible part of the soul can simultaneously perceive different things. He presents two ways.

He presents the first briefly and obscurely, because it has been presented more fully in *On the Soul.*[2]

For evidence on this point, then, it must be considered that, since the operations of the proper senses are referred to the common sense as their first and common principle, the common sense is related to the proper senses and their operations in the way that one point is related to different lines that meet in it. Now a point that is the terminus of different lines is, considered in itself, one and indivisible, and in this way the common sense, *inasmuch as it is* in itself *indivisible, is one power in actuality, able to sense sweet and white,* sweet by means of taste, and white by means of sight. But if the point is considered separately insofar as it is the terminus of this line, and separately again insofar as it is the terminus of another line, it is thus in a way divisible, because we take the one point as two. Likewise the common sense, *when it* is taken as something *divisible*—for instance when it separately judges of white, and separately again of sweet—*is different in actuality.* But inasmuch as it is one, it judges differences among sensible objects. By this the arguments introduced above are dissolved, inasmuch as what senses different sensible objects is in a way one, and in a way not one.

449a13 He presents the second way where he says *Or again, as it is in things themselves.*

He says that *as it is in* external *things, so,* it can be said, it is *in the soul.* For we see that *one and numerically the same* body *is white, and sweet, and many other* such *things* that are predicated of it as accidents—that is, *if* such *affections are not* separated *from one another,* as happens when a body keeps its whiteness and loses its sweetness. But as long as the affections are not thus separated, the white thing and the sweet thing remain the same in subject, but differ in *being.* Likewise, it can be posited of *the soul that the power able to sense all* sensible objects—both those that differ *in genus,* such as white and sweet, and those that differ *in species,* such as white and black—*is one and the same* in subject. And according to this, it will have to be said that the soul senses different sensible objects by means of what in a way is *one and the same,* that is, one and the same in subject, but in a way is *not the same,* inasmuch as it differs *in aspect.*

Difficulties

I

Now an objection to this might be raised. For in what is outside the soul, although the same thing could be sweet and white, nevertheless the same thing cannot be white and black. Thus it would seem that the soul cannot simultaneously sense sensible objects of one genus when they are contraries. Aristotle raises this objection in *On the Soul* when he says, "And it is impossible for white and black to be simultaneous: therefore, neither can their species be experienced simultaneously."[3]

He suggests the solution by what he adds: "if sense and intellect are similar."[4] By this he gives us to understand that the situation in sense and intellect is not completely similar to that in natural bodies. For a natural body receives forms according to their natural and material being, according to which they have contrariety, which is why the same body cannot simultaneously receive whiteness and blackness. But sense and intellect receive the forms of things spiritually and immaterially according to an intentional being, in such a way that they have no contrariety. Hence sense and intellect can simultaneously receive species of contrary sensible objects. Something like this can be seen in the transparent, which in one and the same part of itself can be altered by white and by black, because the alteration is not material or according to natural being, as was said above.

There is also something else to be considered: that sense and intellect not only receive the forms of things, but also make a judgment about them. Now judgment about contraries is not itself contrary, but something one and the same, because by one of the contraries a judgment is taken about the other. To this extent, what was said above is true, that sensible objects belonging to one genus, where judgment about one of the objects is made by means of the other, can more readily be sensed simultaneously than objects of different senses.

II

But there is also another difficulty on this point, because the Philosopher's words presented above (449a13–20) seem to confirm an opinion of the Stoics, who held that color and odor and other sensible objects are not sensed by different powers; and that there are not different sense-powers; but that the soul itself, of itself, knows all sensible objects, and in doing so differs only in aspect.

To this it must be said that the solution of this second difficulty presupposes the first solution. Thus it must be understood that the soul—that is, the common sense, existing as numerically one, and differing only in aspect—knows different genera of sensible objects, which, however, are referred to it by the different powers of the proper senses.

449a20 Then, when he says *Now it is clear that everything that is sensible,* he proves something he presupposed above, namely that nothing is perceived unless it is of some size.

He says that *it is clear that everything that is sensible is a magnitude,* and nothing *indivisible* is *sensible.* To prove this, he introduces the consideration that *there is a distance from which* a thing cannot be *seen;* he says that this distance is *"infinite,"* because if the distance is extended to infinity, nothing is seen from there. And there is a distance *from which* a thing *can be seen,* and this is *"finite,"* because a thing begins to be seen from a finite distance. *It is similar* with the other senses, namely hearing and smell, that sense from some distance through an external medium *without touching the* sensible *things themselves.* Therefore, since the distance from which a thing cannot be seen is infinite in the direction away from sight, but finite in the direction towards sight, it follows that it is possible to identify *a limit from which* nothing is *seen.* But the distance from which a thing can be seen is finite in both directions. Therefore it is possible to identify a terminus *from which* a thing *can first be seen.* But anything intermediate between two quantities continuous with one another is indivisible. Therefore *there is necessarily* some *indivisible* point *beyond which* nothing can be sensed, and *on this side of which* a thing *necessarily* can be sensed. Therefore, *if something indivisible is sensible,* and it *is placed at* that indivisible boundary, it will follow that it is *simultaneously visible and invisible:* invisible inasmuch as it is at the boundary of the distance of the invisible, but visible inasmuch as it is at the boundary of the visible. *But this is impossible.* Therefore the first premise, that something indivisible is sensible, is also impossible. For if something indivisible is placed at the above-mentioned terminus, it will be partly seen and partly not seen, which cannot be said of the indivisible.

Now this proof might seem to fail, because it is not possible to identify a boundary from which all visible things begin to be seen: rather, bigger things are seen from a bigger distance, and smaller ones from a smaller distance.

To this it must be said that every sensible object is visible from some determinate distance. Therefore if the indivisible thing that is held to be sensible is seen from some determinate distance, like a divisible thing, then Aristotle's argument will be conclusive. But if it is not possible to determine a distance from which it begins to be seen at the same time as a divisible thing is, it will again follow that in no way can it be seen. For one must take the proportion of the distance from which divisible things can be seen according to the proportion of the magnitudes that are seen. But there is no proportion of indivisible to divisible magnitude, for instance of a point to a line. Thus it will follow that what is indivisible cannot be seen from any distance, because any distance has a proportion to any other distance. Therefore it will follow that, if the indivisible thing is seen, it is seen by union with sight, which is contrary to the nature of sight and of the other senses that sense without touching. Therefore, an indivisible thing cannot be sensed—except, perhaps, inasmuch as it is the limit of a continuum, for other accidents of continua are also perceived in this way.

449b1 Then, when he says *Something has been said, then,* he makes an epilogue to what was said in this book and establishes continuity with what follows.

He says that *something has been said about the sensitive parts*—that is, the organs of sensing—and about *sensible objects,* and *how they are related* to the senses, *both in general and with respect to each* organ of sense, partly in this book, partly in the book *On the Soul. Of what remains, the first to be considered are memory and recollection and sleep,* because as present things are known by the sense-power, so past things are known by memory, and there is a certain foreknowledge of future things in sleep.

NOTES TO COMMENTARY ON
ON SENSE AND WHAT IS SENSED

Notes to the Translator's Introduction

1. Aristotle, *Parva naturalia*. Rev. text with introduction and commentary by Sir David Ross (Oxford: Oxford University Press, 1955; special edition for Sandpiper Books Ltd., 2001).

2. P. 1.

3. Pp. 2–18.

4. See Bernard G. Dod, "Aristoteles latinus," in *The Cambridge History of Later Medieval Philosophy: From the Rediscovery of Aristotle to the Disintegration of Scholasticism 1100–1600*. Ed. Norman Kretzmann, Anthony Kenny, Jan Pinborg; assoc. ed. Eleonore Stump (Cambridge: Cambridge University Press, 1982), pp. 45–79.

5. Trans. Robert Royal (Washington, D.C.: Catholic University of America Press, 1996). Much of the historical information that follows is taken from this source. On Aquinas's Aristotelian commentaries, see also Joseph Owens, "Aquinas as Aristotelian Commentator," in *St. Thomas Aquinas on the Existence of God: Collected Papers of Joseph Owens, C.Ss.R.*, ed. John R. Catan (Albany: State University of New York Press, 1980), pp. 1–19; and M.-D. Chenu, *Towards Understanding St. Thomas*, trans. A. M. Landry and D. Hughes (Chicago: H. Regnery, 1964), pp. 203–24. On the more general context, see the following articles in *A Companion to Philosophy in the Middle Ages*, ed. Jorge J. E. Gracia and Timothy B. Noone (Oxford: Blackwell, 2003): Charles H. Lohr, "The Ancient Philosophical Legacy and Its Transmission to the Middle Ages," pp. 15–22; and Timothy B. Noone, "Scholasticism," pp. 55–64.

6. See Leonard Boyle, "The Setting of the Summa Theologiae of St. Thomas—Revisited," in *The Ethics of Aquinas*, ed. Stephen J. Pope (Washington, D.C.: Georgetown University Press, 2002), pp. 1–16.

7. See K. White, "St. Thomas Aquinas and the Prologue to Peter of Auvergne's 'Quaestiones super De sensu et sensato,'" *Documenti e Studi sulla Tradizione Filosofica Medievale* 1 (1990), pp. 427–56.

8. Oxford University Press. On the various meanings of "sense" and related terms, see C. S. Lewis, *Studies in Words* (Cambridge: Cambridge University Press, 1990), ch. 6, "Sense (with Sentence, Sensibility and Sensible)," pp. 133–64.

9. Hugh of St. Victor, *Didaskalikon*, III, 9; quoted in M.-D. Chenu, *Towards Understanding St. Thomas*, p. 85, n. 11.

10. "Sententia, secundum Avicennam, est definitiva et certissima conceptio." Book I, division and exposition of the prologue, *Scriptum super Sententiis*, ed. P. Mandonnet and M. F. Moos, 4 vols. (Paris: P. Lethielleux, 1929–1947), vol. 1, p. 24.

11. *Expositio libri Peryermenias* editio altera retractata, Rome-Paris, 1989, p. 84*.

12. See *Sancti Thomae de Aquino Opera omnia,* Tomus 45.2; *Sentencia libri De sensu et sensato cuius secundus tractatus est De memoria et reminiscentia,* ed. R.-A. Gauthier (Rome: Commissio Leonia; Paris: Librairie Philosophique J. Vrin, 1985), pp. 3–9 (hereafter referred to as "Gauthier"). Following the Leonine edition, I have not numbered the first of the commentary's nineteen chapters, but rather called it "Prologue" (which corresponds to the edition's heading *"Prohemium"*). But this chapter in fact consists of two elements: (1) Aquinas's prologue to his commentary, and (2) his commentary on Aristotle's prologue.

13. See Edward P. Mahoney, "Metaphysical Foundations of the Hierarchy of Being according to Some Late-Medieval and Renaissance Philosophers," in *Philosophies of Existence Ancient and Modern,* ed. Parviz Morewedge (New York: Fordham University Press, 1982), pp. 165–257. Aquinas is discussed on pp. 169–72.

14. A. M. Festugière discusses the prologue in "La place du 'De anima' dans le système aristotélicien d'après S. Thomas," *Archives d'Histoire Doctrinale et Litteraire du Moyen Age* 6 (1931), pp. 25–46. He speaks of the prologue's "ferme dessein de tout ordonner sous un principe unique" (p. 44).

15. There are two English translations of Aquinas's commentary on *On the Soul.* The older one, based on the Marietti edition of 1925 and first published in 1951, is *Commentary on Aristotle's De anima,* trans. Kenelm Foster and Silvester Humphries (Notre Dame, Ind.: Dumb Ox Books, 1994); see p. 2 for Aquinas's prologue. The more recent one, based on the critical Leonine edition of the commentary, is *A Commentary on Aristotle's De anima,* trans. Robert Pasnau (New Haven and London: Yale University Press, 1999); see pp. 4–5 for Aquinas's prologue.

16. *Summa theologiae* II-II, Q.53, a.4.

17. On this first and fundamental division of theoretical science, see John F. Wippel, *The Metaphysical Thought of Thomas Aquinas: From Finite Being to Uncreated Being* (Washington, D.C.: Catholic University of America Press, 2000), pp. 4–22.

18. On the Thomistic theme of sense-judgment, see Joseph Owens, "Judgment and Truth in Aquinas," *St. Thomas Aquinas on the Existence of God,* pp. 34–51. For references on the notion of intentional existence, see Owens, *Cognition: An Epistemological Inquiry* (Houston: Center for Thomistic Studies, 1992), p. 57, n. 11.

Notes to the Prologue

1. Aristotle, *On the Soul* III, 4, 429b21–22.

2. Aristotle, *Metaphysics* VI, 1, 1025b3–1026a32.

3. Aristotle, *Physics* I, 1, 184a23–24.

4. *On the Soul* II, 1, 413a7; III, 4, 429a18–b5; III, 5, 430a17–18.

5. See p. ix above.

6. "Virtue" translates the Latin *virtus,* which translated for Aquinas the Greek *dunamis;* "power" translates Aquinas's term *potentia. On the Soul* defines the soul in II, 1–2, then discusses the powers of soul in II, 3–III, 12.

7. *Physics* I, 1, 184a23–24.

8. For more on the distinction of the "internal sense powers," see *Summa theologiae* I, Q.78, a.4.

9. *On the Soul* III, 9, 432b6. Cf. *Summa theologiae* I, Q.81, a.2.

10. The term "concupiscible" is based on "concupiscence" *(concupiscentia)*, which is the name of a kind of desire *(desiderium)*: see *Summa theologiae* I-II, Q.25, a.2, obj.1; Q.30, a.1, ad 2. On the term "irascible," see *Summa theologiae* I-II, Q.25, a.3, ad 1.

11. Aristotle, *Nicomachean Ethics* II, 3, 1104b14–15.

12. *On the Soul* III, 11, 433b31–434a5.

13. The principle is neoplatonic. See Pseudo-Dionysius, *On the Divine Names* VII, 3; *Pseudo-Dionysius, The Complete Works,* trans. Colm Luibheid (New York-Mahwah: Paulist Press, 1987), p. 109.

14. *On the Soul* I, 5, 410a25–26; II, 5, 416b33–34; II, 11, 423b31–424a1.

Notes to Chapter 1

1. "Pleasant" and "unpleasant" translate *delectabile* and *tristabile;* "good-tasting" and "bad-tasting" translate *sapidum* and *insipidum,* which Gauthier (p. 11) indicates as variant translations of the Greek words *to hedu* and *to luperon.*

2. See Preface, p. ix above.

3. P. 18 above.

4. *On the Soul* II, 5, 416b32–35; 11, 423b31–424a1.

5. *On the Soul* II, 12, 424a17–b3.

6. See Alexander of Aphrodisias, *On Aristotle's "On Sense Perception,"* trans. Alan Towey (Ithaca: Cornell University Press, 2000), p. 24. The reader should note that Aquinas's few references to Alexander's commentary do not give sufficient indication of his frequent reliance on it throughout his own commentary.

7. Chapter 8, 440b28–30.

8. *On the Soul* II, 7, 419a11–b3; 8, 419b18–25; 9, 421b8–13; 11, 422b34–423b26; III, 12, 434b24–29.

9. *On the Soul* II, 9, 421a9–13.

10. *Nicomachean Ethics* X, 8, 1178b24–28.

11. *On the Soul* II, 8, 420b29–421a2.

12. *Nicomachean Ethics* VI, 5, 1140a24–b30.

Notes to Chapter 2

1. Empedocles, Fragment 84; Plato, *Timaeus* 45b4–c2, 67e4–68b1.

2. *On the Soul* I, 2, 404b17–18, 405b15–17.

3. *On the Soul* II, 7, 419a11–13, 28–30; 11, 423b20–22.

4. *On Aristotle's "On Sense Perception,"* trans. Alan Towey, pp. 30–31.

5. See Aristotle, *Topics* V, 5, 134b28–135a8; 8, 138b19–21.

6. *On Aristotle's "On Sense Perception,"* trans. Alan Towey, p. 32.

Notes to Chapter 3

1. 437a31–32.
2. 437a32–b1.
3. *On the Soul* II, 7, 418a31–b1.
4. *Ibid.*, 418b13–26.
5. See pp. 36–37 above.
6. See pp. 36–37 above.
7. *Physics* IV, 9, 217a26–b11.

Notes to Chapter 4

1. *On the Soul* II, 7, 418a26–b3.
2. *Ibid.*, 418b9–13.
3. Ch. 5, 439a25–b14.
4. Ch. 5, 439b1–5.
5. See p. 000 above.
6. Cf. *Summa theologiae* I, Q.76, a.8.
7. *On the Soul* III, 1, 425a5–7; 13, 435a14–15.
8. *Ibid.*, 425a4–6.
9. *Ibid.*, 425a5.
10. Gauthier, p. 30, indicates that Aquinas is referring to his own commentary on *On the Soul* II, 9, 421b8–13. See Foster and Humphries, pp. 154–55; Pasnau, pp. 254–56.

Gauthier also notes the contradiction between Aristotle's claim in 438b24 that odor is a smoky evaporation and his argument in 443a21–b2 that it is not; see Ross, p. 194.

11. *On the Soul* II, 9, 421a19.
12. *On the Soul* III, 1, 425a7.
13. *On the Soul* II, 423b26–424a10; III, 435a21–22.
14. *On the Soul* III, 1, 425a6.

Notes to Chapter 5

1. *On the Soul* II, 5, 416b32–418a6.
2. *On Generation and Corruption* II, 2–3, 329b6–331a6.
3. *Meteorologica* IV, 4–8, 382a8–384b23
4. *On the Soul* II, 8, 419b4–421a6.
5. *On the Soul* III, 2, 425b26–426a1.
6. *On the Soul* II, 7, 418a26–28.
7. Ch. 2, 437a31–32.
8. Gauthier, p. 35, points out that this discussion of the levels of the transparent is adapted from Alexander, but is clearer. See Alexander of Aphrodisias, *On Aristotle's "On Sense-Perception,"* trans. Towey, pp. 50–53.
9. *Metaphysics* VII, 5, 1030b14–1031a14; cf. Thomas, *On Being and Essence* ch. 6 (trans. Maurer, pp. 70–71); *Summa theologiae* I-II, Q.53, a.2, ad 3.

Notes to Chapter 6

1. *Metaphysics* VII, 12, 1038a9–26.
2. *Metaphysics* X, 4, 1055a4–10.
3. *Ibid.*, 1, 1052b18–1053b8; cf. V, 6, 1016b17–31.

Notes to Chapter 7

1. *Physics* IV, 14, 223a21–29.
2. *On Generation and Corruption,* I, 10, 327a30–328b22.
3. *Ibid.,* 328a18–b22.
4. Ch. 14, 445b20–29, 446a16–20; see below pp. 000.
5. See above, p. 55.

Notes to Chapter 8

1. *On the Parts of Animals* II, 7, 653a27–28.
2. *On the Soul* II, 11, 423b26–424a10.
3. *Ibid.,* 9, 421a23–26.
4. Gauthier, pp. 48–49, indicates that Moerbeke's translation has *sapor* ("flavor") at 441a4, but that Aquinas follows the reading *insipida* ("flavorless"), which is found both in the older translation and in Moerbeke's translation of Alexander's commentary.
5. Alexander of Aphrodisias, On Aristotle's *"On Sense Perception,"* trans. Towey, p. 70.

Notes to Chapter 9

1. "Learning" translates the term *discere* on which Aquinas comments (p. 000), but at this point in the Aristotelian text Gauthier provides the manuscript corruption *dicere* ("speaking").
2. *Meteorology* II, 2, 354b18–33, 355a32–b6; 3, 357a5–358a27.
3. *On Generation and Corruption* I, 7, 323b29–324a19.
4. *On Generation and Corruption* II, 3, 330a30–331a6.
5. Alexander of Aphrodisias, *On Aristotle's "On Sense Perception,"* trans. A. Towey, pp. 74–75.
6. *Physics* I, 3, 186b4–5.
7. *On the Soul* III, 4, 429b5–22; 6, 430b27–28.
8. *Metaphysics* VIII, 3, 1043b32–1044a11.
9. *Metaphysics* X, 8, 1058a8–16.
10. Gauthier, p. 55, indicates that Avicenna is meant, with reference to the following: Aquinas's *Summa contra gentiles* III, 69, *Summa theologiae* I, Q.115, a.1, and *Questions on the Virtues,* Q.8; Averroes' commentary on the *Metaphysics* (VII 31, XI[XII] 18); and Avicenna's own statements in *Avicenna Latinus. Liber de philosophia prima V–X,* ed. S. Van Riet, Louvain-Leiden: E. Peeters, 1980, tr.IX, c.5, lines 29–48 (pp. 489–90) and lines 94–95 (p. 493).
11. Alexander of Aphrodisias, *On Aristotle's "On Sense Perception,"* trans. A. Towey, p. 74.
12. Gauthier, p. 55, points out that this axiom might be constructed on the basis of *On Generation and Corruption,* I, 5, 320b17–19, and notes that it is common in Aquinas's works.
13. *On Generation and Corruption,* II, 8, 335a10–11.

14. *On the Soul* II, 4, 416b12–13.

15. *On the Soul* II, 3, 414b7.

16. *On Generation and Corruption* I, 5, 320a8–321b33.

17. Gauthier, p. 56, states that no such passage is found in *On the Generation of Animals*, and that Aristotle at 442a3 may have had in mind a treatise *On Nourishment* that he never wrote.

Notes to Chapter 10

1. 439b27–30.

2. *Metaphysics* X, 4, 1055b26–27.

3. See Alexander of Aphrodisias, *On Aristotle's "On Sense Perception,"* trans. Towey, pp. 83–84.

4. *Physics* VII, 2, 244b2–245a22.

5. Alexander of Aphrodisias, *On Aristotle's "On Sense Perception,"* trans. Towey, p. 86.

Notes to Chapter 11

1. 439a18–b14.

2. P. 97.

3. 443a12.

4. 443a9–12.

5. Ch. 7, 440a15–20.

6. Ch. 9, 441b8–442a12.

Notes to Chapter 12

1. Ch. 11, 443bb–16.

2. 443b21.

3. P. 104.

4. Ch. 1, 437a3–17.

Notes to Chapter 13

1. Ch. 12, 444a3–5.

2. Ch. 11, 442b27–443a8.

3. *On the Soul* II, 3, 414b6–14; III, 12, 434b18–19.

4. Ch. 11, 442b29–443a2.

5. 445a4–8.

6. *On Generation and Corruption* II, 8, 335a10–11.

Notes to Chapter 14

1. *Physics* I, 2, 185b10–11; III, 1, 200b18–20; 7, 207b16–17; VI, 8, 239a22.

2. *Categories* 8, 9a28–b27.

3. Ch. 18, 449a20–31.

4. *On the Soul* III, 8, 431b20–28.

5. *Physics* VI, 1–2, 231a21–233b31.

6. Ch. 7, 440b23–25.

7. *Posterior Analytics* I, 20, 82a21–35; 22, 84a29.

8. 445b20–27.
9. *Physics* VII, 5, 249b27–250b6.
10. *Physics* I, 4, 187b37–188a1.

Notes to Chapter 15

1. *On the Soul* II, 7, 418b20–26.
2. *Physics* VI, 1, 232a18–22; 2, 232b20–233a10; 4, 235a11–12.
3. *Ibid.*, 2, 233a10–17.
4. *Physics* VII, 2, 244a3–245b1.
5. *Physics* VIII, 10, 266b27–267a12.
6. *Physics* VI, 1–2, 232a18–233a17.
7. *Posterior Analytics* I, 2, 72a12–13.
8. *Physics* VI, 4, 234b10–20.
9. *Physics* VIII, 7, 261a31–b3.

Notes to Chapter 17

1. Ch. 16, 447b24–25.   2. *Physics* V, 1, 224a21–34.
3. *Physics* VII, 5, 250a12–19.

Notes to Chapter 18

1. Ch. 4, p. 48.   2. *On the Soul* III, 2, 427a9–14.
3. Ibid., 427a7–9.   4. Ibid., 427a9.

ST. THOMAS AQUINAS

Commentary on Aristotle's
On Memory and Recollection

Translated by Edward M. Macierowski

TRANSLATOR'S INTRODUCTION

0.0. Introduction

The occasion for the original draft of this introduction was a conference on Aristotle and Islamic philosophy in honor of Father Joseph Owens's seventy-fifth birthday. For such a commemorative event it seemed not inappropriate, for three reasons, to focus on Thomas Aquinas's Exposition on Aristotle's treatise *De memoria et reminiscentia*.

In the first place, when this paper was originally delivered, Father Owens was present in the audience. Yet it would seem that that was impossible. For, as Aristotle explicitly states,

> . . . memory is of what came to be: no one will say that the present is being remembered when it is at hand, e.g. no one will say he is remembering this white object while he is looking at it. (449b15)

St. Thomas remarks, however, that

> It is obviously not the Philosopher's intention to say that there can be no memory of those things that exist in the present but only of those that exist in the past. For one can remember not only men who have died but also those who are living now, just as one is said to recollect oneself, as Vergil says
>
> > Nec talia passus Ulyxes,
> > Oblitusve sui est Ithacus discrimine tanto.
>
> > 'Neither was Ulysses inexperienced in such things,
> > nor in such a pass has the Ithacan forgotten himself.'
> > —*Aeneid 3. 628–629*

By this he meant it to be understood that Ulysses remembered himself. So the philosopher's intention is to say that memory is of things that are in the past as far as our apprehension of them goes, i.e., that we have sensed or known certain things before, regardless of whether or not those things, considered in themselves, exist in the present.[1]

On that day we happily saw a living verification of Aristotle's intention in Father Owens himself.

My second reason for selecting this text was that St. Thomas explicitly touches upon several points drawn from the Persian philosopher Ibn Sînâ (Avicenna), whose sixth book of the *Physics* from the *Kitāb al-Shifā'* deals with the soul. Thus, Islamic philosophers will be included in dialogue with Thomas.

Finally, owing to the diligent work of Father René Gauthier of the Leonine Commission, a critical edition of Aquinas's text has become available for scientific study, and so it may be of some interest to discuss an old philosophical issue in a new text.

Those reasons still hold good. Today, in addition, we are publishing the results of our translations of two of Aristotle's little treatises on natural things along with Thomas Aquinas's expositions of them. One of the chief tasks of the translator is to accept blame for a task that is in principle unable to be perfectly performed. A good translation should accomplish two things: it should convey the sense of the original and should also be clear and readable in its new linguistic clothing.[2] Here we have two texts: one, itself a quite dense literal translation from Greek to Latin of a text of Aristotle's; the other, a still challenging but much clearer text originally written in technical Latin by Thomas Aquinas. Let us start with a single, relatively simple example, the final sentence of Chapter Five: "whatever things have an ordering, such as mathemes, are more recollectable." Anyone who knows any Greek will immediately detect the hidden presence of the Greek word *mathēmata;* anyone who does not, will be mystified. If the translator renders it clearly as "the theorems of mathematics," then, when he comes to Aquinas's explanation, he is faced with making Aquinas's explanation ("that is, the theorems of mathematics") nugatory. Accordingly, where a linguistic token is opaque, as in such transliterations from Greek, we have attempted to keep them opaque, so that when Aquinas glosses them with a clearer, more linguistically transparent term, his explanation actually explains something. Admittedly, this procedure makes the translation sound rather wooden, but it also has the merit of re-performing or re-activating what Aquinas himself does in disclosing the meaning of an opaque image. Furthermore, though even readers of Latin may, over time, discover some of these practices for himself, we hope that our translations will make these explicative moves easier to follow. Finally, as will become clearer in the next section, some of the key terms used in Aristotle and his successors have themselves suffered such severe thinning that the core elements of meaning must actually themselves be retrieved.

1.0. Uncovering the Distinction between Memory and Recollection

1.1. The Vocabulary of Memory and Recollection

1.11. *The modern thinning of the distinction between memory and recollection.* There seems to be little semantic distinction in ordinary contemporary English between "memory" and "recollection," and, even where a distinction is drawn, modern English gives scant notice to the idea of "recollection." Signs that this is so are easy to find. In the Library of Congress, for example, there are two file drawers of cards for entries on the topic of memory, on the one hand, but less than a knuckle's thickness of cards for recollection, on the other. Again, Richard Sorabji's translation and commentary on Aristotle's *De memoria et reminiscentia* does not bother to include the last half of its title, which names roughly half the text. Accordingly, we may suspect that, even in philosophical discourse, we notice no significant distinction between what goes by the name memory and what is called recollection, or else that we do not find what is called recollection worthy of distinct notice. We may therefore wonder why a distinction that Aristotle felt important enough to name is not important to us. Our wonder increases when we see that the pre-modern philosophical tradition seems to have been maintained fairly consistently between two names as marking out a distinction between two sorts of thing.

1.12. *The pre-modern sorting of terms.* We shall examine a few Greek, Arabic, and Latin philosophical texts that seem to exhibit a contrast between what we shall call "memory" and what we shall call "recollection."

1.121. Greek **mnēmē** *(memory)* versus Greek **anamnēsis** *(recollection).*

1.1211. A rich vocabulary of contrasting memorative and recollective terms is found in the relatively late text of Iamblichus's *Life of Pythagoras.*[3] The report claims that the Pythagoreans used to think that they ought to take hold and preserve in their memory *(mnēmē)* all things taught and explained, and prepare <their> learning and recitations to the point where that which learns and remembers is able to receive that by which he needs to know and that in which he preserves a thought. Indeed they used to honor memory intensely and used to devote much practice and care to it, and, in their learning, did not leave off the <matter> being learned until they could securely encompass the things at their first learning and every day make a recollection *(anamnēsis)* of what was said . . . : a Pythagorean man did not get up out of bed before yesterday's events got recollected *(anamnēstheiē)*. He used to perform his recollection in this way: On rising he used to try to recover in thought what he first said, heard or assigned to those inside, also what he did second, and what he did third. And so on.[4] Again, when going outside, whom he met first and whom he met second, and what speeches got spoken first and second and third. And so on with the rest. For he used to try to recover in thought the happenings during the whole day, striving by means of the order to recollect *(anamimnēskesthai)* just how at some point each of them happened to come about. If he should have more leisure in arousing himself, he would try in the same manner to recover the happenings during the day before yesterday. They used to exercise their memory still more; for there is nothing greater for science and experience and prudence than to be able to remember *(mnēmoneuein)*.[5]

In the light of this instructive text from Iamblichus, we may also wonder whether Plato's *Republic* might fruitfully be read as a Socratic version of a Pythagorean *anamnēsis*.[6]

1.1212. Plato himself explicitly distinguishes between *mnēmē* or memory, as keeping a sensation *(sōtērian aisthēseōs)*, and *anamnēsis* or recollection, as a recovering of "what the soul experienced with the body when it recovers these things by itself without the body."[7]

1.1213. Similarly, Aristotle in the *Historia animalium* (A, 1, 488b24–26) sharply distinguished memory from recollection: "Man is the only one of the animals able to deliberate. Many share as a common character both memory and teachability, but no other, except for man, is able to recollect *(anamimnēskesthai)*." He is no less explicit in *De mem. et rem.* 453a6–10: "Recollecting differs from remembering not only with respect to time but also because many of the other animals participate in remembering *(mnēmoneuein)*, but none, so to say, of the known animals, except man, participates in recollecting *(anamimnēskesthai)*."

1.122. Arabic philosophical discourse preserves a corresponding distinction between *dhikr* and *tadhakkur.*

1.1221. The Aristotelian dicta of §1.1213 are echoed almost word for word in Avicenna (Ibn Sînâ, A.D. 980–1037), *De anima* 4.3 (ed. Rahman, p. 185): "Memory *(dhikr)* may be found in the other animals; but recollection *(tadhakkur)* is the technique for recalling what has been obliterated *(al-ihtiyâl li-istiʿâda mâ indarasa),* and so, in my opinion, it will not be found except in man."

1.1222. Averroes (Ibn Rushd, A.D. 1126–1198), the great commentator on Aristotle, likewise contrasts memory with recollection in the very same Arabic terms:

> He begins with an inquiry into memory <*dhikr*> and recollection <*tadhakkur*> in this book. . . . Man can indeed remember only that which he has had a knowledge of previously at some time in the past. Recollection is the search for the thing by volition, after a person has forgotten it, and reinstating it after it has disappeared, by cogitating upon it. It is apparent, therefore, that recollection will be peculiar to man alone. As for memory, it will occur generally in all animals endowed with imagination, for he is of the opinion that many classes of animals, such as crustaceans and worms, do not possess imagination.
>
> The difference between memory and recall is that retention is applied to that which has not ceased existing in the soul from the time it was perceived in the past until the present moment. As for recall, it is applied to that which has already been forgotten; hence, recall is a discontinued retention, while retention is a continuous recall. This faculty, then, is one in substrate but two in aspect. Memory, in general, is the cognition of something already known, after the knowledge thereof has been discontinued. Recollection is the search for this knowledge when it is not present and the exercising of the cogitative faculty in order to reinstate it. It is apparent that this action must belong to a faculty that is neither sense nor imagination and this is what is called the memorative faculty.[8]

1.123. Latin philosophical texts also are careful to preserve the same distinction.

1.1231. The Latin version of Avicenna's *De anima* 4.3 (ed. Van Riet, p. 40.61–64) preserves the same distinction under the terms *memoria* and *recordatio:* "*Memoria* autem est etiam in aliis animalibus. Sed *recordatio* quae est ingenium revocandi quod oblitum est, non invenitur, ut puto, nisi in solo homine." (Cf. 1.1221, above, for an English translation directly from the Arabic.)

1.1232. The two Latin versions of *Averrois Cordubensis Compendia Librorum Aristotlelis Qui Parva Naturalia Vocantur* edited by A. L. Shields with the assistance of H. Blumberg (Corpus Commentariorum Averrois in Aristotelem, Versio. Lat., vol. 7 [Cambridge, Mass.: Mediaeval Academy of America, 1949]) also preserve the distinction between memory and recollection, albeit with slightly differing terms.

2.12321. The "vulgate" version (cf. §1.1222), ed. Shields, pp. 47–49 at top, thus denominates what we call "memory" *(re)memoratio* and what we call "recollection" *investigatio per rememorationem:*

> It is clear that remembering is in them: for we do not call <something> remembering unless <it is> of what was already known in the past. For remembering *(rememoratio)* is a turning back, in the present, <to> a notion *(intentio)* comprehended in the past. Investigation through remembering *(investigatio . . . per rememorationem)*, however, is a search for that notion through the will and making it present after <its> absence. Hence it is seen that investigation through remembering is proper to man. Memory *(memoratio)*, however, is in all the imagining animals: for it is thought that many kinds of animals do not imagine, e.g. worms and those having shells. Remembering *(rememoratio)*, however, differs from conservation, since conservation is of that which has always been in the soul, after it had been comprehended; whereas remembering is of that which <p. 49> had been forgotten. Hence remembering is an interrupted conservation; but conservation is a continuous remembering. Therefore that power is one in subject and two in manner. Therefore remembering is a knowledge of that which was known after knowledge of it had been interrupted. To investigate through remembering is the acquisition of knowledge and to work and to make the cogitative <power> working in the representation of that knowledge. That action belongs to the power that is called rememorative.[9]

1.12322. The "Parisian" manuscript contradistinguishes *memoria* and its act *(re)memoracio* from *reminiscencia* (ed. Shields, pp. 48–49 bottom):

> And if such knowledge were from the very first continuous comprehension, then it would be called memory *(memoracio):* for it is the preservation of what always was in the soul after it had been comprehended; whereas remembering *(rememoracio)* is of what had been interrupted after its comprehension. Hence conservation is continuous remembering, and remembering is interrupted conservation. Hence it is clear that this pow-

er is one in subject and two in manner. Recollection *(reminiscencia)*, however, is the voluntary investigation of a once-comprehended notion *(intentio)* which has been given over to forgetfulness.[10]

This power seems to be proper to man, because in this sort of investigation man makes the cogitative power work to represent the notion which was erased through forgetting. For the other animals do not seem to have this investigation, although memory is in all those having imagination. For there are many animals that do not seem to have an imagination, e.g. worms, shellfish, and many others.[11]

The terms accordingly are regularly contradistinguished, even where the contours of the distinction are obscured somewhat through translation. A vestige of the phrase *investigatio per rememorationem* seems to be present.

1.1233. In the Latin text under our special consideration, St. Thomas is reading a translation that distinguishes consistently between *memoria* and *reminiscentia*.

1.124. Unlike the polarity in Greek and Arabic, which is marked by words of the same root (see §1.2, below: **Etymologies,** for the technical details), the terms for memory and recollection in Latin and English do not share the same etymology and therefore do not come equipped with built-in semantic pointers to connote each other. Even so, the examples given above ought to be sufficient to establish a context of discourse.

The distinction between memory and recollection—and also why it is elusive—is nicely summarized by the Platonic scholar Jacob Klein:

> (1) it is the *past* status of the objects of recollection *as well as* of memory which makes *anamnêsis* appear akin to *mnêmê;* (2) that is why so often the terms "recollection," "reminiscence," "remembrance," "memory," are used synonymously albeit imprecisely; (3) the faculty of *eikasia* seems to play a role in both *anamnêsis* and *mnêmê;* (4) and most importantly, the phenomenon of "recollecting" cannot be considered without taking into account its "opposite," the phenomenon of "forgetting," while the phenomenon of "having something in one's memory" does not have "forgetfulness" as its "opposite": we either have or do not have memories, we either keep them or lose them, but we lose them without being aware of our forgetting. To become aware of our having forgotten something means to begin recollecting.[12]

These remarks ought to suffice to show that an intelligible distinction between memory-terms and recollection-terms has been developed at least in the Aristotelian philosophical community, that we ordinarily neglect to distinguish the things designated by these terms, and that there is something puzzling about this distinction.

1.2. Etymologies.

Etymological roots are listed in Julius Pokorny, *Indogermanisches etymologisches Wörterbuch*, I. Band (Bern und München: Francke Verlag, 1959), especially pp. 726–728 under "3. men" for Gk *mimnōskō, mnaomai,* Lat. *memini.*

Liddell-Scott-Jones's *Greek-English Lexicon* refers *mnêmē,* "memory," to *mnaomai,* a middle verb taking the genitive "be mindful of"; *anamnêsis,* a "calling to mind, reminiscence," derives from the verb *anamimnēskō* taking a double accusative "remind one of thing," which in turn is derived from the causal verb *mimnēskō* "remind" one, "put" one "in mind," also taking the accusative. The passive form *anamimnēskomai,* usually with the genitive, means to "be reminded of" and thence "remember, call to mind." Richard Sorabji, *Aristotle on Memory* (Providence: Brown University Press, 1972), p. 35, n. 1, emphasizes the point: "It is passive rather than middle, as can be seen from the formation of the future and aorist tenses." In Greek both *mnêmē* and *anamnêsis* have the same root.

On the Latin side, A. Ernout and A. Meillet, *Dictionnaire étymologique de la langue latin* (Paris: Klincksieck, 1959), report distinct roots for *memor* (q.v.), from which we have *memoria,* and *meminî* (q.v.), from which we have *reminiscentia.* To *memor* Pokorny, pp. 969–970, assigns the root *(s)mer,* found in the Sanskrit verb *smárati,* "remembers"; *meminî,* however, has the same root as *mnêmē* and *anamnesis,* viz. "3. men-." Thus the derivative English words "memory" and "reminiscence" are not etymologically related (see the *Oxford English Dictionary* [*OED*], s.vv.).

The Greek *ana-* in compounds such as *anamnêsis* suggests upward movement or repetition and improvement (see Liddell-Scott-Jones, s.v. "*ana*") and therefore connotes something over and above *mnêmē.* The verbal prefix *re-* in the Latin word *reminiscentia,* like its Greek counterpart *ana,* denotes "movement back or in reverse, reversal of a previous process, restoration, response or opposition, repeated action."[13] But, as we have seen just now, the Latin words *reminiscentia* and *memoria,* unlike their Greek equivalents, have no common root.

In the Arabic tradition, Avicenna and Averroes, two of St. Thomas's major sources, use _dhikr_ as the Arabic equivalent of _mnēmē_ and _ta-dhakkur_ for _anamnēsis_. Like the Greek original, these Arabic renderings share a common root, namely _DH K R;_ the deverbal noun of the first form _dhikr_ signifies "memory" and the corresponding deverbal noun of the fifth form "recollection." The formation of the Arabic terms captures much of the sense of the Greek original.[14] The fifth form adds the notion of _reflexivity_ to the second form. For example, the root _KSR_ appears as _kasara_ (Form I), "to break" something; _kassara_ (Form II), "to break" something "in pieces"; _takassara_ (Form V), "to be broken in pieces." Accordingly, _tadhakkara_ (_DH K R_ Form V) can express the passive sense of _anamimnēsketai_ as "he is being reminded"; but, like the Greek middle voice, the Arabic can also convey the more basic notion of some sort of reflexivity or reflectiveness. Such precision betokens thoughtfulness, sophistication, and care in the translators from Greek to Arabic.

In the absence of words in English that have both the correct meanings and the same etymology, English philosophical discourse conventionally assigns "memory" to render _mnēmē_ and "recollection" for _anamnēsis;_ e.g. Benjamin Jowett, in Plato's _Meno,_ and J. I. Beare, in the Oxford translation of the _De memoria et reminiscentia._ The English verb "recollect" includes even a note of contemplation in some senses (_OED,_ s.v., second entry, **4**).

For our purposes, however, it is more important to attend to the meaning of terms than to their etymology. For "the etymology of a term is one thing and its meaning another: Etymology considers the source from which a term is assigned a meaning; whereas the meaning of a term looks to the thing that the term is supposed to signify. These are sometimes distinct; for the term 'stone' _(lapidis)_ is assigned its meaning from hurting the foot _(a laesione pedis),_ but that is not what it means; otherwise, since iron hurts the foot, it would be stone" (_Summa theologiae_ II-II, q.92, a.1, ad 2[m]).

Though Jowett and Beare are not always consistent in their rendition of the terms, there is enough consistency to make our convention recognizable. We shall use "memory" and its derivatives to designate _mnēmē_ and its associated word-forms and "recollection" and its derivatives to mark _anamnēsis_ and its associated word-forms.

2.0. Aquinas's Exposition of Aristotle's
De memoria et reminiscentia

Let us finally turn to Aquinas's exposition of Aristotle's treatise *peri mnēmēs kai anamnēseōs,* so as to introduce the chief philosophical themes of that text and to touch on a few directly related issues. Aquinas divides Aristotle's text into its two main parts, a treatment of memory (Chs. 1–3) and another on recollection (Chs. 4–8).

The part on memory takes up three questions: first, "What is memory?" (Ch. 1); second, "To what part of the soul does memory belong?" (Ch. 2); and third, "What is the cause of remembering?" (Ch. 3).

The part on recollection also has three major divisions, which do not, however, perfectly line up with the chapter divisions. The first question on recollection is "What is recollection in comparison to other apprehensions?" (Ch. 4). The second question is "How does recollecting take place?" (Ch. 5–7). The question is subdivided, however, into two: first, "How does recollecting arise from the things to be recollected?" (Ch. 5–6); second, "How does recollecting arise from time?" (Ch. 7). The third question is "What is the difference between memory and recollection?"

The text and notes have been enriched through the generosity of the Leonine Commission, which is charged with critically editing and publishing the Latin works of St. Thomas Aquinas.

The following table will orient the reader to the text, its divisions, and the topics and issues discussed:

Subdivisions of the Aristotelian Lemmata according to Leonine Chapters, Spiazzi Paragraphing of Aristotle's text in the Marietti edition, and Standard Bekker Pagination, with a Decimal Outline of the Chief Divisions of the Text

Leonine edition chapters	Spiazzi's para-graphing	Bekker edition, page, column, lines	Division of the Text	Topical Heading For the Division Of the Text
II,				
Chap. **1**			0.0	Proem: Division of the Text
	159	449b03		The Treatise Itself
			1.01	Three Questions on Remembering
	160	b09	1.1	What is remembering?
			1.11	The object of memory
	161	b10	1.111	Not future things
	162	b13	1.112	Not present things
	163	b15	1.113	Past things
	164	b24	1.12	The definition of memory
Chap. **2**			1.2	What is the seat of memory?
	165	b30	1.21	Preliminary remark: Understanding does not exist without an image
	166	450a01	1.211	Exemplification
	167	a07	1.212	Why understanding requires a continuum has to be discussed elsewhere.
			1.22	Which part of the soul does memory pertain to?
	168	a09	1.221	Memory belongs properly to the primary sensitive but accidentally to the intellect
	169	a15	1.2221	Other animals besides man remember. So memory cannot be an intellective power.
	170	a18	1.2222	Memory is not in all animals, but only in those that sense time.
	171	a22	1.223	Memory accompanies imagination.
Chap. **3**			1.3	What is the cause of remembering?
	172	a25	1.31	Why not remember the present psychic affection rather than the absent thing?
	173	a27	1.311	A presupposition of the objection.
	174	a32	1.312	Signs, indications, or examples

Leonine edition chapters	Spiazzi's para- graphing	Bekker edition, page, column, lines	Division of the Text	Topical Heading For the Division Of the Text
	175	450b11	1.313	Disputation of both sides of the question.
			1.32	Solution to 1.31
	176	b20	1.321	Why remembering occurs.
	177	451a02		Three relations between image and object of memory
	178	a12	1.322	Why memory is preserved well.
	179	a14	1.02	Epilogue in answer to 1.01.
Chap. **4**			**2.0**	**Recollecting**
	180	a18	2.01	Proposed intention
			2.1	What is recollection in comparison with other ways of apprehending?
	181	a20	2.11	Thesis: What recollection is not: neither a repeated remembering nor an original grasp of a knowable object
	182	a21	2.111	The difference between recovering and acquiring a memory
	183	a23	2.1111	Memory is not the original grasping.
	184	a25	2.1112	Nor does memory yet exist in the first instant of getting a notion, since it is not yet habitual.
	185	a31	2.112	Further, recollection is neither the recovery of a memory nor a new acquisition.
	186	451b02	2.12	What recollection is: a movement or a path toward remembering, a recovery of the original reception
	187	b06	2.13	Recollection, like relearning or rediscovering, occurs after knowledge has been lost; but it requires a further special principle beyond what is required to learn.
Chap. **5**			2.2	How does recollection come about?
			2.21	How is recollection related to the things recollected?
	188	b10	2.211	The cause of recollecting: psychic movements.
	189	b16	2.2111	How one proceeds in recollecting.
	190	b25	2.21111	Solution to a difficulty
			2.21112	Confirmation of the solution

Leonine edition chapters	Spiazzi's para- graphing	Bekker edition, page, column, lines	Division of the Text	Topical Heading For the Division Of the Text
	191	b31	2.211121	First indication
	192	452a02	2.211122	Second indication
Chap. **6**			2.2112	The difference between recollecting and learning
	193	452a04	2.21121	Recollecting and relearning from another
	194	a07	2.21122	Recollecting and rediscovering for oneself
			2.2112	That a recollector needs starting-points.
	195	a12 But	2.21121	Statement of thesis.
	196	a12 Hence	2.211211	An indication *that* it is so: loci aid recollection
	197	a13	2.211212	The cause *why* it is so
	198	a17	2.211213	The sort of starting-point that is needed: universal and intermediate
			2.21122	Why we sometimes fail to recollect
	199	a24	2.211221	Failure to recollect at all
	200	a30	2.211222	Failure to recollect accurately
Chap. **7**	201	452b07	2.22	How is recollection related to time?
	202	b08	2.221	How does the soul distinguish between greater and lesser measures of time? By proportional motion.
			2.222	An impasse.
	203	b13 By what	2.2221	Query
	204	b13 Either	2.2222	Solution: Proportion.
	205	b17	2.2223	Exemplification
			2.223	Proof of the principal thesis:
	206	b23	2.2231	One who recollects must know time.
	207	b29	2.2232	Measured vs. unmeasured time
Chap. **8**	208	453a04	2.23	What is the difference between memory and recollection? (Three)
			2.3	What sort of affection is recollection?
			2.30	Implicit objection: incorporeal, because syllogistic.

Leonine edition chapters	Spiazzi's para-graphing	Bekker edition, page, column, lines	Division of the Text	Topical Heading For the Division Of the Text
	209	a14	2.31	Evidence to the contrary: unsuccessful recollectors are physically disturbed.
			2.32	Why they are disturbed.
	210	a20	2.321	If the cause were purely intellectual, they could stop their inner movement at will, but not if a bodily organ is involved
	211	a23	2.322	Those with moisture near the organs of sense are most affected.
			2.323	Illustrations: Even against our will
	212	a26	2.3231	Emotions, once started, persist.
	213	a28	2.3232	Intense activities persist
	214	a31–b11	2.32	Bodily indispositions affecting recollection

CHAPTER 1

449B4–30

449b4 *About memory*[1] *and remembering we must say what it is, and owing to what cause it comes about, and in which of the parts*[2] *of the soul this affection*[3] *occurs; and we must do the same about recollecting. For those who are good at remembering are not the same as those who are good at recollecting; rather, as frequently happens, those who are slow to learn are more able to remember, while those who are quick and learn easily are able to recollect.*

449b9 *Since the question "What sort of things are memorable?" is frequently misleading, this is the first point to be taken up.*

449b10 *For the future is not remembered, but it can be thought about and expected. Moreover, there will also be a science of expectation,*[4] *which some call divination.*

449b13 *Nor is memory of the present, but sense is. For by sense we know neither the future nor what's been done, but only the present.*

449b15 *But memory is of what has been: now no one will say that the present is being remembered while it is at hand, e.g. this white object while someone is seeing it, no one will say he is remembering it; nor will he say that he is remembering what is being considered while he is considering or understanding it; but they generally call the first act sense and only the second knowing. But since one may have knowledge and sense without the <corresponding> acts,*[5] *one may remember that a triangle has three angles equal to two right angles in this way: This occurs in the one case since he has learned or speculated upon it, and in the other since he has heard or seen it or some other such thing. For when one acts according to memory, one always speaks thus in one's soul—that one has heard or felt or understood it before.*

449b24 *Therefore there is a thing called memory, and it is neither sense nor opinion, but with any of these there is a habit or an affection once time has passed. But of the now itself there is no memory in the now itself, as has been said. Rather sense is of the present; expectation, of the future; and memory, of the past. For this reason, only those animals that sense time remember, and they do so by the very thing by which they sense it.*

Commentary

As the Philosopher says in the seventh book on the *Histories of Animals*,[6] nature proceeds from inanimate to animate things little by little, so that the genus of inanimate things comes before the genus of plants. For plants, when compared to other bodies, seem to be animate, even though when they are compared to the genus of animals they seem to be inanimate. In the same way, nature proceeds from plants to animals in a continuous order; for certain immobile animals—those that adhere to the earth—seem to differ little from plants. So, too, in the order of progression from animals to man, some animals are found in which something like reason appears.[7] For although prudence—"the right reason of things one can do," as it is called in the sixth book of the *Ethics*[8]— is a virtue proper to man, some animals are found to participate in a sort of prudence.[9] This is so not because they can reason, but because they are moved to act by a natural instinct.[10] Such acts result from an apprehension by the sensitive part[11] of the soul, as if they were done from reason.

The role of prudence is to direct the prudent man to do what ought to be done by considering not only the present but also the past. This is why Cicero[12] sets down as the parts of prudence not only foresight, through which future things are attended to, but also understanding, through which present things are considered, and memory, through which past things are apprehended. Accordingly, even other animals that seem to have something like prudence must have not only a sense-awareness of present things but also a memory of past things. Therefore, at the beginning of the *Metaphysics*[13] the Philosopher says that in the case of certain animals memory comes from sensation, and for this reason they are prudent.

Just as these animals have an imperfect sort of prudence compared to that of man, so is their memory likewise imperfect. For other animals only remember, while men both remember and recollect.[14] Now Aristotle proceeds step by step, and, after the book in which he treats sensation,[15] which is common to all the animals, he now treats of memory and recollection, the latter of which is found only in men, and the former both in men and in the perfect animals.[16]

449b4 Accordingly this book is divided into two parts. In the first place Aristotle gives his prologue, in which he presents what he sets out to do; in the second, he begins to treat the things he has in mind, where he says *Since the question* (449b9).

As to the first point, he says that there are two things *to be discussed.* The first is *concerned with memory and* its activity, *remembering.* About this he promises to discuss three points, namely *what* memory or remembering is, what *its cause* is, and to which part *of the soul the affection* of remembering belongs. For all the operations of the sensitive part of the soul are affections,[17] in as much as sensing is somehow to be affected.[18]

In the second place, he promises to discuss *recollecting.* Now lest recollecting and remembering appear to be identical, he indicates their difference: they are each found in different sorts of men. For we do not find that *the same* men have good *memories* and good powers of *recollection. Rather,* as *frequently* happens, *those* who are *slow* at discovering and learning have better *memories;* whereas those who are quick-witted at discovering things on their own and in learning things from others are better at recollecting.

The reason for this is that the diversity of man's capacity to perform various acts of the soul arises from the diverse dispositions of the body. We see that those bodily things that receive an impression slowly and with difficulty, such as stone, retain the impression well; while those, such as water, that take an impression easily, do not retain it well.[19] Since remembering is merely keeping in good condition the things that have once been received, it follows that (a) those who are slow to receive an impression retain it well once they have accepted it, and this is to remember it well; whereas (b) those who accept something with ease often lose it just as easily. Recollecting, on the other hand, is a sort of rediscovery of things that were previously accepted but no longer preserved, and so those that are quick to discover things and to receive instruction are also good at recollecting.

449b9 Then, when he says *Since the question* (449b9), he pursues what he set out to do.

First he treats of remembering; second of recollecting, at *It remains, however, for us to talk about recollecting* (451a18).

In regard to the first topic, he does three things. In the first place he shows what remembering is; second he shows to what part of the soul it belongs, at *We have spoken however, about imagination* (Ch.2, 449b30); third he shows the cause of memory, at *One might perhaps wonder* (Ch.3, 450a25).

Since operations, habits, and powers are specified by their objects,[20] he does two things concerning the first topic. First he asks what the object of memory is; second he concludes with a definition of memory, at *Therefore there is a thing called memory* (449b24).

As to the first he does two things. First he tells us what he wishes to discuss; second he explains what he has set out to do, at *For the future is not* (449b10).

As to the first of these points, he says that to explain memory one must, to begin with, grasp *what sort of things are remembered*, because objects are prior to acts, and acts prior to powers, as has been observed in the second book of *On the Soul.*[21] It is necessary to settle this matter since it is *frequently* deceiving: some think that there is memory of things about which actually there is not.[22]

449b10 Then when he says *For the future is not*, he explains what he has set out to do.

First he says that memory is not of future things; second he says it is not of the present, at *Nor is memory of the present* (449b13); third he says it is of the past, at *But memory is of what has been* (449b15).

Accordingly, in the first place, he says that *future things are not remembered, but* of them there is opinion. Such things belong to the cognoscitive power of opinion, as when one thinks[23] that something is going to happen, or to the appetitive power of hope or expectation,[24] as when expectation extends to something in the future.

He says that there can also be *a sort of science* of future things, something that can be called a "science *of expectation.*"[25] Some call this *divination*, because through it certain persons can know what is going to happen in the future; for expectation is concerned with the future.

But since expectation is of future things that can be acquired by man, and since such things are future contingents, about which there cannot be any science,[26] it seems that there can be no science of expectation about future things.

So we must say that there cannot be a science of future contingents considered in themselves. When they are considered in their causes, however, there can be a science about future contingents inasmuch as some sciences know that there may be inclinations to such-and-such effects. In this sense, there is a natural science dealing with things subject to generation and corruption. This is how astronomers are able, through their science, to foretell certain future events, like fertility or sterility,[27] because of the disposition of the heavenly bodies toward such effects.

449b13 Then, when he says *Nor is memory of the present*, he shows that memory is not concerned with *the present,* for that, he says, pertains to sensing, through which *we apprehend neither the future nor what's been done,* i.e. a past thing, but *only what is present right now.*

449b15 Then, when he says *But memory is,* he shows that memory is concerned with past things. He proves this claim from the common way of speaking.

For *while* something *is* actually *at hand,* e.g. *while someone is* actually *seeing* something *white, no one would say that* he *is remembering the white* thing; similarly, too, no one would say that he is remembering that which *is* actually *being considered* by the intellect, *while* he is actually considering and understanding it; *but* when people are seeing something white they commonly call it *sensing;* and they use this "considering" something actually *only* when they are *knowing* it right now.

While one has habitual *knowledge*[28] or a sensitive power *without their acts or operations,* one is said to remember past acts. For example, when one has considered with one's intellect that a triangle has three angles *equal to two right angles* and perhaps at the level of sense has seen a diagram of the figure, then, *in the one case* from the standpoint of the intellectual operation one also remembers either *that he learned* something from another or that he thought it up for himself; while *in the other* from the standpoint of sense-apprehension one remembers that he has *heard* or *seen* or perceived something by one of the other senses. *For whenever* the soul remembers, it always judges that it heard or felt or understood something *before.*

From this it is obvious that it is not the Philosopher's intention to say that there can be no memory of those things that exist in the present but only of those that existed in the past. For one can remember not

only men who have died but also those who are living now, just as one
is said to recollect oneself, according to the dictum of Vergil:

> *Neither was Ulysses unmindful of such things nor in such a pass did the Ithacan*
> *forget himself.*[29]

By this he meant it to be understood that Ulysses remembered himself. So the Philosopher's intention is to say that memory is of things
that are in the past as far as our apprehension of them goes, i.e. that we
have sensed or known certain things before, regardless of whether or
not those things, considered in themselves, exist in the present.

449b24 Then, when he says *Therefore there is,* he draws a conclusion
from the premises on the nature of memory.

It is *neither sense,* because this is only of things present, *nor* is it *opinion,* which can also deal with things future. *But* it must pertain to something belonging to both *of these*—either as a habit, if there is a permanent power,[30] or as an affection, if there is a transient impression.
Memory pertains to sense or opinion in this way *when* some *time* shall
have intervened between the prior apprehension of the sense or of the
intellectual opinion and the subsequent memory,[31] in such a way that
there can be a memory of a past apprehension, since right now there is
no memory of what is being apprehended right now, as *has been said.*[32]
But sense-apprehension is of the present, expectation of the future, and *memory*
of the past. Therefore *every memory* must exist *with* some *time* intervening
between it and the prior apprehension.

From this he concludes that *only* those animals that can sense *time remember,* and they remember by means of that very part of the soul by
which they also *sense* time. About this he inquires in the sequel.[33]

449b30 *We have spoken, however, about imagination in the books on the soul, and said that understanding does not exist without an image.*

450a1 *For the same affection occurs in the case of the intellect as in the case of drawing: though using a triangle without determinate quantity we will still draw it quantitatively finite; and likewise even if one who understands something does not understand how big it is, nevertheless something of some size is put before his eyes, even though he understands it not according to how big it is. Even if nature contained things of infinite size, nevertheless something of determinate size is put before him and he understands it only as being of some size or other.*

450a7 *Hence the reason why it is not possible to understand anything without a continuum nor to understand beings without the notion of time is another argument.*

450a9 *It is necessary, however, to know magnitude and motion, whereby time, too, is known. And the image is an affection of the common sense. Hence clearly knowledge of these belongs to the prime sensitive power. Memory, however, and that which is of the intelligibles, does not exist without an image. Hence it will belong to the intellective part of the soul only by accident, but to the first sensitive by itself.*

450a15 *Hence it also exists in certain other animals and not just in man and in those that partake of opinion and prudence. If, however, it were any of the intellective parts of the soul, it would not exist in many of the animals other than man, perhaps indeed in none of those that are mortal.*

450a18 *As it stands, it does not belong to all, because not all have the sense of time. For, as we have said before, whenever memory acts, it at the same time always senses that it has seen or heard or learned this thing before. The before and the after, however, are in time.*

450a22 *Hence it is clear to which part of the soul memory belongs, because in fact it is the same as that to which imagination belongs, and there are some things that are memorable by themselves, namely, those of which there is imagi-*

nation; and others are memorable by accident, namely, whatever do not exist without imagination.

Commentary

449b30 After the Philosopher shows what memory is, he goes on to show to what part of the soul it belongs.

He does two things in this regard. First he presents what is needed for explaining what he has set out to do. Second he explains the thing he set out to do, where he says *It is necessary, however, to know* (450a9).

Concerning the first of these topics he does three things. First he sets out his intention. Second, by using an example, he explains what he has said, where he says *For the same affection occurs* (450a1). Third, he points out a related matter that must be considered elsewhere, where he says *Hence the reason why* (450a7).

Accordingly he first brings up *what was said in On the soul*[1] about what the imagination is, namely that it is a motion brought about by an activated sense-power. It was also said in the same book[2] that it is *not* possible for a man to *understand* anything *without an image.*[3]

450a1 Then, when he says *For the same affection occurs,* he explains what he has just stated.

For it might seem unreasonable to someone for a man to be unable to understand anything without an image, since an image is a likeness of a bodily thing, whereas understanding is of universals, which are abstracted from particulars. To explain this difficulty he introduces an example, saying that what *occurs* in the case of the intellect with reference to its needing an image is like what occurs in the drawings of geometrical figures. In the latter a triangle of some determinate quantity is indeed drawn even though in its demonstration geometry does not use any *determinate quantity* of triangle. *Likewise,* too, in the case of a man who wants to understand some things, namely, an image of a definite quantity, i.e. of a singular, is set *before* his *eyes;* for example, an image of a man two cubits tall might come to mind when one wants to understand *man,* but the intellect understands man inasmuch as he is man, not inasmuch as he has this quantity.

But since the intellect can understand the nature of quantity, he adds that if the things to be understood are, in their own nature, quantities, e.g. line, surface, or number, but are not finite (i.e. determined as singulars), an image of a definite size is nevertheless set before one's eyes. In this way, an image of a line two feet long comes to mind in one who wants to understand line, but the intellect understands it only in its nature as a quantity and not its being two feet long.

450a7 Then, when he says *Hence the reason why,* he shows what will be set aside for another consideration.

He says that it is the task of another discussion to identify the cause of a man's being unable to understand anything apart from the continuum and time.

✧○✧

This happens in fact insofar as man can understand nothing without an image; for an image is necessarily accompanied by the continuum and time, because an image is a likeness of a singular thing existing here and now. The reason why man cannot understand without an image can easily be identified in the case of his first acquisition of intelligible species, which, according to Aristotle's teaching in the third book of *On the Soul*,[4] are abstracted from images. But it is clear from experience that he who has already acquired intelligible knowledge through an intellectually understood species also cannot actually consider that of which he has his knowledge, unless some image comes to mind. This is why a man with a damaged organ of imagination is kept not only from knowing things for the first time, but also from considering the things he knew before, as is clear in the case of the insane.[5]

Now at this point someone[6] might wish to say that the intelligible species do not remain in the human possible intellect except while a man is actually understanding something; but after one ceases[7] actually to understand, they vanish and the intelligible species cease[8] to be in the intellect, just as light ceases to be in the air in the absence of any illuminating body,[9] and hence if the intellect wishes to renew its understanding, it must turn again toward the images in order to acquire the intelligible species.

But this expressly contradicts the words of Aristotle in the third book of *On the Soul*,[10] where he says that when the possible intellect becomes each of the intelligible things (which is accomplished through their species) at that point it is able to understand them in act. This position is also repugnant to reason, because the intelligible species are received in the possible intellect unchangeably, as is characteristic of an intellectual principle.

Now the way in which the possible intellect possesses the intelligible species, even when it is not actually understanding anything, is not the same as that in which the sensible species are possessed in the sensitive powers: in them, owing to the composition of the bodily organ, it is one thing to receive an impression, which makes for actual sensing, and another to retain it even when the things are not actually being sensed, as Avicenna objects.[11]

The possession of the intelligible species comes about rather because of the diverse levels of being of the intelligible forms: either according to pure potency, e.g. in discovering or learning; or according to pure act, as when one is actually understanding something; or else in a manner intermediate between potency and act, as in a habit.[12]

Hence the human possible intellect needs an image not only to acquire intelligible species but it also in a way looks at them within the images. This is also what is said in the third book of *On the Soul:* "The intellective power therefore understands the species in the images."[13]

The reason for this is that activity is proportionate to power and essence. But the intellective power of man does exist in the sensitive part of the soul, as is said in the second book of *On the Soul.*[14] Hence its proper operation is to understand intelligible things in images, just as the activity of the intellect of a separate substance is to understand things known in themselves.

This is why the cause of this must be assigned by the metaphysician, to whom the task of considering the various levels of the intelligences belongs.

❖o❖

450a9 Then, when he says *It is necessary, however,* he shows to what part of the soul the memory belongs.

He does so first by an argument; second through signs, where he says *Hence it also exists* (450a15). Third he draws the intended conclusion, where he says *Hence it is clear* (450a22).

Accordingly he says first that it is *necessary* that magnitude and the motion by which time *too* is known should be known by the same part of the soul. For these three follow each other both in division and in being finite and infinite, as is proven in the sixth book of the *Physics*.[15]

Now magnitude is known by the sense-power, since it is one of the common sensibles;[16] and likewise motion, too, especially local motion, is known inasmuch as the distance of a magnitude[17] is known; and time is known inasmuch as a before and an after in motion is known.[18] Hence these three can be perceived by the sense-power. Now there are two ways in which something is perceived by the sense-power. In one way, it can be perceived through the very changing of the sense-power effected by the sensible object; both the proper and also the common sensibles are known in this way both by their proper senses as well as by the common sense. In the other way, something is known by a sort of secondary motion that is left over from the first change of the sense-power by the sensible object; this movement sometimes remains even after the disappearance of the sensible objects and pertains to the imagination, as is held in *On the Soul*.[19] Moreover, the *image* that appears through such a secondary change *is an affection of the common sense:* for it is consequent upon the whole change of the sense-power. Such a change begins with the proper senses and ends at the common sense. Hence *clearly* these three, viz. magnitude, motion, and time, are known through the common sense, since they are grasped in an image.

Memory, however—not only the memory of sensibles, as when one remembers that he has sensed something, but also *of intelligibles,* as when one remembers that he has understood something—*does not exist without an image:* for after the sensibles are gone, they are not perceived by the sense-power unless they exist in an image. There is also no act of understanding without an image, as was held above.[20] Hence he concludes that memory belongs to the intellective part of the soul by *accident,* but by *itself* it belongs to the *first sensitive,* i.e. the common sense. For it was said above[21] that a certain determinate size is put before the intellect although the intellect by itself considers the thing absolutely; but it does pertain to the memory to apprehend time with respect to a certain determinateness, namely a distance in the past from this present moment. Hence memory by itself pertains to the preparation of an image, but by accident it pertains to the judgment of the intellect.

From what is being said here one might think that imagination and memory are not powers distinct from the common sense but are affections of it.

But Avicenna shows, using the method of reason,[22] that they are different powers.[23] For since the sensitive powers are acts of bodily organs, the reception of sensible forms, which belongs to the sense-power, and the conservation of those forms, which belongs to the imagination, must pertain to diverse powers, just as in the case of bodily things we see that reception and conservation belong to distinct principles: for wet things are good receivers, while dry and hard things are good conservers.[24] Likewise, too, it pertains to a distinct principle to receive a form and to conserve the form received through a sense as well as some meaning[25] not apprehended through a sense. This meaning or interest is something that the estimative power, even in animals other than man, perceives, but the memorative power retains it; it does not belong to the memorative power to remember a thing absolutely but rather to do so inasmuch as the thing has been apprehended in the past by the intellect.[26]

Nevertheless one of the diverse powers of the soul may be, as it were, the root and origin of the other powers, the activities of which presuppose the activity of this potency; thus, the nutritive power is, as it were, the root of the powers of growth and generation, both of which require nourishment. Similarly, the common sense is the root of the imagination and the memory, both of which depend upon the activity of the common sense.

❧o❧

450a15 Then, by means of two signs, when he says *Hence it also exists in certain other animals* (450a15), he explains what he had said.

The first of these signs is taken with regard to the animals that have memory. He says that since memory by itself belongs to the first sensitive part of the soul, *it exists in certain* other animals that have sense and lack intellect, and *not only in man but also* in any other animals *that partake of "opinion,"* which can also belong to the speculative intellect, *and "prudence,"* which pertains to the practical intellect.[27] *Now if* memory *were one* of the intellective powers, *it would not exist in many of the animals other than man* that obviously do have a memory but do not have an intellect, and *perhaps* memory would not exist in any *of the mortals* except man, since man alone among the mortals has an intellect.

Now he says "perhaps" for the benefit of those who might have been in doubt whether any animals other than man have an intellect. Such a doubt might have arisen owing to certain activities similar to those of reason, such as some of the activities of apes and certain other such animals.[28]

450a18 He offers the second sign where he says *As it stands, it does not belong to all.* This second sign is drawn from the animals that do not have memory.

He says that it is clear that memory belongs by itself to the sensitive part of the soul, because even *as the case stands,* while we suppose that man alone among the animals has an intellect, memory is not found in all animals, but only those that sense time have memory. For there are some animals that perceive nothing except in the presence of sensible things; e.g. certain immobile animals, which have an undetermined imagination, as is said in the third book of *On the Soul,*[29] and hence cannot recognize the before and the after, and consequently cannot recognize time either. This is why they do not have memory. *For when* the soul acts through the memory, as was said *before,* the soul *always at the same time senses that it saw or heard or learned this before; and the before and the after* pertain to time.

450a22 Then, when he says *Hence it is clear to which part of the soul,* he concludes with what he had set out to do.

He is saying that from what has been said it is *clear* to which part of the soul *memory* pertains, since it is the same as the one to which *imagination* pertains. It is also clear that those things *are memorable in themselves of which there is imagination,* namely sensible things; intelligibles, however, which are not apprehended by man *without the imagination,* are memorable by accident.

This is also why we are less able to remember things that have subtle and spiritual aspect, while those that are gross and sensible are able to be remembered. We must tie down intelligible natures with certain other images, as it were, as Cicero teaches in the *Rhetoric.*[30]

Nevertheless some put memory in the intellective part of the soul, inasmuch as by memory they understand all the habitual conserving of the objects that pertain to the intellective part of the soul.[31]

CHAPTER 3

450A25–451A17

450a25 *One might perhaps wonder why it is that when the affection is present and the thing is absent, what is not present is remembered.*

450a27 *For it is clear that one must understand some such to have been made by the senses within the soul and in the part of the body having it as a sort of picture, the having of which we say is memory; for the motion that has been made impresses, as it were, a figure of the sensible thing, like those who impress seals with their signet rings.*

450a32 *Hence, too, for those who are in great motion because of an affection or because of age, memory does not come into being, as motion and a signet-seal falling into flowing water. For others it does not come into being owing to their being cold, like the old parts of buildings, and the impression does not take because of the hardness of the recipient of the affection. For this reason, the extremely young and the extremely old are deficient in memory; for the young are in flux owing to their growth and the old owing to their deterioration. Similarly, again, neither the excessively quick nor the excessively slow seem to have memories. For the quick are moister than they ought to be, and the slow are harder. Thus, in the case of those who are too quick, the image does not remain in the soul; whereas it never touches the others.*

450b11 *But if such is the case with respect to memory, does one remember the affection or the thing from which it was generated?*

450b13 *For if we remember the affection, we could remember nothing of the things that are absent.*

450b14 *If, on the other hand, we remember that absent thing, how is it that while sensing this affection we remember what we are not sensing, which is absent?*

450b15 *Also, if it is similar in the way that a figure or picture is in us, why would there be memory of another thing and not rather of this very impression? For the one acting by memory sees this affection and senses this affection.*

450b18 *How then does he remember what is not present? For he would be able both to see and to hear what is not present.*

450b20 *Or is it the case that this happens and occurs? For just as an animal inscribed on a tablet is both an animal and also a likeness, and one and the same thing is both, although the being is not the same for both, it is possible to consider it both as an animal and as a likeness. So too one must take the image that exists in us to be both itself something existing in its own right and also as an image of another. In its own right it is an object of speculation or an image, but inasmuch as it is of another, it exists as a likeness and an object that can be remembered. Hence, too, when the motion of that thing acts, there is a corresponding two-fold result. On the one hand, with regard to the motion taken in its own right, the soul will have sensed it in such a way that something intelligible or an image would seem to be present to it. On the other hand, insofar as it is of another and exists as in a picture, it considers it as a likeness, and he who does not see Coriscus considers it as Coriscus's likeness; here it is another affection of this speculation. When one considers what has been drawn as an animal, then, on the one hand, in the soul this picture becomes an intelligible object only, and, on the other hand, as there, because it is a likeness, it becomes a memorable object.*[1]

451a2 *For this reason, when such motions are engendered in our soul by what we have previously sensed, we sometimes do not know whether this happens because of having sensed it; and we sometimes are in doubt whether there is memory or not. Understanding and recollecting sometimes happen since we have heard or seen something before; but this comes about when the one who is looking as though at it is changed and considers it as of the other. Sometimes, however, even the contrary comes into being, as occurs in the case of Antipheron of Oreita and others affected by ecstasy; for they used to speak of images as facts and of themselves as remembering them. This comes into being when someone considers what is not a likeness as a likeness.*

451a12 *Meditations, however, preserve the memory in recollecting, and this is nothing other than to consider something frequently as a likeness and not as something in its own right.*

451a14 *So then what memory is, as well as what remembering is, has been stated: it is the having of an image as a likeness of that of which it is the image; and to which part of those in us it belongs, since it belongs to the first sensitive part and that by which we sense time.*

Commentary

450a25 After the Philosopher shows what memory is, and to what part of the soul it belongs, here he shows the cause of remembering.

In this regard he does two things. First he presents a difficulty.[2] Second he resolves it, where he says *Or is it the case* (450b20).

With respect to the first point he does three things: first he raises the difficulty; second, he makes one of its presuppositions explicit, where he says *For it is clear* (450a27); third he brings up the arguments bearing on the question, where he says *But if such is the case* (450b11).

Accordingly he first says that since in remembering there is an affection affecting the soul by its presence,[3] but the thing that we remember is absent, *someone* might wonder *why* we remember *what is not present*, namely the thing, and why we do not rather remember the affection which is present.

450a27 Then, when he says *For it is clear*, he makes explicit something that he had presupposed, namely, that while we remember, there exists an affection within the soul.

First he explains this through its cause; second through examples,[4] where he says *Hence, too, for those who are in great motion* (450a32).

Accordingly he first says that it is *clear* that one *must understand some such* affection to be *made* by the sense-power *within the soul and within* an organ of an animated body; we say that *memory belongs to* the soul *of this* body as *a habit*, and that this affection is, so to speak, a sort of picturing,[5] since the sensible object imprints its likeness upon the sense, and since this sort of likeness persists in the imagination even when the sensible object goes away. This is why he adds that the *motion* that is engendered by the sensible object upon the sense-power *impresses* upon the imagination *as it were* a sensible *figure* that remains when the sensible object goes away in the same way as that whereby those who seal things *with their signet rings* impress within the wax a figure that remains even when the seal or the ring has been removed.

He says "in the soul and in a part of the body" since, although an affection of this sort pertains to the sensitive part of the soul, a part that is the actuality of a bodily organ, nevertheless such an affection does not belong to the soul alone, but to the composite of body and soul together. He calls memory a "habit" of this part, since memory is in the sensitive part and since we sometimes do not actually apprehend the things that we keep in our memory, but retain them, as it were, habitually.

450a32 Then, when he says *Hence, too, for those who are in great motion*,

he uses signs or examples to clarify what he has set out to prove, namely that this affection is present in remembering.

He says that precisely since such an affection is necessary for memory, *memory* may not be produced in some people, because they are un-
dergoing much change: whether this comes about *because of an affection*
(either of the body, as in those who are sick or drunk, or of the soul, as
those who are moved to wrath or desire), *or because of* a time of life characterized by growth or decay. Thus, for reasons of this sort, the body of a
human being is in quite a flux and so cannot retain the impression that
comes into being from the motion of the sensible thing, as would happen if a motion or even a signet seal were impressed *into flowing water:*
for the figure would perish immediately owing to the flow.[6]

In certain *others,* however, the impression is not received at all. *Sometimes* this happens *because of* a chill that thickens the humors; thus, it
may not be possible for anything to be impressed upon the soul of those
who are in a state of great fear because of this "freezing up." He even
gives the example of old buildings: a wall can easily be changed when it
is fresh, before the casement sets, but not after it is aged. Sometimes,
however, the impression fails to be received, not through a "freezing
up" but *because of* the natural *hardness* of that which is to receive the affection: for earthly bodies possess hardness even if they are hot, but watery bodies are hardened by being frozen. It is *for* these causes that those
who are *extremely "new,"*[7] viz. children, *and* also *the old,* are *deficient in
memory,* since the bodies of children are in flux *because of growth, while*
those of the old are such *because of* their wasting away; hence in neither
of these is an impression well retained.

Yet it does happen that one firmly retains in his memory things that
he encounters[8] as a child. The vigor of a motion may cause things we
marvel at to be more deeply impressed upon our memory. We chiefly
wonder about new and unusual things;[9] and newborn children tend to
marvel at things still more because they are not used to them, and for
this reason too they remember firmly.[10] On the other hand, with respect
to the fluid condition of their body, children are naturally liable to slips
of memory.

He adds that *similarly* for the reasons just mentioned, *neither* those
who are *very*[11] quick at apprehension nor those who are *very* slow *seem*

to be *good at remembering*. For those who are *very quick* are of a more humid constitution than is fitting, since it is easy for something moist to receive an impression. On the other hand, those who are *slower* also have a harder constitution. Thus, in the case of those with a quick constitution, the impression of an image does *not* remain *in the soul*, whereas *it does not even touch* those with a hard constitution, i.e. they do not receive an impression of the image.

However, what he said can also be explained otherwise. Thus, in the first way, we may understand him to have assigned the cause for the failure of memory to the onset of a change, which he later illustrated by the example of the young and the old; in the second way, on the other hand, he assigned the cause on the basis of natural constitution: either because in some things the watery humor, which is cold and wet, is predominant and consequently the impressions of the images in them are easily dispersed, just as old buildings crumble easily;[12] or because the earthy humor predominates in certain things, and these do not take on any impression owing to their hardness. He subsequently clarified this point by using the example of the quick and the slow.

One must also note that he first stated that the impression of the images comes into being "in the soul and in a part of the body,"[13] so that later he might show that men are related in various ways to such an impression owing to the various dispositions of their bodies.

450b11 Then when he says *But if such is the case,* he presents arguments on both sides of the previously posed question.[14]

In the first place he takes up the question once again, as if what had been supposed were now manifest. He says that *if with respect to memory,* this happens, namely, that there is an affection present within it as a picture, this question must be asked: *Does* anyone remember this *affection* which exists as a presence[15] within the rememberer, or does one remember the sensible thing *by* which the impression *has been made?*

450b13 In the second place, where he says *For if we remember the affection,* he presents an objection to one side of the question.

He says that if anyone should state that a human being remembers the affection present to him, it follows that we would remember *none* of the things that are absent, which is contrary to what has been previously determined.

450b14 In the third place, at *If, on the other hand, we remember that ab-*

sent thing, he presents objections to the other side of the question, using, as it were, three arguments.

The first of these arguments he presents by saying that if one remembers the thing by which the affection was brought into being, it would seem unfitting that a man should sense that which is present, namely, the affection, and at the same time along with this should remember that *which* is *absent,* which he cannot sense. For it was said[16] that memory pertains to the "first sensitive" part; and in this fashion it would not seem that there should be a sense-act of the one and memory of the other.

450b15 The second argument he presents at *Also, if it is similar in the way that a figure.*

He says that if the sort of affection that is present to a rememberer is *in us in the way that the sense's own figure or picture* is (i.e. as representing the first change of the sense-power induced by the sensible object), then why *will memory be of the other* (i.e. the thing), and not of the figure or picture itself? For since it is a figure belonging to the sense-power, it can clearly be apprehended. This is obvious from experience, since he who remembers *gazes at* something bearing upon *this affection* through his intellect, or else *senses* it through his sensitive part. But it would seem unfitting that, while that which falls under the apprehension is present, not it but rather something else should be apprehended.

450b18 The third argument he presents at *How then does he remember.*

He asks *how* one might remember through an interior sense that which is *not present.* For since the exterior sense "*con*-forms" to the interior sense, it would follow that even the exterior sense would be of a thing not present, in such wise that it might *see and hear* a thing not present, which would seem awkward.

450b20 Then, when he says *Or is it the case,* he solves the difficulty he had posed.

He first points out the reason why memory occurs. In the second place he points out the cause for something being well preserved in the memory, where he says *Meditations, however, preserve the memory* (451a12). Third he adds an epilogue, where he says *So then what memory is* (451a14).

On this first topic he does two things: first he solves the difficulty; second he illustrates his solution by means of signs or examples, where he says *For this reason* (451a2).

Accordingly, first he says that it is possible to explain how what had been stated—that one may sense a present affection and remember an absent thing—can and does occur. He gives the example of an animal that is painted *on a tablet. It is both* a painted *animal*[17] *and* is *also a likeness*[18] of a real[19] animal. Now although that to which these features both belong is the same in subject, nevertheless, the two differ in character; and so the consideration of it inasmuch as it is a painted animal is other than the consideration of it inasmuch as it is a likeness of a real animal. So *too the image that* is *in us* can be taken either as it is *something* in itself or as it is an *image of the other.* Now *in its own right it is* a certain *object of speculation,* concerning which the intellect speculates, or else an *image,* inasmuch as it pertains to the sensitive part of the soul. *But* according as it is an image *of the other,* which we have previously sensed or understood, it is considered *as a likeness* leading to something else and a principle of remembering.

Consequently since the soul's remembering accords with the motion of an image, (1) if the soul be turned to the image *in its own right, in this way there would seem to be present* to the soul either *something intelligible* (which the intellect inspects within the image), or simply an *image* (which the imaginative power apprehends); (2) *if,* however, the soul turns itself to the image *inasmuch as* it is an image *of the other* and considers it *as a likeness* of what we previously have sensed or understood (as was said about the picture). Moreover, just as (i) *he who is not seeing Coriscus* considers an image of Coriscus *as a likeness of* him, *here,* now *this* consideration is *affected in another way,* because now the situation pertains to memory.

And (ii) just as an image of an individual man like Coriscus may sometimes be considered in its own right and sometimes as a likeness, so too does this occur in the case of intelligible objects. For if *when* the intellect looks at an image *as a painted animal,* it inspects it in itself, the image is considered *only an intelligible* object; if on the other hand the intellect inspects it inasmuch as it is a *likeness,* then it will be a principle of remembering, as occurs *there,* i.e. with respect to the particulars.

✤०✤

So then it is clear that when the soul turns itself toward an image as it is a form preserved in the sensitive part of the soul, in this way there is an act of the imagination or phantasia,[20] or even of the intellect considering the universal involved in this image. If, however, the soul should be turned toward the image inasmuch as it is a likeness of what we have previously seen or understood, this belongs to an act of remembering. In addition, since to be a likeness marks an interest[21] with respect to this form, Avicenna fittingly observes[22] that the memory focuses on the interest, whereas the imagination focuses on the form apprehended through the sense.

451a2 Then when he says *For this reason,* he clarifies what he had said by means of signs or examples.

He says that since we remember when we attend to an image as a likeness of something we have sensed or understood before, human beings can be related to the act of memory in three ways.

For sometimes, although there may be within us motions of the images that were made *by what we have sensed before,* motions that are left over from the first immutation[23] of the sense by the sensible object, nevertheless *we do not know whether* these motions happen to be in us *because of* the fact that we have sensed something before, and consequently *we are in doubt* as to whether we are remembering or not.

Secondly, it *sometimes* happens that a human being understands and recollects that *"we have heard or seen something before"* whose image is occurring to us now. This is remembering in the proper sense, and *this happens* when he who is looking at an image is being moved by the image that is present but is considering it inasmuch as it is a likeness *of the other* thing that he had sensed or understood before.

In the third way, the *contrary* of the first *sometimes* occurs: a human being believes that he is remembering but in fact does not. This is the sort of thing that *happened* to a fellow who was called Antipheron and was originally from Oreita;[24] similar things happen to others who lose their mind. For they reckon the images that occur to them for the first time as though they were images of previous deeds, as if they were remembering things that they had never seen or heard. This happens *when someone* considers what is not a likeness of another prior fact as if it were a likeness of it.

451a12 Then when he says *Meditations, however, preserve the memory,* he indicates how memory is preserved.

He says that frequent *meditations* upon what we have sensed or understood conserve the *memory* so that anyone may recollect well what he has seen or understood; "meditating," *however, is nothing* else than *frequently* considering certain things *as a likeness* of previously apprehended things *and not* only *in their own right,* and it is meditating which is the mode of considering that pertains to the character of memory. Moreover, it is clear that the habitual grasp of memorable objects is consolidated by frequently engaging in the act of memory, just as any other habit is strengthened by similar acts, and, when the cause is brought to bear many times,[25] the effect is made stronger.[26]

451a14 Then, when he says, *So then what memory is,* he adds an epilogue to what was said above.[27]

He says that *what memory and remembering are has been stated,* since memory is a *having,* i.e. a habitual conservation, *of an image,* not in its own right (for this pertains to the imaginative power) but inasmuch as the image is a likeness of something previously apprehended. It was also stated[28] to which part of the soul *of those that* are *in us* the memory pertains, since it was said that it belongs to the first sensitive part, inasmuch as it is through it that we are cognizant of time.

CHAPTER 4

451A18–451B10

451a18 *It remains, however, for us to talk about recollecting; first it is necessary to set out as being whatever things in the argumentative discourses are true.*

451a20 *For recollection is neither the recovery of a memory nor its acquisition.*

451a21 *For when one first learns or is affected, one does not recover any memory at all: for none has come into being before.*

451a23 *Nor does one acquire it from the beginning. For when a habit or an affection is engendered, then there is memory. Hence memory is not engendered along with the affection that is being engendered.*

451a25 *Further, when it has first come to be in the individual and the ultimate, the affection or knowledge already does indeed exist in the one affected, if one must call knowledge a habit or an affection. Nothing, however, prevents us from remembering by accident certain things that we know; but remembering by itself does not exist before time having come into being: for one remembers now what one has heard or seen or been affected by before; one does not remember now what he has experienced now.*

451a31 *Further it is clear that there is remembering for one that is not now recollecting but sensing or being affected from the beginning.*

451b2 *But when one recovers what he had before—knowledge or sense or the habit of that which we called memory—this is recollecting and it exists then, and is not any of the things that have been stated; but remembering is concomitant and memory follows.*

451b6 *Nor then do these come about without qualification if, although they were before, they come about again, but it is so in one way and in another is not. For it is possible for the same <person> to learn and discover twice; hence recollecting must differ from these, there also being a further principle than that from which they learn for recollecting.*

Commentary

451a18 After the Philosopher has settled his determination on memory and remembering, he turns to the topic of recollecting.

First he states the object of his interest; second he pursues the goal set out, where he says *For recollection is neither* (451a20).

Accordingly, first he says that after he has spoken[1] about remembering *it remains for us to talk about recollecting,* in order that whatever truths might be taken up by means of the dialectical discussions may first be supposed as being true. In this way he excuses himself from a long disputation about things pertaining to recollection.[2]

451a20 Then, when he says *For recollection is neither,* he pursues the goal he had set out.

In regard to this he does three things. First he shows what recollection is by comparing it to other apprehensions. Second he determines the mode of recollecting where he says *Recollections happen* (Ch.5, 451b10). Third he shows what sort of affection recollection is where he says *Now, then, that those with good memories* (Ch.8, 453a14).

In regard to the first of these he does two things. First he shows what recollection is not. Second he shows what it is where he says *But when one recovers* (451b2).

On the first of these points he does two things. First he sets out what he intends to do. Second he explains what he set out to do where he says *For when one first learns* (451a21).

Accordingly, first he says that recollection is neither *the recovery of a memory,* in the sense that recollecting would be nothing but a repeated remembering; *nor* again is recollection the first *acquisition* of a knowable object, namely the acquisition that arises through the sense or the intellect.

451a21 Then when he says *For when one first learns,* he explains what he had said.

In regard to this he does two things. First he shows the difference between the two terms he had set out, namely, the recovery of a memory and the acquisition of one. Second he shows that recollection is not the recovery of a memory and also not an acquisition, where he says *Further it is clear that remembering* (451a31).

On the first point he does two things. First he shows that the acquisition is not memory, since he who acquires is not remembering. Second, where he says *Nor does one acquire it from the beginning* (451a23) he shows that the converse is not true either: memory is not acquisition, because he who remembers is not acquiring something new.

Accordingly, he first states that when one first *learns* something, with respect to one's intellective apprehension, *or is affected* by it, with respect to one's sensitive apprehension, at that point one *recovers no memory,* because nothing is recovered except something previously existing; but *no* memory has preceded. Therefore to learn or to sense something for the first time is not to recover a memory.

451a23 Then, when he says *Nor does one acquire it from the beginning,* he shows that remembering is not the first acquisition.

In regard to this he does two things. First he shows that remembering does not consist in acquiring a notion for the first time. Second he shows that it does not consist in having been acquired for the first time, where he says *Further, when it has first come to be* (451a25).

Accordingly, he first says that neither, too, does the one remembering *acquire* his notion of the remembered thing from *the beginning.* For, since memory is of the past, as was maintained above,[3] *then there is memory,* when a notion is already existing by way of habit or at least of passion as it does in a past existence; but when the affection itself comes into being, i.e. in the very acquiring of the notion, it is not yet in a past existence; hence memory does not yet come into being in the man.

451a25 Then, when he says *Further, when it has first come to be,* he shows that there is also no memory in the first instant in which a notion has just come into being, whether by way of habit or of passion, as when the notion has not yet been converted into a habit.

At this point one ought to consider the fact that something is first said to have come into being in the indivisible instant that is the ultimate moment of the measuring time, as is proved in *Physics* VI.[4]

Hence he says that *when* a notion *has first come into being* in an indivisible instant, which is the last movement of the time of the generation of the notion, in that instant it can *indeed* be said that *the affection and the knowledge* is *already* in *the one affected,* i.e. in the one acquiring the notion, yet in such a way that we do not give full force to the term "knowledge," which properly speaking signifies a habit, but rather we take the term in a general sense in the sense of habit as well as that of passion. (The reason for his saying this is that in the last instant of generation it is always true to say that that of which there is generation exists; as in the last instant of the generation of fire, there is already fire.) Given that knowledge exists, however, *nothing prevents us from remembering* those things inasmuch as we have a knowledge of them in the present. But *re-membering* does *not* occur in its own right *before time having come into being*, that is, before some time intervenes between the previously existing notion and the memory itself; *for one remembers now what one has heard or seen* or in some fashion or other *been affected by before*, but one *does not remember now what he has experienced now*. Moreover, it is obvious that one is first said to be "already affected" at the last instant of the affection. Hence there cannot be memory at that instant.

451a31 Then, when he says *Further it is clear that there is remembering*, he shows further that recollection is neither recovery of a memory nor an original acquisition.

He states that it is *clear* from what has been said before that one who is *not now recollecting* may *remember*, i.e. he does not remember what he is now recollecting, *but* that which he has sensed or in some fashion or other experienced *from the beginning*. Thus, recollection is not recovery of a memory but is related to something that someone has apprehended before.

451b2 Then, when he says *But when one recovers*, he shows what recollection is.

First he says that recollection is the recovery of the first acquisition. Second he shows that recollection is not just any such recovery, where he says *Nor then do these come about without qualification* (451b6).

Accordingly, he first says that recollection is not a recovery of a memory, but is when someone recovers what he has known or sensed *before*, whether by a proper or by the common sense, *the habit of which* we say is *memory* (for just as remembering is related to a previously generated notion, so also is recollecting), *and recollecting exists then*, viz. when in some way we recover a prior apprehension, but *not* in such a way that recollection be *any of the things that we have stated*, whether sense or memory or imagination or knowledge, but through recollection *remembering is concomitant*, because recollection is a sort of movement toward remembering, *and* thus *memory follows* recollection, just as the terminus follows its movement.

Or, according to another manuscript,[5] recollection follows *memory*, since, just as the enquiry of reason is the way to know something and yet it proceeds from something known, so too is recollection the way to remember something and yet it proceeds from something that is re-membered, as will become clearer later on.[6]

451b6 Then, when he says *Nor then do these come about without qualification,* he shows that recollection is not just any recovery of a sensation or of knowledge.

He says that it is not universally true that there is recollection wherever an awareness of a knowledge or a sensation that had been there before comes about again, but in one way he who recovers the science or the sensation recollects and in another way he does not. <Aristotle> shows that it is not universally true, because *it happens that the same* man may learn *the same* thing a second time after his knowledge had been lost, or may *discover* what he had before, but yet this is not recollecting. *Hence recollecting must* be different *from these,* i.e. from repeated learning or discovery, and there must be something more to be a starting-point of recollecting than is required for learning. What this something more is will be explained in the sequel.[7]

CHAPTER 5

451B10–452A4

451b10 *Recollections happen since this motion is now naturally apt after this one; for if it is of necessity, it is manifest that, when it is moved with that one, it will be moved by this; but, if not of necessity but from custom, it will be moved as it were much. It comes about, however, that certain ones have become accustomed more quickly once, than others moved several times. Hence we remember some things more on seeing them once, than others many times.*

451b16 *Hence, when we recollect we are moved according to one of the prior motions, until we be moved after that one was customary. Hence, too, we are made to come to what is subsequently by meditating from now or some other point and from the similar, the contrary, or the proximate. Recollection comes about because of this: for the motions are of these, of these, the same; of others, however, at the same time; of others, they have a part, so that the remainder is little which has been moved after that one. Therefore they seek in this way, and, not seeking, they still recollect in this way, when that motion comes into being after the other one; but it used to come about when the other motions such as we have spoken of had come about, as it were, much.*

451b25 *It is not at all necessary to attend to how we remember those that are distant but not those that are near; for it is obvious that the method is somehow the same. Now I say how it says "that consequently", neither inquiring in advance nor recollecting; but this motion is by custom consequent after this one; and therefore when he may want to recollect, this is what he does: he tries to grasp the starting point of a motion after which there will be that one.*

451b31 *Hence recollections come about in the quickest and best way from the starting point: for as things are related to each other in that which is consequently, so too are the motions.*

452a2 *And whatever things have an ordering, such as mathemes, are more recollectible; but those that are badly, with difficulty.*

Commentary

451b10 After the Philosopher has inquired into how recollection is related to the other things that pertain to cognition, here he begins to explain the manner in which recollecting takes place.

First he explains the manner of recollecting. Second he points to the difference between memory and recollection where he says *Now, then, that those with good memories* (Ch.8, 453a4).

Concerning the first topic he does two things. He shows how recollecting takes place first with regard to the things one remembers; and second with regard to the time (for recollection is concerned with time, just as memory is), where he says *It is most necessary, however, to know time* (Ch.7, 452b7).

With respect to the first topic he does two things. First he sets out the cause of recollecting. Second he points out the manner in which one proceeds in recollecting where he says *Hence, when we recollect* (451b16).

The cause of recollecting is the order of the motions that remain in the soul from the first impression of what we first apprehend.

Accordingly, in setting out this cause, he states that *recollections happen* because one *motion is naturally* disposed to occur to us *after* another. This may happen in two ways. In one way, when the second motion follows the first *of necessity,* as apprehending "animal" *of necessity* follows on apprehending "man"; and thus it is *manifest that,* when the soul is moved by the first movement, *it will be moved* by the second, too. In the other way, the second motion may follow after the first *not of necessity but from custom,* since one is accustomed to think, say, or do that thing after this one, and then the second motion follows after the first not always *but as it were much,* i.e. for the most part, as natural effects also follow from their causes for the most part, not always. The custom under discussion is not, however, established equally in all men, but *it comes about* that some *more quickly* establish the custom within themselves on thinking *once, than* do others if they think this after that *several times* (which can happen either because of greater attention and deeper cogitation or because of a nature that is better able to receive and retain an impression). Hence, too, it may come about that *we remember some things more seeing them once than* others seen *many times* (since those things that we are more vehemently intent upon remain more in the memory, whereas those that we see or think of superficially or lightly slip quickly from the memory).[1]

451b16 Then, on the supposition of this order of motions, he shows how recollection proceeds, where he says *Hence, when we recollect.*

Concerning this point he does two things. In the first place he shows the manner of proceeding in recollecting. In the second place he points out whence a recollector ought to proceed, where he says *A beginning-point, however* (Ch.6, 452a12).

With regard to the first topic he does two things. In the first place he shows the manner in which one proceeds in recollecting. In the second place, from this he points out how recollecting and relearning differ, which is a matter he had left unsettled above; he does this where he says *Recollecting also differs from relearning* (Ch.6, 452a4).

With regard to the first topic he does three things. In the first place he sets out how recollecting occurs. In the second place on the basis of this he resolves a difficulty, where he says *It is not at all necessary to attend* (451b25). In the third place he uses examples[2] to clarify what he had set out to show, where he says *Hence recollections come about* (451b31).

Accordingly, in the first place, he concludes from the premises[3] that, since one motion follows after another either of necessity or by custom, it must be that, when we recollect, we are moved *according to* some one *of the prior movements, until* we come to the point that *we are moved* by the movement to be apprehended, which *is accustomed* to be after the first, namely, the movement that we intend to rediscover by recollecting, since recollection is nothing other than a search for something that has fallen from memory.[4] Hence in recollecting *we hunt,* i.e. we search, for *what* is *consequently* from something prior that we do remember (for just as he who searches through demonstration proceeds from something prior, which is known, from which he is made to come to something posterior, which was unknown; so too the one who recollects proceeds from something prior, which he remembers, to rediscover what had fallen from his memory).

The "first" from which a recollector begins his search, however, is sometimes a time that is *known* and sometimes a thing that is known. With respect to the time, he sometimes begins *from now,* i.e. from the present time proceeding into the past, the memory of which he is seeking (e.g. if he is seeking to remember what he did four days ago, this is how he meditates on the matter: "I did this today, that yesterday, and something else the day before," and in this fashion he arrives at what he did three days ago by tracing things back according to the sequence of the customary motions). Sometimes, however, he begins from *some other* time (e.g. if someone remembers what he did a week ago and has forgotten what he did three days ago, he will proceed by coming down to the sixth day and will proceed in the same way until he reaches the third day before, or he may also go up to a day two weeks ago also starting from a week ago, or to any other past time).

Sometimes, in like fashion, one may also recollect beginning with something that he remembers and from which he proceeds to another one for three reasons: (1) sometimes one recollects by reason of similitude (e.g. when one remembers Socrates, and from this Plato, who is like him in wisdom, comes to mind); (2) sometimes, by reason of contrariety (as when one remembers Hector, and Achilles therefore comes to mind); (3) and sometimes one recollects by reason of some proximity (as when the son comes to mind when one remembers the father, and the same reason holds for any other sort of proximity, whether of association, of place, or of time).[5]

And recollection comes about because the motions corresponding to these cases follow them.

For the motions of some of the aforementioned items are the *same*, as is especially so of the similars; of others, viz. the contraries, *however, at the same time*, since when one of the contraries is known, the other is known at the same time; and sometimes certain motions *have a part* of others, as happens in things that are in proximity to each other, since something is considered in one of the neighbors which pertains to the other; and so, although the residue that is missing from one's apprehension be *small*, it follows the motion of the prior one, so that, once the first has been apprehended, the second consequently comes to mind.

There is, however, a further point to consider: sometimes those who *seek* to rediscover a consequent lost motion arrive at a later motion from a prior one in the manner described: this is properly recollecting just when one intentionally[6] seeks for the memory of a thing. Sometimes, however, it happens that even those who do not seek to remember come upon the memory of a thing when they proceed unintentionally[7] from the prior to the posterior movement in the manner described:[8]

when that movement of the forgotten thing *comes into being* in the soul *after the other* and this was unintentional[9] but *as it were much,* i.e. as *that* motion which occurs arises in many *other motions such as we have spoken of,* viz. the like, the contrary, or the proximate; but the latter unintentional movement is called recollecting by way of a departure from proper usage; it is rather a chance remembering with a certain resemblance to recollection.

451b25 Then, when he says *It is not at all necessary to attend,* he solves a certain difficulty on the basis of these premises.[10]

For one could come to wonder why we frequently remember the things *that are distant,* i.e. those that happened many years ago, and we do *not* remember the ones *that are near,* i.e. those that were a few days ago.

But he claims that *it is not necessary to attend* to this, i.e. to take the question seriously, since it is *obvious* that it *somehow* happens in the same way as was set out before.[11] He explains this by reviewing what he had said, namely, that sometimes it happens that the soul may say what it had forgotten by apprehending something *that* exists *consequently* and do so without inquiring in advance or intentionally recollecting. The reason for this is that one motion follows on another by custom, and so when the first motion arises the second follows even if the man does not intend it; and just as this happens unintentionally from custom, so, too, *will* one *do this when* he intentionally *wills to recollect:* for he *tries to grasp* the first motion, at which the later motion follows. Since it sometimes happens that the motions of the thing that are remote are by custom more established, we sometimes remember them either with or without seeking for them.

451b31 Then, when he says *Hence recollections come about,* he shows how this is so by means of two examples.

He presents the first of these signs by saying that since one customarily proceeds from the prior toward the subsequent motion either by inquiring or by not inquiring for it, *recollections come about in the quickest and best manner* when one begins meditating *from the starting point* of the whole business. The reason for this is that it is according to the order in which the *things* follow each other that their motions are engendered in the soul with this order; thus, when we are looking for a particular verse of a psalm, we begin at the top.

452a2 He presents the second example where he says *And whatever things have an ordering.*

He states that *whatever* things are well ordered, *such as mathemes,* i.e. the theorems of mathematics, *are more recollectible;* the second of these is concluded from the first, and so on for the rest; but those that are badly ordered, we recollect with difficulty.

Accordingly, we can in this way learn four results useful for remembering or recollecting well:[12] first to strive to reduce what one wants to retain into some order;[13] second to set one's mind upon them deeply and intently;[14] third to meditate frequently according to the order;[15] fourth to begin to recollect from the starting point.[16]

CHAPTER 6

452A4–B6

452a4 *Recollecting also differs from relearning in this: that one will be able somehow to be moved to what is after the starting point; but when not, but through something else, one no longer remembers.*

452a7 *Often, however, one cannot any longer recollect but can seek and does find. This, however, comes about for one who is moving many things, if he should be moving with the sort of motion as that upon which the thing follows. For remembering is to be a moving potency within; and this is so in such a way that one is being moved from himself and the motions by which he is held, as has been said.*

452a12 *A beginning-point, however, must have been taken.*

452a12[bis] *For which reason they sometimes seem to recollect from places.*

452a13 *The cause of this is that they come quickly from one thing to another, as from milk to white, from white to air, and from the latter to the moist—from which one remembers autumn while seeking this season.*

452a17 *A universal, moreover, seems to be the beginning-point and the middle of them all. For if one does not do so before, when he gets to this point, he will recollect, or he will not do so from anywhere else, either. Thus, if someone should have understood something in which there are A B G D E Z I T: for if one does not recollect at E, he remembers at T; for from there one can be moved to both— both to D and to E. But if one is not seeking one of these, one will recollect on coming to G, if one is looking for I or Z; and if not, he will go on to A, and so on always.*

452a24 *The cause of one's sometimes remembering from the same and sometimes not remembering is that one happens to have been moved from the same starting-point to many places, as, for example, from G to E or to D. Hence, if one is not being moved through the old one, he is being moved in a more uncustomary way: for custom already serves as nature. Hence we quickly recollect things that we have frequently understood. For, just as this thing is by nature after this one, so too does action make a nature by doing this many times.*

452a30 *But since just as in things that exist by nature there comes to be what*

is both outside nature and also by chance, still more is this the case in those that
exist by custom, in the latter of which nature does not exist in the same way
whereby sometimes to be moved both there and in one way and in another, and
when he is drawn hence in any case; and for this reason when one needs to recol-
lect a name we commit a solecism dissimilar to the one we know against it.

Commentary

452a4 After the Philosopher shows how recollecting takes place,
here he explains two points that were touched upon above.[1]

In the first place, he shows how recollecting differs from relearning.
Second[2] he shows that one who recollects must begin from starting-
points, where he says *A beginning-point* (452a12).

With respect to the first topic he does two things. First he shows how
recollecting differs from relearning. Second[3] he shows how recollecting
differs from rediscovering, where he says *Often, however, one cannot any
longer recollect* (452a7).

With respect to the first point, we must bear in mind that both he
who recollects and also he who relearns recover a notion that they lost;
but the one who recollects recovers it under the aspect of memory, i.e.
in a relation ordered to something that had been known before, whereas the one who relearns it, recovers the notion absolutely, i.e. not as
pertaining to something previously known. Now since we do not arrive
at a notion of things unknown except from previously known principles, the principles from which we proceed to know anything unknown
must belong to the same genus, as is clear from the *Posterior Analytics*.[4]
Hence he who is recollecting necessarily proceeds to recover the notion
under the aspect of memory from starting-points that have been remembered, but this is not the case with one who is relearning something.

Accordingly he says that *recollecting differs from relearning in this: that*
he who is recollecting has the power *somehow* to be moved to something
that is consequent upon a starting-point that has been retained in the
memory (for instance, when someone remembers that such and such a
thing was said to him but has forgotten who had told him, one therefore
uses what he has in the memory to recollect what he has forgotten). But
when one does *not* arrive at the recovery of a lost notion through a
starting-point that has been retained in the memory *but through* some-

thing *else* that is newly handed on to him by a teacher, that is *not* memory or recollection but new learning.

452a7 Then, when he says *Often, however, one cannot any longer recollect,* he explains how recollecting and rediscovery differ from each other.

He says that a human being *often cannot any longer recollect* what he has forgotten, because the particular movements from which he could arrive at what he is seeking to remember do not remain in him, but, if he should seek the notion of that thing in a new way, he *can* proceed and often *does find* what he is seeking as though he were acquiring the science anew.[5] Now that happens when a soul, while thinking out diverse things, is moved by many movements: if, in addition, it should happen that it arrive at a movement at which a cognition of the thing follows, then one is said to be discovering it. Though one can be discovering something, one cannot, however, be recollecting it, since recollecting comes about because a human being retains within himself a certain *potency* or power of guiding himself toward the movements that he is seeking of the thing. *This* recollecting, *however,* comes about when one can arrive at what is being moved with the movement that he lost through forgetfulness, doing so *both from himself,* not from someone teaching him, as happens when one relearns something, *and* from previously held *movements, as has been said,*[6] not from new movements, as when one rediscovers something.

452a12 Then, when he says *A beginning-point, however, must have been taken,* he shows that one who is recollecting must start from a beginning.

Concerning this topic he does two things. First he points out the claim under discussion. Second he assigns the cause for a defect that we sometimes suffer in recollecting[7] where he says *The cause of one's sometimes remembering* (452a24).

With respect to the first point he does two things. In the first place he shows that one who is recollecting must start from a beginning-point. In the second place[8] he indicates what sort of starting-point he must begin from, where he says *A universal, moreover, seems to be the beginning-point* (452a17).

Concerning the first topic he does three things.

In the first place he sets out what he intends to claim.

He says that he who wants to recollect *must* take a *beginning-point* from which he has begun to be moved either by thinking, by saying, or by doing something.

452a12 In the second place, he illustrates what he had said by using an example where he says *For which reason they sometimes seem to recollect* (452a12).

For since he who is recollecting must take hold of a starting-point from which he may start proceeding to recollect, human beings *sometimes seem to recollect from* the *places* in which certain things have been said, done, or thought. They do so using a place as a sort of starting-point for recollecting, because the entrance to a place is a sort of starting-point of all the things that are done in that place. This is also why Tully in his *Rhetoric*[9] teaches that, to remember easily, certain places are imagined to be arrayed in order, and by means of these places we distribute the images of the things we want to remember.

452a13 In the third place he illustrates his claim through its cause where he says *The cause of this is that they come quickly* (452a13).

He says that the *cause* whereby he who is recollecting must get hold of a starting point is that human beings, through a kind of wandering of the mind, *come* easily from one thing *to another* by reason of its likeness, its contrariety, or its proximity.[10] Thus, if we think or speak about *milk* we come easily to *white*, because of the whiteness of milk, and from *white to air* because of the clarity of the transparent, which causes whiteness, and from air *to the moist* because air is moist,[11] and from the moist one comes to recollect the season of autumn, which one was seeking, by reason of contrariety, since that season is cold and dry.[12]

452a17 Then, when he says *A universal, moreover, seems to be the starting-point,* he indicates what sort of starting-point one who is recollecting ought to get hold of.

He says that what is *universal seems* to be the *beginning-point and the middle,* through which one can be brought to all things (but here the universal that is spoken of is not that which is predicated of many, as in logic, but rather that by which one is accustomed to be moved to various things; it is as if after milk one is being moved to whiteness and sweetness, and again from whiteness to other things, as has been said,[13] and again from sweetness to the digesting heat, to fire, and to other things thought of in due sequence, milk will be, so to speak, the universal with respect to all these motions). In addition, one must run back to this universal if one wants to recollect any of the consequent items; since *if* one does *not* recollect any of the consequent terms previously through other posterior beginning-points, one will at least *recollect* it *when* he has come to the first universal beginning-point; *or,* if one does not recollect it then, one will *not* be able to do so *from any other.*

In addition he gives an example about various thoughts by the various letters A B G D E Z I T (he reckons these letters according to the order of the Greek alphabet;[14] yet the order is not the same in the recollecting, but we must take it that in thinking or speaking about B one may come to A; in thinking about A, however, sometimes one comes to T, sometimes to G; now from T one sometimes comes to D and sometimes to E; in thinking about G, on the other hand, sometimes one comes to I and sometimes to Z).

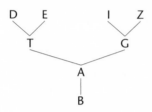

FIGURE 6.1

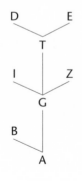

FIGURE 6.2

If, therefore, one should *not* recollect what is in E, he will be able to recollect it if he should come to T, from which he used to be moved to the two, viz. to E and to D. But perhaps one was not seeking E and not D, either, but rather was seeking I or Z, then *coming* to G one *will recollect.* But since we do not know whether what we are seeking is contained under T or under G, one must run back to A, which is, as it were, the universal with respect to them all. *And* one must *so* proceed *always;* for instance if at that point B is still more universal than A.

The aforesaid arrangement can, however, also be understood in another way, so that one is made to come from A to G directly, but to B laterally (although there is no mention of B in the text); moreover, one may be led from G laterally to I on the one hand and to Z on the other, but directly to T, from which one is led to D and E. And so he says that if one does not remember in E, which is last, he comes into T, which is prior; and if perchance one does not remember in T, because what he is seeking is not contained under it, he must run back to G, under which certain other thoughts are contained, namely I and Z, and from there to A, under which, as has been said before,[15] B is also contained.

452a24 Then, when he says *The cause of one's sometimes remembering,* he assigns the cause for a deficiency that is experienced by those who recollect.

He explains this defect in their recollection first to the extent that they do not recollect at all; and second to the extent that they recollect corruptly,[16] where he says *But since just as in things that exist by nature* (452a30).

Accordingly, in the first place he says that *from the same* given starting-point human beings sometimes recollect and sometimes do not, *since* it *happens* that *from the same starting-point* from which one is moved toward various things, one is more often moved to one than to another; e.g. if *from G* one is moved *to E* and *to D* more often to the one than to the other, then, once one has got hold on the starting point, one easily recollects the one to which one is more often accustomed to be moved. But *if* one is *not* moved *through the old* one, i.e. through that by which one was more accustomed to be moved, then one *is being moved* in a less customary way,[17] and therefore one does not recollect easily, because *custom is,* as it were, a certain *nature. Hence,* just as those things that exist naturally come into being and are restored easily, inasmuch as things quickly return to their own nature because of the inclination of nature, as is clear in heated water, which quickly returns to coolness, so too do we easily *recollect* those things *that* we have *often* considered, because of our inclination of custom.

Moreover, that custom exists as nature does, he explains through this: that *just as* in *nature* there is a certain order whereby *this* thing comes into being *after this* one, so also when many operations follow each other through an order, they make a certain *nature.* Now this happens especially in the animal operations in whose principles there is a something impressing and a something receiving an impression, as for example the imagination receives an impression of a sense. And so things that we have frequently seen or heard are the more firmly established in the imagination in the manner of a nature in the same way as the repetition of the impression of a natural agent eventually also leads to a form which is the nature of a thing.

452a30 Then, when he says *But since just as in things that exist by nature,* he points out the cause whereby we sometimes recollect corruptly.

He says that *just as in things that exist* according to nature something happens that is *outside of nature,* i.e. *by fortune* or chance, such as monsters in the parts of animals,[18] so much the *more* does something unordered and unintentional happen *in those that exist* according to *custom,* which, even if it does imitate nature, yet falls short of its stability. Consequently, *there,* too, i.e. in those things that we recollect through custom, recollecting happens sometimes *in one way* and sometimes *in another;* this occurs because of some impediment, as *when* one draws back *hence,* i.e. from one's accustomed course, toward any other, as is clear in those who recite something from memory: if their imagination be distracted to something else, they lose what they have to say or they say it corruptly. *And for this reason, when one needs to recollect a name* or a speech, we make a grammatical error with respect to another in a manner unlike the one that we *know.*

452b6 Finally he adds as an epilogue that *recollecting occurs* in the manner just described.

CHAPTER 7

452B7–453A4

452b7 *It is most necessary, however, to know time, either with a measure or infinitely.*

452b8 *There is, however, something by which one judges the greater and lesser: moreover, it is able to be put into a ratio,[1] just like magnitudes. For one understands great ones even far off, not by extending one's understanding out yonder, as some might say of sight (for even when they are not, it similarly understands), but by a proportional motion. For there are similar figures and motions in it.*

452b13 *For[2] by what does it differ when it understands the greater ones?*

452b13 *Or is it that[3] it understands those that are less? For all those that are within are lesser; and those that are outside are also proportionately. But perchance it is able to get a proportional just as also with the species, but in it, so too with the distances.*

452b17 *So just as if something is moved according to AB, BE it makes GD: for AG and GD are proportional. What then makes GD rather than ZI? Or as AG is to AB, so is KT to TM; hence it is being moved with respect to those together; but if one wants to understand according to AZ, ZI, he understands similarly to GB, BE. But instead of TC, he will understand KL. For these are related as ZA to BA.*

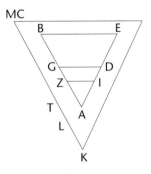

FIGURE 7.1

452b23 *So when a motion of both the thing and of the time comes about together,* then memory is acting. If, however, he thinks he remembers while not doing so; for nothing keeps someone from being deceived and to seem to remember even while not remembering. It is not, however, possible for one acting in his memory not to think that he does so but rather not to notice what is remembered: for this was just what remembering is. But if the <motion> that belongs to the thing *should come into being without the one that belongs to the time, or the latter without the former, he does not recollect.*

452b29 *But the one that belongs to time is twofold. For sometimes he does not remember it with a measure, e.g. that it was two days ago, but that he did do it at some time or other. Sometimes however also with a measure. But he does remember although not with a measure; for men are accustomed to say that they remember <something> but do not know when, whenever they do not know its quantity with a metron.*

Commentary

452b7 After the Philosopher has shown the mode of recalling from the side of the things to be recalled, here he determines the mode of recalling from the side of time.

And first he sets out what he intends to do. Second he clarifies what he had set out, where he says *There is, however, something by which one judges* (452b8).

He says first, therefore, that in recollecting *it is most necessary to know time,* namely the past, which memory is concerned with, which recollection is a search for; past time is known by one who is recollecting sometimes under a determinate *measure,* for instance when one knows that one has sensed this item two days ago, and sometimes it is known *infinitely,* that is indeterminately, for instance if one remembers that he has sensed this item at some unspecified time.[4]

452b8 Then, when he says *There is, however, something by which one judges,* he clarifies what he had set out.

First he shows how the soul knows the measure of time. Second he clarifies the principal point which he had set out, namely that the person who recollects must know time, where he says *So when a motion of both the thing and of time* (452b23).

In regard to the first he does two things. First he clarifies what he had set out. Second he solves a certain question where he says *For by what does it differ* (452b13).

For he says first that *there is something* in the soul *whereby it judges* a greater or lesser measure of time. And this is to be *able to be put into a ratio* with respect to time *just as* it is *also* in respect to bodily *magnitudes:* which the soul *understands* to be both *large* with respect to the quantity of the bodies seen, *and far off* with respect to the quantity of local distance, to which the quantity of time is made proportionate, which is grasped according to its distance from the present moment. The soul knows such magnitudes *not by extending one's understanding out yonder,* as if the soul knows magnitudes by getting in contact with them according to the intellect (which is something that he seems to be saying on account of Plato,[5] as is clear in the first book of *On the Soul*[6]); and in this way *some* people also *say* that *vision* comes into being because a visual ray crosses the whole distance up to the thing seen, as is said in the book *On Sense and What Is Sensed.*[7] But it cannot be that magnitudes are known by the soul through contact with the intelligence, since in that way the soul could understand only existent magnitudes, but as the case now stands we see that it understands magnitudes that do not exist. For nothing keeps the soul from understanding a quantity twice that of the heavens. Therefore the soul does not know a magnitude by extending itself to it, but because a certain movement left in the soul by the sensible thing is proportional to an exterior magnitude: *for there are in* the soul certain forms *and motions similar* to the things through which it knows things.

452b13 Then, when he says *For by what does it differ,* he settles a question about what was set out before.

And concerning this he does three things. First he proposes a question. Second he solves it, where he says *Or is it that it understands those that are less* (452b13). Third he gives an example of the answer in letters where he says *So, therefore, if one is moved* (452b17).

So first he asks this question: when the soul knows a magnitude through the likeness of the magnitude which it has, in *what does* that by which it knows a greater or lesser magnitude *differ?* For they seem not to have a different likeness, in that they do not differ in species.

452b13 Then, when he says *Or is it that it understands those that are less,* he resolves the question.

And he says that the soul, through a similar figure or form, knows the *lesser* ones, that is, a smaller quantity, just as through a similar form it also knows a larger magnitude. For the interior forms and movements correspond proportionately to the exterior magnitudes, and *perchance* the same thing happens with magnitudes or *distances* of places and times as also happens in regard to the *species* of things, so that just as *in it,* the one knowing, there are various likenesses and movements correspon-

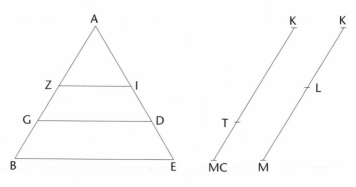

FIGURE 7.2

ding proportionately to the various species of things, for example to a horse or a cow, so also do they correspond to various quantities.

452b17 Then, when he says *So just as if something is moved,* he shows such a various proportion through an example with letters.

To make this clear one must realize that since he said above that there are in the intelligence figures similar to and movements proportional to the things, he uses here, for the sake of an example, the similarity of figures as the geometers use them, amongst whom figures are called similar whose sides are proportional and angles equal, as is clear in the sixth book of Euclid.[8] Therefore, let triangle BAE be described, the base of which is BE. Then from a point G marked in the side BA let a line be drawn equidistant from the base and right up to the other side; this line is GD. And, similarly, in the triangle GAD let a line ZI be drawn equidistant from the base. It was demonstrated in the first book of Euclid[9] that a straight line falling upon two equidistant lines makes the opposite angles equal. Therefore, angle AGD is equal to angle ABE, and angle ADG is equal to angle AEB. But angle A is common; therefore, the three angles of triangle GAD are equal to the angles of triangle BAE. Therefore the lines that subtend the equal angles are proportional, according to the fourth proposition of the sixth book of Euclid;[10] therefore, what the proportion[11] of AB to AG is the same as the proportion of BE to GD; therefore, alternately, the proportion from AB to BE is the same as the proportion from AG to GD; and thus the two aforementioned triangles are similar figures. Through the line AB and its parts are understood the movements of the soul by which the soul knows; and through the lines BE, GD, and ZI, which are the bases of the triangles, are understood the various quantities differing in greatness and smallness.

Therefore, by way of example, he concludes that *if* the soul is moved *according to* movement AB, *it is moved* to know the quantity BE, this movement will also make quantity GD be known according to something belonging to itself, since the movement AG, which is contained in AB, and the magnitude GD are in the same proportion as the movement AB and the magnitude BE. But then the question that was raised above will return: *what* more is required for knowing the quantity GD, which is greater, than for knowing the quantity ZI, which is less? And in order that this might be seen more plainly, he takes indistinct movements, one of which is not contained in the other: therefore, let there be one line KM and let it be divided at point T in such a ratio[12] that there is the same proportion of KT to TM as that of the line AG, according to which the quantity GD is known, to the line AB, according to which quantity BE is known; in this way, therefore, *it is being moved with respect to these* movements, since just as according to the movement AG the quantity GD is known, so according to the movement KT, and, just as according to the movement AB the quantity BE is known, so according to the movement TM. *But if* someone *wants, according to* the movement AZ, to know the quantity ZI, then GZ will have to be subtracted from AG, just as GB was added to it in order to know the quantity BE. *But*, if we wish to take distinct movements, we must take in place of the two movements KT and TM (in place of which he now puts TC, C and M may be inscribed on the same point) two other movements, one of which is KL and the other LM, so that the line KM is divided at point L according to this ratio,[13] so that the proportion of KL to LM is as the proportion of AZ to AB. Hence, just as through the movement LM one knows the quantity BE, so through the movement KL one knows quantity ZI.[14]

452b23 Then, when he says *So when a motion of both the thing and of the time comes about together,* he goes on to explain the principal thing he had set out to do.

And first he shows that the one who recollects must know time. Second he shows two ways of knowing time where he says *But that which is of time* (452b29).

Accordingly he says first that when the movement of the *thing* to be remembered *and of* the past *time* occur in the soul *together, then* there is the act of memory. *If,* however, someone should *think* that it is so relat-ed and yet memory should not come into being in this way—because it lacks either the movement of the thing or the movement of the time—then there is no object remembered; *for nothing keeps* deception from ex-isting in the memory, as when it seems to someone that he remembers something and he actually does not, since the past time occurs to him but not the thing that he saw, but another instead.[15] In addition, some-times one remembers and does not think that he does so, but it escapes his notice, because the thing occurred to him but not the time <corre-sponding to it>; since, as noted above,[16] remembering is to be intent on the phantasm of a thing inasmuch as it is the likeness of something pre-viously apprehended.[17] Hence, *if* movement *of the thing should come about without* the movement *of the time, or* vice versa, *one does not recollect.*

452b29 Then when he says *But the one which belongs to time,* he shows the diverse manner in which those who recollect know time.

For sometimes one does *not* record the time under a determinate *measure;* for example, *that* he did something *two days ago,* but rather *that he did it at some time or other; however,* sometimes he records it even under a certain *measure* of time; *but* it is in the memory if one records a past time, *although not* under a determinate *measure. For* men *are accustomed to say* that they do record a thing as past but *do not know when* it was, since they do not know the *metron,*[18] that is, the measure, of the time. And this happens because of a weak impression, as occurs in things that are seen by those who are far away and which are known indeterminately.

CHAPTER 8

453A4–B11

453a4 *Now, then, that those with good memories and those with good recollections are not the same, has been said before. But remembering differs from recollecting not only with respect to time, but also since even many of the other animals take part in remembering, whereas not one of the known animals, so to speak, except the human being, takes part in recollecting. The cause for this is that recollecting is, as it were, a sort of reckoning. For the one who is recollecting reckons that he saw or heard or was affected by some such thing before, and it is something like a search.[1] But this affection accrues only to those animals in which the deliberative element in addition is present by nature; for deliberating, too, is a sort of reckoning.*

453a14 *A sign that this affection, viz. recollection, is something bodily and an inquiry for an image within such a thing is the fact that some people get very upset whenever they cannot recollect. And, even though they strain intensely to hold back their thought from cogitating and are no longer trying to recollect, they are none the less distressed—especially those of melancholic temperament, since images move these persons most of all.*

453a20 *The cause for recollecting's not being in their own control is that, just as in the case of those who throw something have no longer within themselves the stopping of it, so too one who is recollecting and tracking something down is moving something bodily in which the affection exists.*

453a23 *Those in whom there happens to be moisture around the seat of sensation are the ones most upset; for moisture on the move is not easily put to a stop until it reaches what it is in quest of and the motion proceeds in a straight line.*

453a26 *This is also why, when instances of anger and fear move against each other, and these in turn engender a counter-movement, they do not settle down, but rather engender another movement contrary to the same.*

453a28 *This affection is related to names, tunes, and discourse whenever any of these comes from the mouth a lot. For those that stop singing or speaking may involuntarily go to it again.*

453a31 *Moreover, those who have their upper parts too large and also* *dwarves are of inferior memory to those of contrary disposition because they have a lot of weight on their sensitive organ and because the motions are from the beginning unable to move easily in a straight line in their recollecting. Whereas those that are utterly new to the world and the very old are devoid of memory owing to motion; for the old are waning and the young waxing greatly. And furthermore, such children as are dwarf-like are so for a long period.*

453b8 *So then concerning memory and remembering we have said what their nature is, and by which of the parts of the soul it is that animals remember, and concerning recollecting, we have said what it is and how it comes to be and owing to what cause.*

Commentary

453a4 After the Philosopher has shown how recollecting takes place, he now shows the difference between memory and recollection.

He refers to three differences. The first of these stems from one's aptitude for each of the other two. For *it was said* above[2] that *the same* men *are not* good rememberers *and* good *recollectors.* The second difference stems from time, since recollection, because it is a path to memory, precedes it in time, as is apparent from what has been said already.[3] The third difference stems from the subject in which each of them can be found. For *many* other animals besides man *participate* in *remembering,* as was also noted above;[4] but *no* animal that is known to us recollects except man; he says this because some people are in doubt whether some animal besides man might be rational. *But the cause* why recollecting belongs to man alone is this—*since* recollection bears a likeness to a sort of syllogism: for just as in the syllogism one arrives at a conclusion from some principles, so also in recollecting one *syllogizes,* in a way, that he has seen something *before,* or in some other manner perceived it, arriving at it from some starting point. *And* recollection *is,* as it were, *a search,* since the one recollecting does not go by way of chance from one thing to another; rather he proceeds with the intention of arriving at a memory of something. *But this,* namely that one should be in quest of something else, *comes about only* in those *in whom there is* a natural power for deliberating, since deliberation also comes about in the manner of a syllogism. Deliberation however belongs to human beings alone; the other animals work not from deliberation, but from a natural instinct.[5]

453a14 Then when he says *But that it is a bodily affection,* he shows what sort of affection recollection is.

For since he had said that recollection is, as it were, a sort of syllogism, and since moreover to syllogize is an act of the reason, which is not an act of a body, as is proved in the second book of *On the Soul,*[6] hence it might seem to some that recollection is not an affection of the body, that is, an operation exercised through a bodily organ, but the Philosopher shows the contrary.

And firstly he does this through something that happens to those who recollect; second through those who have something that obstructs their recollection where he says *Moreover, those who have their upper parts* (453a31).

In regard to the first he does three things. First he introduces the happenstance just mentioned. Second he assigns the cause for the happenstance where he says *The cause for recollecting's not being in their own control* (453a20). Third he explains it by means of an example where he says *This is also why, when instances of anger and fear* (453a26).

Accordingly he says first that a *sign* that recollection is *a bodily affection,* and is a *search of a phantasm* existing *in such*—that is, in some particular—or *in such,* in some bodily organ, is this: that *when* some people *cannot recollect,* they are agitated, that is, they are made restless with a kind of uneasiness, *and with a great effort* they apply their mind to recollecting, and if it should happen that as if ceasing from what they had set out to recollect, that uneasiness of thought remains in them. This happens especially in melancholiacs,[7] who are to the greatest degree moved by phantasms, since, in them, because of their earthy nature, the impressions of the phantasms are more fixed.

453a20 Then, when he says *The reason that recollection is not within them,* he assigns the cause for the happenstance under discussion.

First he gives the cause. Second he points out those in whom it most especially has its place, when he says Now those people are especially disturbed (453a23).

In regard to the first point, it must be observed that the activities that belong to the intellective part of the soul aside from any bodily organ fall within one's own choice, so that one can cease from them whenever one wishes to do so, but such is not the case with the activities that are performed through a bodily organ, since it is not in the power of man that his being affected—precisely insomuch as the organ is purely corporeal—should cease at once.

Thus he says that the *cause of the fact that recollecting does not* seem *to be in* the recollectors *themselves,* that is, in their power, such that they could cease whenever they wanted, is this—*since, just as* it happens with those who throw something, after they have set in motion the body that they have thrown, it is *no longer in* their power that it stop, *so* also the recollector *and* anyone else *tracking* something down by using a bodily organ *moves the bodily* organ, *in which the affection exists;* hence the movement does not cease as soon as the man wishes it to.

453a23 Then, when he says *Those people are especially disturbed,* he shows those in whom the cause under discussion especially has its place.

He says that in recollecting those in *whom* there is an abundant *moisture around the place* where the organs of the senses are located, namely around the brain and around the heart, *are especially disturbed,* that is, they are made to share in the movement, since moisture that has been set in motion is not easily brought to rest *until* the thing *that is being sought* presents itself, *and the movement* of the search *proceeds in a straight line* up to its endpoint. This does not contradict what was said above,[8] that this happens especially in melancholiacs, who are persons of a dry nature, since in them it takes place owing to a violent stamping of an impression, while in these others it happens because of the ease with which they are moved.

453a26 Then, when he says *This is also why, when instances of anger and fear,* he clarifies what he had said by means of examples.

He sets down two similar instances.

The first of these is concerned with the affections of the soul, by which the bodily organ undergoes a certain corresponding movement. He says that when anger or fear or desire or something else of this sort is moved *against* a given object, even if men want to move in the contrary direction by holding themselves back from anger or fear, the affection is not put to rest, but keeps being moved against the same object. This happens because the corresponding movement[9] of the bodily organ is not quieted at once.

453a28 Then, when he says *This affection is related to names,* he sets down the second point of similarity.

He says that this *affection* that comes about in recollecting *is related to names and melodies* and arguments, *when one* of them is uttered *through the mouth* intentionally, as happens to those who recite or name or sing with great intensity, since when they wish to stop it nevertheless *happens* that, in spite of their intention, they sing or utter something anyway because the corresponding movement of the original imagination still remains in the bodily organ.

453a31 Then, when he says *But those whose upper parts are larger,* he clarifies his point by stating that recollection is hindered by a bodily disposition.

He refers to two bodily dispositions that hinder recollection.

He presents the first of these, saying that those whose *upper* parts are larger than their lower parts—which is the disposition of dwarves since they have short legs, and the upper part of their body is proportionately larger[10]—*are worse at remembering than* those who have the opposite disposition, *because of* this—that the sensitive organ, which is in the upper part, is oppressed by a surplus of matter, and because of this the *motions* of sensible objects *can* not remain in them for very long, but are quickly dissipated owing to a confusion of humors; this disposition pertains to a failure of memory, *nor* can they easily proceed *rightly in recollecting,* since they are not able to control the motion of matter, which pertains to a failure of recollection.

453b4 The second hindrance is that those who are *completely new,* such as newborn children, *and the very old are lacking in memory because of the movement* of growth that is in children and that of decay that is in the old, as was said above.[11] This disposition is in partial agreement with the first, to the extent that it refers to children who *for a rather long period are dwarf-like,* as having an unusually large upper part of the body.

Thus it is clear that recollection is a bodily affection and it is not an act of the intellective, but of the sensitive part of the soul, which in man is nobler and more powerful than in the other animals, because of its conjunction with the intellect. For that which is of an inferior order always becomes more perfect by being joined to its superior, as partaking of its perfection.[12]

453b8 Finally, by way of epilogue, he concludes that *it has been said of memory and remembering, what their nature is,*[13] and through what part *of the soul the animals remember;*[14] and likewise *of recollecting what* it is,[15] *and how* it comes into being *and because of what cause.*[16]

NOTES TO COMMENTARY ON
ON MEMORY AND RECOLLECTION

Notes to the Translator's Introduction

1. See note 29 to Chapter 1 of the *DM* translation, below.

2. See the prologue to Aquinas's *Contra errores Graecorum,* Leonine ed., v. 40, pp. A 69–105.

3. Iamblichus, *Vita Pythagorae* (ed. Nauck), pp. 164–66, cited in Diels-Kranz, 1968, *Die Fragmente der Vorsokratiker,* 13th ed., 58, D, 1, pp. 467–68, from Aristoxenus's *Pythagorean Sayings and Life of Pythagoras.* My translation.

4. Literally: "The same account obtains also concerning future things *(ta esomena)*"; the text has the neuter plural of the future middle participle of the verb to be *(einai)* rather than *ta mellonta.* The reference is not entirely clear: does it refer to the subsequent items after the first, second, and third things I did yesterday (like *"kai ta loipa"* = "and the rest"? Or does it refer to actions I am planning to embark upon today (like *"ta mellonta"* = the things that are going to occur)? The translation given above takes the first interpretation.

Though less plausible in context, the second interpretation is in its own way also suggestive. We may note in passing that recent time-management literature would adapt Pythagorean practice—with an emphatic turn toward the future, expressing interest in the past chiefly as providing a list of yet-to-be-accomplished actions. For example, Alan Lakein, *How to Get Control of Your Time and Your Life* (New York: Penguin (Signet), 1973, p. 35: "Take your Lifetime Goal list in hand and spend one minute selecting your top three goals. Label the most important of these A-1. The second most important is A-2. The third is A-3. Do the same for your three-years list, and your six-months list."

Similarly, we may recall that in his *Spiritual Exercises,* St. Ignatius of Loyola suggests two *examina,* but later in the day—an *examen* after noon and another one in early evening rather than at waking—looking back at our past deeds with a view to doing better in the future.

Athletes using video recordings of their performance as an aid to improving future performance are using an external device; only when such reflection is actually internalized and activated from within the performers themselves will there be properly recollective activity. Such recollective activity can contribute mightily to the formation of good habits or virtues.

These examples would seem to confirm Cicero's belief that memory is the first part of prudence, but there is nothing in the immediate context of the passage to emphasize the future value of memory so explicitly.

5. This and all subsequent translations are our own, unless otherwise noted.

6. Note that the first sentence of the *Republic* uses an *aorist* verb, i.e. an aspect

that focuses on the act-character of the verb rather than on its stage of completion. The aorist seems to mark no definite time. Accordingly, the whole dialogue may be taken as a recollection of what Socrates said and did *yesterday (chthes)*, whenever "yesterday" might happen to have been. Thus, whenever the dialogue is being read is the day after yesterday, i.e. today. Accordingly, the dramatic representation of the dialogue is simultaneously also a "re-presentation" or making present again of what was past.

7. *Philebus* 34a–c. I owe this reference to the extraordinarily useful, but little-known study by J. Castonguay, O.P., *Psychologie de la Mémoire: Sources et Doctrine de la* memoria *chez saint Thomas d'Aquin* (Montréal: Les Éditions du Lévrier, 2ème ed., 1964), p. 35. On this passage see Carlos Huber, S.J., *Anamnesis bei Plato* (Pullacher philosophische Forschungen, VI), München: Max Hueber, 1964, sect. 533 (p. 612) and its cross-references.

8. *Epitome of Parva Naturalia*, translated from the original Arabic and the Hebrew and Latin versions by Harry Blumberg (*Corpus Commentariorum Averrois in Aristotelem, Versio Anglica*, vol. 7 [Cambridge, Mass.: Medieval Academy of America, 1961]), pp. 22–23. For the Arabic, see the edition of Helmut Gätje, *Die Epitome der Parva Naturalia des Averroes*, I, Text (Wiesbaden: 1961), pp. 40–41. A useful paraphrase of Blumberg's English version checked against Shield's edition of the Latin can be found by Janet Coleman, *Ancient and Medieval Memories: Studies in the Reconstruction of the Past* (Cambridge: Cambridge University Press, 1992), ch. 18, "Averroes: *The 'Epitome' of the 'Parva Naturalia'; the 'De Memoria,'*" pp. 401–15.

9. "Et manifestum est quod rememoratio est in istis: non enim vocamus rememorationem nisi illius quod presciebatur in preterito. Rememoratio enim est reversio in presenti intentionis comprehense in preterito. Investigatio autem per rememorationem est inquisitio istius intentionis per voluntatem et facere eam presentari post absentiam. Et ideo visum est quod investigatio per rememorationem est propria homini. Memoratio autem est in omnibus animalibus ymaginantibus: existimatur enim quod multa genera animalium non ymaginantur, sicut vermes et habentia conchas. Rememoratio autem differt a conservatione, quia conservatio est illius quod semper fuit in anima, postquam fuit comprehensum; rememoratio autem est eius quod fuit oblitum. Et ideo rememoratio est conservatio abscisa; conservatio autem est rememoratio continua. Ista igitur virtus est una in subiecto et due secundum modum. Rememoratio igitur est cognitio eius quod fuit cognitum, postquam cognitio eius fuit abscisa. Investigare autem per rememorationem est acquisitio cognitionis, et laborare et facere cogitativam laborantem in representatione illius cognitionis. Et ista actio est virtutis que dicitur rememorativa." Ed. Shields, pp. 47–49, upper text.

10. "Et si noticia huiusmodi fuerit ab ipsa prima comprehensione continua, tunc diceretur memoracio: conservacio enim est illius quod semper fuit in anima, postquam fuit comprehensum; rememoracio vero eius quod post suam comprehensionem fuit abscisum. Unde conservacio est rememoracio continua et rememoracio est conservacio abscisa; propter quod patet <p. 49, bottom> quod ista virtus est una in subiecto et due secundum modum. Reminiscencia vero est voluntaria investigacio intencionis olim comprehense, que est oblivioni data." Ed. Shields, pp. 48–49, lower text.

11. "Hec autem virtus videtur propria esse hominis, eo quod in huiusmodi investigacione facit homo laborare virtutem cogitativam ut representet intencionem illam que per oblivionem deleta est. Nam alia animalia non videntur istam investigacionem habere, licet memoria sit in omnibus habencibus ymaginacionem. Multa enim sunt animalia que non videntur habere ymaginacionem, sicut vermes et conchilia et alia plura." Ed. Shields, p. 49, lower text.

12. Jacob Klein, *A Commentary on Plato's Meno* (Chapel Hill: University of North Carolina Press, 1965), pp. 111–12. This text is a philosophical commentary.

13. *Oxford Latin Dictionary,* ed. P. G. W. Glare (1982), s.v. "re-," p. 1578a.

14. See the discussion of the formation of the Arabic verb in W. Wright, *A Grammar of the Arabic Language,* vol. 1 (Cambridge: University Press, 1896–1898), pp. 30–38: §36 "The *first* or ground form is generally transitive . . . or intransitive . . . in signification. . . ." §§39–40 "The *second* form (fa^ccala) is formed from the first *(fa^cala)* by doubling the second radical . . . The signification agrees with the form in respect of being intensive . . . or extensive . . ." §§47–48 "The fifth form *(tafa^ccala)* is formed from the second *(fa^cala)* by prefixing the syllable *ta-* . . . This form annexes to the second the reflexive force of the syllable *ta-.*" Accordingly, the fifth form of the Arabic verb often has the sense of the Greek medio-passive voices; see H. W. Smyth, *A Greek Grammar for Colleges* (New York: American Book Company, 1920), p. 107, §356: "**Voices.**—There are three voices: active, middle, and passive. **a.** The middle usually denotes that the subject acts *on himself* or *for himself . . .* **b.** The passive borrows all its forms, except the future and aorist, from the middle."

Notes to Chapter 1

1. For a discussion of the key terms *mnēmē* (memory) and *anamnēsis* (recollection), see the Translator's Introduction.

Though the Latin text of the Leonine critical edition renders that published in earlier Marietti manual editions obsolete, so much scholarly literature refers to the paragraph numbers of Spiazzi's edition of the *De memoria et reminiscentia* commentary that a concordance of passages may well be useful to readers of the secondary literature. A tabulation is provided on pp. 000–000.

2. "Tini . . . moríōn."

3. Greek: *"to pathos":* Lat. *"passio."* See *Webster's Third International Dictionary* (Springfield, Mass.: G. & C. Merriam, 1964), s.v. "^1passion . . . **4 a:** the state of being subjected to or acted on by what is external or foreign to one's true nature. . . . **b:** a capacity of being affected or acted upon by external agents or Influences . . . **5 a** (1): EMOTION, FEELING." An Aristotelian *pathos* expresses any way of being affected, and also, more specifically, the ways the soul can be affected by an exterior mover, including emotionally. The entry "^3affection" gives the generic sense "an action of affecting or state of being affected," and "^1affection" touches on the way that being affected plays out In the present context: "**4** *psychol* **a:** the feeling aspect of consciousness . . . **b:** ^1AFFECT"—here mainly in its obsolete sense of "feeling or emotion" rather than in its narrower psychological sense of "the conscious subjective aspect of an emotion considered apart from

bodily changes." Broadly speaking, the Greek pair of terms *(poiein* and *paschein)* provides the point of analogy for the usage found both in Latin *(agere* and *pati),* and in English *(acting* and *being affected)* where the pairs of terms are used analogously.

4. *"epistēmē . . . elpistikē":* On "elpis," see Karl M. Woschitz, *Elpis-Hoffnung: Geschichte, Philosophie, Exegese, Theologie eines Schlusselbegriffs* (Wien: Herder, 1979).

5. In the last paragraph of his commentary on this paragraph, Aquinas will contrast these acts of knowing and sensing with habitual knowledge and having a sensed power without actually using it (see under 449b15.).

6. Aristotle, *Historia animalium* VIII, 1, 588b4–17. Aquinas's text refers to "the seventh book of the *History of Animals*"; more recent editors use "eighth." Greek authors will be cited according to the abbreviations given in Henry G. Liddell, Robert Scott, and Henry S. Jones, *A Greek-English Lexicon* (Oxford: Clarendon Press, 1940). Father René Gauthier compiled a massive collection of notes for the Leonine edition; his notes to the *De sensu et sensato* commentary (Leonine "Tractatus I") will be cited hereafter according to treatise, chapter, and Leonine edition line (e.g., Gauthier's final note on the *De sensu* is given at I, 18, Leonine ed., p. 101, lines 313–314); those to the *De memoria et reminiscentia* commentary (Leonine "Tractatus II") will be cited similarly (e.g. his final note to the *De memoria* is at II, 8, Leonine ed., p. 133, lines 162–163).

7. Lat. "aliqua similitudo rationis."

8. Aristotle, *EN* VI, 1, 1144b26–28. Cf. Thomas, *In 6 Eth.* 7, 1141b22–1142a32 (Leonine ed., pp. 356–59); *In 7 Eth.* 10, 1152a6–36 (Leonine ed., pp. 420–22). Cf. Gauthier's note to the *De sensu* commentary Tractatus I, c. 1 (Leonine ed., p. 15, line 298), for a broader notion of "prudence" found in Albert the Great.

9. Cf. *Summa theologiae* II-II, Q. 47, a.15, arg. 3. See Gauthier's note to *De sensu* commentary Tractatus I, c. 1 (Leonine ed., p. 169), for references to *Historia animalium* Book VIII. Modern editors refer to Book IX rather than Book VIII.

10. Cf. Thomas, *In 3 Eth.* 19 (Leonine ed., p. 182, lines 205–6), with Gauthier's note on the terms "instinctus naturae" and "instinctus naturalis." See George Klubertanz, *The Discursive Power* (St. Louis, Mo.: Modern Schoolman, 1952), pp. 150 and 160–61.

11. Since the soul is not divisible into quantitative parts, the term "part" is used in some other sense, e.g. a "virtual" part, i.e. the soul as distinguished according to its various capacities for action, its "virtues" or active powers.

12. M. Tullius Cicero, *Rhetorici libri duo De inuentione*, II, liii, 160 (ed. Stroebel, p. 147b–148b.); also cited by Augustine, *De Trinitate* XIV, xi, 14 (ed. Mountain, CCL, t. 50A, p. 441); cf. Thomas, *De veritate*, Q.10, a.2, s.c.2 (Leonine ed., vol. 22, p. 300, lines 67–71).

13. Aristotle, *Metaphysics* I, 1, 980a27–981a1. Thomas, *In 1 Metaph.,* lect. 1, 980a21–982a3, nos. 10–14.

14. Cf. II, 8, 453a6–14.

15. *De sensu et sensato,* 436a1–449b3.

16. Perfect animals have three parts—a receptor for nourishment, a part for expelling wastes, and an intermediate part, viz. a "chest" or something analogous. Aristotle, *Juv.* II, 468a13–17; *PA* II, 10, 655b28–32. Gauthier's cross-refer-

ence to II, 2 at 450a18–22 makes no explicit mention of "perfect animals" but speaks of non-human animals that sense time.

17. Latin: *"passiones."*

18. Latin: *"pati."* Cf. above, I, 1, 26–27, where Aquinas says Aristotle calls sensing (sentire) an affection (passio) with Gauthier's note citing Aristotle, *On the Soul* II, 10, and II, 23.

19. Cf. below II, 3, 450a32–b11, as well as Avicenna, *De anima* I, 5 (ed. Van Riet, p. 88, 25–29): "You ought to know that receiving proceeds from one power which is other than the one from which there is retaining; and consider this in water, which has the power of receiving 'insculpations,' depictions, and figure in general, and has no power for retaining them"; IV, 2 (p. 32, 48–51): "for although he who is of a dry constitution retains things well, he does not receive them so well; but though he who is of a humid temperament quickly receives one, he quickly loses it and it is as though he had never received it." Cf. Averroes, *Compendium libri De memoria* (ed. Shields-Blumberg, p. 69–70); Albert the Great, *De anima* II, iv, 7 (ed. Col., VII, 1, p. 157, 22–25): "We know that the power that retains well is other than the power that receives well, since one who retains well is perfected by the cold and the dry while one who receives well is perfected by the moist"; Albert the Great, *De memoria* I, 1 (p. 98a): "In the De anima we have established that it is impossible for the same organic power to receive well and to preserve well"; St. Thomas himself, *Quaestiones disputatae De anima*, Q.13 (Leonine ed., p. 117, lines 254–57): "for in bodily things the principle of receiving is other than that of preserving; for the things that are able to be received well are sometimes badly preserved"; *Summa theologiae* I, Q.78, a.4: "In bodily things receiving and retaining are reduced to diverse principles: for moist things receive well and keep badly, whereas the opposite holds for dry things"; cf. II, 2, (Leonine ed., p. 108, lines 87–92, p. 110, lines 171–179, with annotations).

20. Albert the Great, *De memoria*, I, 2 (p. 99b): "But since one has to learn the powers *(virtutes)* and acts of the soul . . . from their objects." Cf. Thomas, *In 1 De an.* 8 (Leonine ed., p. 38, lines 47–48), with notes); *In De memoria* I (Leonine ed., p. 105, line 99, note).

21. Aristotle, *On the Soul* II, 4, 415a18–22. Thomas, *In 2 De an.* 6 (Leonine ed., pp. 91–94).

22. See below II, 3, 451a2–12; II, 7, 452b24–26. Gauthier reports an alternative explanation from Adam of Bocfeld, *In De memoria*, 2a rec. (Vat. lat. 5988, f. 26va): "since every cognition is of some presently beheld object of cognition, one might believe that memory is either not a cognition at all, or else it is the cognition of something present."

23. Latin: "opinatur." The cognoscitive power, then, would seem to aim at expressing some truth, in contrast with the appetitive power, which anticipates some good. (Cf. *De ver.* I, 1, Leonine ed., vol. 22.1, p. 5, lines 155–61.)

24. Neither Aristotle nor the Stoics included "hope" or "expectation" *(spes,* Gk. *elpis)* among the passions, and so the source of this doctrine is obscure; cf. R. Gauthier, *Magnanimité* (Paris: J. Vrin, 1951), p. 33; p. 195, n. 2; p. 321, n. 1. This issue is not addressed in K. M. Woschitz, *Elpis. Hoffnung Geschichte, Philosophie, Exegese, Theologie eines Schlusselbegriffs* (Wien: Herder, 1979).

25. Latin: "sperativa scientia."

26. Compare Aristotle, *APo* I, 44, 88b30–35; *EN* VI, 3, 1139b20–24; and Thomas, *Summa theologiae* I, 86, 3, arg.1.

27. Compare Aristotle, *Pol.* I, 9, 1259a10–12.

28. Latin: "scienciam."

29. Vergil, *Aeneid* 3, 628–629: ". . . nec talia passus Vlixes / Oblitusue sui est Ytacus discrimine tanto." St. Thomas does not cite the authority of St. Augustine, *De Trinitate* XIV, 11, 14 (ed. Mountain, *CSEL* 50A, 442.15–23), who uses the same Vergilian text to show that there is a memory of the present. Compare the standard medieval theological textbook of Peter Lombard, the *Sententiae in IV Libris Distinctae*, 3rd ed. (Rome: Editiones Collegii S. Bonaventurae ad Claras Aquas, 1971–1981), I, 3, 2, n.5 (I, 73, 17–20): "It is also known that memory is not only of things absent or past, but also of things present, as Augustine says in Book XIV *On the Trinity;* otherwise it would not grasp itself." Augustine's criticism does not refer to Aristotle by name but only to "the secular literature *(in ipsis saecularibus litteris)."*

A more literal-minded criticism of Aristotle's mode of expression than that of Aquinas can be found in Norman Malcolm, *Memory and Mind* (Ithaca, N.Y.: Cornell, 1977), pp. 13–14: "A little reflection on our actual use of language reveals that Aristotle was mistaken in supposing that 'No one would say that he remembers the present, when it is present.' . . . I may, . . . if I spot a familiar face . . . think to myself, 'I remember that man.'" Neither Aquinas nor Malcolm offers a counter-example to Aristotle's dictum based on Greek usage, which might not coincide with "our actual use" of English. Yet by appealing to Aristotle's "intention," Aquinas can make Aristotle agree with Augustine and Malcolm. Compare Thomas, *De veritate* Q.10, a.2, s.c.2 (Leonine ed., v. 22, p. 300.67–71): "But, memory, even taken in its proper sense, is equally related to every time, as Augustine says in XIV *De Trinitate* and proves through remarks of Vergil, who used the name memory and forgetfulness in their proper sense."

An Aristotelian defense might go something like this: Even sentences such as "Remember to take out the garbage" demand that the addressee recall an antecedent resolution or obligation to take out the garbage, even though this obligation may be past only relative to a future act of remembering. Though the act of taking out the garbage is itself future with respect to the act of remembering one's intention to do so, the remembering here properly marks the antecedent obligation and only incidentally involves the future act consequent on one's past resolution. The primary meaning of remembering accordingly points to something as experienced before the now in which remembering occurs. Other uses can be expanded by *pros hen* equivocation (cf. Aristotle, *Metaphysics* IV, 2, 1003a34–b5, and Joseph Owens, *The Doctrine of Being in the Aristotelian Metaphysics*, 3rd ed. [Toronto: Pontifical Institute of Mediaeval Studies, 1978], pp. 118–23).

30. Latin: "vis permanens."

31. Gauthier's note (185–95) cites Averroes's *Compendium libri De memoria* (ed. Shields-Blumberg, p. 59, Versio Parisina): "memoria proprie dicta est *continua* conservacio intencionis forme ymaginabilis, rememoratio uero est *intercisa* conservatio eiusdem intentionis," i.e. properly speaking, memory is the *continuous* preser-

vation of the intention of the imaginable form, whereas recollection is an *inter-rupted* preservation of the same intention. (See also p. 65 of the Averroes text.)

Peter of Spain, *Sciencia libri De anima*, 7.5 (ed. Alonso, 2nd ed., p. 271, 23–32): "Set uirtus retentiua formarum et intentionum est duplex: quedam est eas *continue* retinens; alia est retinens *intercise*, et prima dicitur simplex conseruativa, secunda uero memoria. . . . Est enim rememoratio intentionis in preterito comprehense, cuius intercisa est retentio, reuersio in presenti . . . ," i.e. there are two sorts of power for retaining forms and intentions, one power "retaining things *continually*" and the other "retaining them *interruptedly*. The first is called the simple power of conservation; the second, memory. . . . For recollection is a returning in the present of a notion that has been grasped in the past when the retention of <that notion> has been interrupted."

Again, Gauthier quotes an anonymous commentator *In De memoria* (Milano Ambro. H 105 Inf., f. 19ra–rb): "Quecunque enim animalia hoc tempus retinent et apprehendunt, apprehendunt etiam fluxum illius temporis ad tempus in quo actu memorantur et etiam apprehendunt interpolationem inter alias apprehensiones, omnia, dico, huiusmodi animalia memorantur; ex quo patet quod memoria non est ubi semper est apprehensio siue consideratio *continua* et in actu, immo ubi est consideratio siue apprensio *intercisa*, ut scilicet cum aliquis prius apprehendit aliquid et postea, quiete et intercisione apprehensionis interueniente, postea apprehendit se prius apprehendisse illud, et hoc uult Commentator. . . .": "For whatever animals retain and apprehend this time and also apprehend the flowing of that time to the time in which they actually remember and also apprehend the 'interpolation' between the other apprehensions—all such animals, I say, remember; from this it is clear that memory does not <just> exist where there is always a *continuous* actual apprehension or consideration, but also where there is an *interrupted* consideration or apprehension, such that when one has apprehended something previously and later, quietly, when a break in the apprehension intervenes, he later apprehends that he had previously apprehended that thing: this is what the Commentator means. . . ."

". . . Ex hoc etiam notificari potest quod, cum anima fuerit in ultima prosperitate sicut in patria, non memorabitur, et hoc quia semper erit tunc continue et actu considerans, cognoscens et sciens; nec tamen propter hoc putandum est quod anima non recolat ibi siue sciat que hic passa fuit et sciuit dum fuit in corpore, immo et sciet ea, set non sciencia que sit in potencia ad actum, immo erit semper actu sciens ea, et ita, licet sciet ea, non tamen erit hoc per memoriam eorum, set continua et actuali consideratione.": "From this it can be noted that, when the soul shall have attained ultimate happiness in heaven, it will not remember, because then it will always continually and actually be considering, thinking, and knowing; yet one ought not for this reason think that the soul does not recollect or know there what it has experienced here and has known while it was in the body; no, it will know them, but not with a knowledge that is in potency to an act, but rather it will always be actually knowing them, and so, though it will know them, this will not obtain through a memory of them but by means of a continuous actual consideration."

One may wonder what sort of non-human animals have such powers of reflection as the Anonymous author of this passage seems to suppose. In humans, continuous retention would seem to be memory; when memory returns after interruption, this might be called recollection in a general sense, but further conditions may well be required.

32. 449b13.

33. II, 2, 450a18–22.

Notes to Chaper 2

1. Aristotle, *On the Soul* II, 30, 429a1–2 in the old Latin translation; cf. Thomas's commentary to Aristotle at 429a2.

2. Aristotle, *On the Soul* III 6, 431a16–17.

3. We consistently render the Greek term *phantasma*, which is merely transliterated in the Latin version, as "image"; by way of contrast, in Chapter III, the Greek introduces the term *eikōn*, which the Latin translates as "imago" and we render "likeness." For a fuller rationale, see our note at 450b20 below. Our rendering "image" follows Aquinas's strictly consistent employment of the Aristotelian technical term *phantasma*, which refers to a sort of psychic image existing in the sensitive part of the soul.

4. Aristotle, *On the Soul* III, 7, 431b12–17; cf. Thomas, *In 3 De an.* 6 (Leonine ed., pp. 229–34). See also Aristotle, *On the Soul* III, 8, 432a3–14; cf. Thomas, *In 3 De an.* 7 (Leonine ed., p. 236, lines 62–96).

5. Lat. "in freneticis." Cf. Thomas, *In 3 De an.* 7 (Leonine ed., p. 236, lines 95–96).

6. "Someone": Avicenna, *De anima* V, 6 (ed. Van Riet, pp. 146–47, lines 6–15; ed. Rahman, p. 245, line 13–p. 246, line 2): "Or shall we say that the intelligible forms themselves are things existing by themselves, each one of which is a species or a thing existing in itself, and the intellect sometimes looks at those forms and sometimes turns away, so when it does look at them they become a likeness in it, and when it turns away from them, they do not become a likeness? So the soul will be like a mirror, while <the forms> are like external things so as sometimes to appear in it and sometimes not to do so. This comes about depending on the relations obtaining between the soul and <the forms> or the agent principle will keep emanating form after form upon the soul in accordance with the soul's seeking them out, and when the soul turns away from that principle will the emanation cease? And if that were so, would it not be necessary to be learning from the start all the time?" For a brief appreciation of the place of Avicenna's psychology in Aquinas's account, see the conclusion of A. C. Pegis, *St. Thomas and the Problem of the Soul in the Thirteenth Century* (Toronto: Pontifical Institute of Mediaeval Studies, 1934), pp. 188–202. See also how Aquinas deals with Avicenna's position in the following note.

7. Lat.: "*desinit.*"

8. The word *pereunt*, "perish," appears in the MSS right before *cessant*, "cease"; Gauthier judges that Thomas corrected himself but forgot to delete the first word: St. Thomas was already well aware of Avicenna, *De anima* V, 6 (ed. Van Riet, p. 146–147, lines 6–14); he summarized it at the beginning of his career *In Sent.* IV,

d.50, Q.1, a.2 as follows: "and when <the intellect> ceases *(desinit)* to turn to the agent intellect, those forms cease to be in it, just as the visible form ceases to be in the eye when the eye ceases to turn to the thing that is seen."—Gauthier notes that the species themselves, according to Avicenna, do not utterly "perish," since the change is wholly on the part of the intellect, which turns away from them; hence he takes St. Thomas's second thought as the right one to follow here.

9. This is Avicenna's doctrine (cf. Thomas, *In 3 De an.* 2, 36, and also 7, 90–92).

10. Aristotle, *On the Soul* III, 4, 429b5–7; cf. Thomas, *In 3 De an.* 2 (Leonine ed., p. 209, lines 32–59): ". . . Avicenna's opinion . . . about intelligible species is false and anti-Aristotelian. For Avicenna claims that intelligible species are not kept in the possible intellect and do not even exist in it except when one actually understands; according to him, whenever one actually understands, one must turn to a separate agent intelligence whence intelligible species flow into the possible intellect. Against this . . . Aristotle says that the intellect, even when actually specified with actual knowledge, is still an intellect in potency. For, when the intellect actually understands, the intelligible species are in it in a perfectly actual manner, but when it has habitual knowledge, the species are in the intellect somehow between pure act and pure potency. . . . <O>nce an intellect is somehow actualized regarding the singular <objects> to which it was in potency, it can understand, but <since> it was in no way in potency in regard to itself, some might believe that, even when actualized, it would not understand itself. So to exclude this possibility, he adds that an actualized intelligence can understand not only other things but 'can understand itself' even 'then'."

11. Avicenna, *De anima* V, 6 (ed. Van Riet, pp. 147–48, lines 16–39; ed. Rahman, p. 246, line 3–p. 247, line 2): "So we shall say that the last part of the division is true. For we cannot say that this form exists in the soul in perfect actuality nor that it is understood in perfect actuality; for 'the soul understands the form' means nothing except 'the form exists in the soul'. Now it is impossible for the body to be the storehouse of the form; and it is impossible for the essence of the soul to be storehouse of the form, since its becoming the storehouse of the form would be tantamount to that form's being understood and existing in the essence of the soul along with the consequent act of understanding. But this is not so for the memory and the formative power, because apprehending the form does not belong to the storehouse but only retaining it does. Its apprehension belongs only to some other power. That remembered or 'beformed' forms should exist in a thing is not the same as apprehension any more than the existence of sensed forms in a thing would be sensation: that is why bodies in which the forms of the sensibles exist are not characterized by apprehension. Apprehension requires something that can take on that form with an impression appropriate to an apprehensive power. The memory and the formative power, however, can be impressed with forms only inasmuch as they are instruments and have a body that keeps those forms near the bearer of the apprehensive power, which is estimation *(wahm)*, so that it can consider them whenever it wants to in the same way as it keeps the sensible forms near the sense so that it can consider them whenever it wants to. This explanation is applicable to the memory and the formative power but not to the soul, because for an intelligible form to exist in the soul is

the same as the soul to apprehend it. We shall also explain in first philosophy that this form does not subsist separately."

12. Aristotle, *On the Soul* II, 1, 412a10–11,22–23; II, 11, 417a22–30; III, 2, 429b5–10; cf. *Physics* VIII, 8, 255a33–b5; *Metaphysics* IX, 5, 1048a30–35.

13. Aristotle, *On the Soul* III, 7, 431b2.

14. "The intellective . . . in the sensitive": Gauthier notes that Aristotle puts it the other way around at *On the Soul* II, 3, 414b28–32, according to Thomas, *Quaestiones disputatae De anima*, Q.2, arg.8 (Leonine ed., vol. 24.1, lines 57–60): "The Philosopher in II De anima says that just as the triangle is in the tetragon and the tetragon is in the pentagon, so the nutritive is in the sensitive *and the sensitive in the intellective*" (St. Thomas adds the expression in italics); *Quaestio disputata De spiritualibus creaturis*, a.3 (Leonine ed., vol. 24.2, p. 44, lines 419–423): "Hence too in II De anima Aristotle says that the vegetative is in the sensitive and the sensitive in the intellective, just as the triangle is in the quadrilateral and the quadrilateral in the pentagon"; St. Thomas more fully explains this view of Aristotle in *De unitate intellectus*, 1, lines 811–844 (Leonine ed., vol. 43, pp. 300–301). Here however St. Thomas seems to have had another notion of Aristotle in mind, namely that in human beings the intellect cannot be without the vegetative and the sensitive powers. See *On the Soul* II, 6, 415a1–14, with Aquinas's comments.

15. Aristotle, *Physics* VI, 1–2, 232a18–233a21, especially 233a10–21; Thomas, *In 6 Phys.*, 1–3 (Leonine ed., vol. 2, pp. 267–76).

16. Cf. above, I, 1, 437a8–9; *On the Soul* II, 13, 418a17–18; II, 25, 425a13–16.

17. Aristotle, *Physics* IV, 3, 209b6–7.

18. Aristotle, *Physics* IV, 11, 219b1–2.

19. Aristotle, *On the Soul* II, 3, 428b10–429–a2. See Thomas, *In 2 De an.* 30 (Leonine ed., pp. 197–200).

20. See above, Leonine ed., p. 107, lines 15–17, citing Aristotle, *On the Soul* III, 6, 431a16–17.

21. Above: 450a4–6.

22. Latin "rationabiliter"; cf. Thomas Aquinas, *Expositio super librum Boethii De Trinitate*, ed. Bruno Decker (Leiden: Brill, 1955; corrected reprint, 1959), Q.6, a.1, trans. Armand Maurer under the title *The Division and Methods of the Sciences* (Toronto: Pontifical Institute of Mediaeval Studies, 4th ed. rev., 1986), pp. 65–66. The new Leonine critical edition of the *Super libros Boethii De Trinitate* and the *De hebdomadibus* appeared in 1992.

23. Avicenna, *De anima* I, 5 (ed. Van Riet, pp. 87–88, lines 10–29; ed. Rahman, p. 44, lines 3–11): "Of the interior apprehensive vital powers, the first is fantasy *(banṭāsiyā)* which is the common sense *(al-ḥiss al-mushtarika)*; it is a power situated in the first cavity of the brain, receiving through itself all the forms impressed upon the five senses leading back to it. Then there is the imagination *(al-khayâl)* and the forming power *(al-muṣawwirah)*, which is also a power situated at the end of the anterior cavity of the brain, a power that retains what the common sense received from the five particular senses and remains in it after the disappearance of the sensible objects. Know that reception *(qubûl)* belongs to a power other than that by which there is retention *(ḥifẓ)*. Thus, consider this bit of water: it has

the power to receive engraving, marking, and, in general, shape; yet it does not have the power to retain it."

Again, Avicenna, *De anima* IV, 1 (ed. Van Riet, pp. 5–6, lines 56–72; ed. Rahman, p. 165, lines 6–18): "This power is what is called the common sense and is the center of the senses; from it they branch out and to it they return. It in truth is what does the sensing. But to hold what this power apprehends belongs to the power which is called imagination *(khayâl)*, as well as formative *(muṣawwira)* and imaginative *(mutakhayyila)*. There may be a conventional distinction between the imagination and the imaginative, and we are among those who draw it. The common sense and the imagination are, as it were, one power and not, so to speak, diversified in subject but rather in form. For receiving is not the same as preserving. For the power that is called the formal and the imagination preserves the form of the sensible object without exerting judgment upon it in any way but only preservation. The common sense and the exterior senses, however, somehow judge or distinguish. For <the common sense> says that this mobile object is black or that this red thing is sour. One does not judge anything of a being through this conserving feature except what exists in it in the sense that it contains a form of this sort."

Corresponding to the exterior sensory judgment there seems also to be a synthesis by the inner sense, according to Avicenna, *De anima* IV, 1 (ed. Van Riet, p. 6, lines 73–78; ed. Rahman, p. 165, line 19–p. 166, line 4): "Then we know with certainty that within our nature we compose some sensible objects with others and that we distinguish some of them from others—not in accordance with the form that we find outside and not with the belief that any of them exists or does not exist. So there must be a power by which we do this, and this is called cogitative *(mufakkira)* when the intellect uses it and is called imaginative *(mutakhayyila)* when an animal power uses it."

The distinction between a sensed "form" or *ṣūrah* and a non-sensed "intention" or *maʿnà* (which we shall render into English by the word "interest") is also derived by way of Avicenna, *De anima* IV, 1 (ed. Van Riet, pp. 6–7, lines 79–94; ed. Rahman, p. 166, lines 5–16): "Then we may make judgments about the sensibles in terms of interests (plur.: Arabic *maʿāni*; Latin *intentiones*) that we do not sense, either in that their natures are not sensed in any way or in that they are sensible but we do not sense them at the time of judgment. As for the notions that are non-sensible in their very natures, they are things like the enmity and malice and disagreeability that a sheep apprehends in the form of a wolf, and in general the interest (sing.: *al-maʿnà*) which scares <the sheep> away from it; and the agreeability that it apprehends in its fellow and in general the interest that leads it to get along with it. These are things that the animal soul apprehends without the sense indicating anything about them. Hence the power through which these <interests> are grasped is a distinct power and is called the estimative *(al-wahm)*. As for the sensibles, we see something yellow, for example, and so we judge that it is honey or sweet, even though this is not yet known by the sense. It is in the class of sensibles although the judgment itself is not at all a sensible object; but it does not apprehend it in the present. Nevertheless it is a judgment that perhaps contains an error; it also belongs to that power. Now in man the estimation has proper judgments on the basis of which the soul makes it deny the existence of things that are not imagined or are not inscribed within <the estimation> and which <the soul> is not willing to believe in. There is no doubt that this power exists in us and is the sovereign chief in the animal, judging not with a division, in the manner of an intellectual judgment, but with an imaginative judgment joined to particularity and the sensible form, and from this most of the animal activities emerge. It is customary to call what is apprehended by the sense a form (Arabic *ṣūrah;* Latin *forma*) and to call what is apprehended by the estimation an interest (Arabic *ma'nà;* Latin *intentio*)."

Cf. Leonine ed. lines 171–179 and 179–186 with annotations ad loc.

There is an analogous contrast between what Avicenna calls "form" and what he calls "intention" in David Hume's *Treatise of Human Nature,* ed. Selby-Bigge (Oxford, 1888), Book I, section 7, p. 20: ". . . to form the idea of an object, and to form an idea simply is the same thing; the reference of the idea to an object being an extraneous denomination, of which in itself it bears no mark or character." Hume's term "reference" would seem to answer to Avicenna's "intention."

For a survey of "grammatical texts of the first four Muslim centuries" attempting to answer the question "what things are *ma'nàs?*" see R. M. Frank, "Meanings Are Spoken in Many Ways: The Earlier Arab Grammarians," *Le Muséon: Revue d'études orientales* 94 (1981): 259–319.

24. Cf. above, II, 1, (Leonine ed., p. 104, lines 68–71, with the notes), as well as Avicenna, *De anima* IV, 1 (ed. Van Riet, pp. 5–6, lines 56–66): "and this power is what is called the common sense . . . and it is truly what senses. But to retain the things that it apprehends belongs to the power that is called imagination . . . this is because what receives is not what retains."

25. Latin: "intentio."

26. Avicenna, *De anima* I, 5 (ed. Van Riet, p. 86.93–06; p. 89–90.44–60); IV, 1 (p. 6.79–80; p. 7.87–88; p. 8.2–5; p. 9.8–12): "Then we sometime judge sensible things through intentions that we do not sense . . . hence the power by which they are apprehended is another power <aside from the sense> and is called the estimative . . . Normal usage is that what the sense apprehends is called the form, and what the estimation apprehends is called an intention. But each of these has its own storehouse. The storehouse of what the sense apprehends is the imaginative power, which is located in the frontal part of the brain . . . The storehouse of what apprehends the intention, however, is the preservative power, which is located in the rear part of the brain . . . this power is also called the memorative power." Cf. below, II, 3, (Leonine ed., pp. 115–16, lines 215–226).

27. On the contrary, Aristotle teaches that opinion and prudence belong to the same opining part of the soul, *Nicomachean Ethics* VI, 4, 1140b25–28, but had taught that opinion can also be about eternal things, *ibid.* III, 6, 1111b30–33.

28. Some thought that pygmies, for example, were subhuman but above monkeys. Gauthier at Leonine ed., p. 110, lines 211–215 cites Albert the Great, *De memoria* I, 3; *De animalibus,* XXI ɪ 2, §11, §14; I ɪɪ 4, §175; II ɪ 1, §12; IV ɪɪ 2, §96; VII ɪ 6, §62 for references. For other references to pygmies, see also Pliny, *Historia naturalis* VII, 2, 26–27; Augustine, *De Civitate Dei* XVI, 8 (CCL 48, p. 508, 10).

29. Aristotle, *On the Soul* III, 11, 434a4–5; Thomas, *In 3 De an.*, lect. 16, 433b27–434a21, nos. 838–839 (Leonine ed. III, 10 *(sic)*, pp. 249–50, lines 28–60). Also *On the Soul* II, 1, 415b10–11; Thomas, *In 2 De an.*, lect. 6, 414b32–415a22, no. 302 (Leonine ed. II, 6, pp. 92–93, lines 85–103).

30. Pseudo-Cicero, *Ad C. Herennium Libri IV de ratione dicendi* III, 16–24.28–40, especially 33–37 (ed. H. Caplan, p. 214). This famous passage is quoted and discussed by Frances A. Yates, *The Art of Memory* (Chicago: University of Chicago Press; London: Routledge and Kegan Paul, 1966), p. 11.

31. St. Augustine would seem to be the one whom St. Thomas has in mind; e.g. *In 4 Sent.*, d. 44, Q.2, a. 3, qla. 2, a. 4; d. 50, Q. 1, a. 2; *De Ver.*, Q. 10, a. 2, s.c. 2 and the body; *Summa theologiae* I, 79.6, s.c.; 1.79.7 ad 1.

Notes to Chapter 3

1. Here, at 450b20, it is important to discuss our rationale for using the term "likeness" to render the Latin *imago*, which, in turn, is used to translate the Greek *eikōn*.

Until now in the third chapter of the Aristotelian text we have translated *phantasia* and *phantasma* regularly as "imagination" and "image"; the Latin lemmata of the *De memoria*, however, consistently keep these transliterated Greek terms. Both of these Greek words, as Aristotle himself recognized (*On the Soul* III, 3, 429a3), are etymologically connected with *phaos*, the Greek word for light. It is almost impossible to bring out the full resonance of such expressions as *phantasma phainetai* (450b29), which would connote something like this: "something illuminated brings itself to light"; in Latin, as in English, etymology must be sacrificed for sense: *phantasma videtur*, "an image is seen" or "an image appears."

At this point (450b20–451a17) it is necessary to note that Aristotle introduces a new and contrasting term rather emphatically into the treatise: in the Greek text of the *De memoria* there are only nine occurrences of forms of the word εἰκών, which Aristotle elsewhere glosses as "that whose emergence comes through imitation" *(hou hē genesis dia mimēseôs)* (*Topics* VI, 2, 140a14–15). It is noteworthy that Richard Sorabji in *Aristotle on Memory* (Providence, R.I.: Brown University Press, 1972) translates *eikōn* as "copy" but ignores the text from the *Topics*. It is also worth checking Aristotle, *Metaphysics* V, 14, 1020b4, on the mimetic character of composite numbers. How is it that the Greeks could call certain numbers (which are discontinuous magnitudes) "square" numbers, since squares are continuous magnitudes? If we represent, say, sixteen points as our number, we can reconfigure the points in such a fashion as to make them look like a square; the number will have a square shape as a product of its imitating *(mimêma)* a square. But are the sixteen points ever properly a "copy," as Ross's Oxford translation renders *mimêma*, of a square? Sixteen items do not come ready-made as squares; they are able to be rendered isomorphic or conformed to a square, but are squares only metaphorically. Mimetic numbers are still properly numbers. For a thoughtful discussion of the relation between *eikon* and *eikasia* in Plato, see Jacob Klein, *A Commentary on Plato's Meno* (Chapel Hill: University of North Carolina, 1965), pp. 112–25. Aristotle does not use the word εἰκασία. Although St. Thomas did not have direct access to the *Republic,* whose central books alone among the genuine works of Plato mention *eikasia,* the translator of his base-text, the *De memoria et reminiscentia,* has faithfully translated *eikôn* into Latin by *imago,* which designates concretely something that is like something else. The tenth occurrence of *imago* is supplied by the Latin translator where, in 450b20–451a2, the context requires Coriscus to have one.

Since no instance of *eikôn* occurs in Aristotle's treatise except here in Chapter III, there will be no danger in translating it by the concrete work "likeness," as when we say that a portrait is a good likeness of someone. Elsewhere in this translation where the word "likeness" occurs, except where explicitly noted, it designates the abstract relation of similarity (Greek ὁμοιότης, Latin *similitudo*), rather than the concrete thing that has this relation to something else. It should be noted that our rendering of *imago* by "likeness" is an improvisation required by the context; Aquinas's own usage distinguishes four characteristics of an image, the first of which is likeness *(similitudo),* an adequation at least of proportion, an expressed and proximate sign of the species or form, and an ordering or relation *(Sent.* I, d.28, Q.2, a.1, c.). See also *Summa Theologiae* I, 35, 1–2; I, 93, 1; *Sent.* 2, d.16, Q.4.

In *Summa Theologiae* III, 25, 3, c. it is also clear that the Latin word *imago* (which, since in this context there is no need to contrast it with *phantasma,* we shall here merely transliterate) corresponds to Aristotle's Greek term *eikôn* or "likeness": "As the Philosopher states in his treatise on memory and recollection [450b27], the soul has two sorts of motion toward an image. There is one motion toward the image itself as a thing; in the other way, the motion is toward the image inasmuch as it is an image of another. The difference between these two motions is that the first motion, by which one is moved toward an image inasmuch as it is a thing, is other than the motion toward the real thing; the second motion, however, which is toward the image inasmuch as it is an image, is one and the same as that which is toward the real thing. In this sense therefore one ought to say that no reverence is shown to the image of Christ inasmuch as it is a thing such as carved or painted wood, since reverence is not owed to anything except a rational nature. Hence it remains that reverence is exhibited to it only inasmuch as it is an image, and thus it follows that the same reverence is shown to an image of Christ as to Christ Himself. Hence, since Christ is adored with the honor and service due to God alone, His image is consequently to be adored with the honor and service due to God alone." For other discussions of the distinction between the motion toward a thing and the motion toward an image as such, compare *Summa Theologiae* II-II, 81, 3, ad 3m; II-II, 103, 3, ad 3m; III, 8, 3, ad 3m; *Sent.* I, d.27, Q.2, a.3; II, d.4, 1, ad 4m; II, d.12, 3, ad 5m; III, d.9, Q.1, a.2.

2. Aquinas's term "difficultas" tracks reasonably well with Aristotle's Greek *aporia.*

3. Latin: "praesentialiter."

4. Latin "signa."

5. *Pictura:* The word may connote a verbal force to correspond with *passio,* "affection": "picturing" intends the product being pictured within the soul. Cf. the *Oxford English Dictionary* on the *-ure* suffix; cf., e.g., a "tracing." *Kinēsis* (motion),

praxis (action), *poiēsis* (production) and other action nouns marked by the Greek suffix *-sis* normally mark the act in contrast to the product of the act; the English suffix *-ing* can mark both an act (e.g., "tracing") or the product of an act ("a tracing").

6. See Father Gauthier's note to Chapter 1, p. 104, lines 68–71. Anonymous, *In De memoria* (Milan Ambr. H 105 inf., f. 20ra). Cf. Aristotle, below, 450a9–11, for Gauthier's textual notes, as well as II, 1, above, (Leonine ed., p. 104, lines 68–71).

7. Latin: "novi."

8. *Accipit:* cf. Averroes's *sensit* in Gauthier's note to lines 80–87, quoted in our note 14, below.

9. Gauthier's note on wonder at Leonine ed., p. 114, lines 83–84, compares *Summa Theologiae* III, Q.15, a.8: "Wonder is properly about something new and unusual (admiratio proprie est de nouo aliquo insolito)"; the object of "admiratio" St. Thomas gathers from the presumption of novelty described by St. Gregory the Great, *Moralia in Job* XXXI, 45 (P.L. 76, 621); cf. *De malo,* Q.9, a.3; II-II, Q.21, a.4; Q. 132, a.5; the term "insolitum" seems to be drawn from Augustine's definition of miracles in *De util. credendi* XVI, 34 (P.L. 42, 90, line 7), cf. *In Sent.,* 2, d.18, Q.1, a.3, arg.2; or Augustine's *Tr. in Ioannem* XXIV, 1 (P.L., 35, 1593; cf. "inusitatum," VIII, 1, ibid., 1450; *De Trinitate* III, 5 (CCL 50, p. 137–138), cf. 1–2, Q.32, a.8; *De pot.,* Q.6, a.2. Other interpretations are offered in Aristotle, *Metaphysics* I, 3, 982b12–19, 983a12–21 (the object of wonder is that whose cause is not known); John Damascene, *De fide orthodoxa,* in Burgundio's translation, c. 29 (ed. Buytaert, p. 122): "Wonder is a fear arising from a *great* imagination."

10. On remembering the experiences of youth, see the pseudo-Ciceronian *Ad Herennium,* 3. 22. 35–36 (ed. Caplan, p. 218): "For if in life we see small, usual, day-to-day matters, we do not usually remember them, because the mind is not moved by a new or admirable thing; and if we see or hear anything outstandingly base, dishonest, unusual, great, unbelievable, laughable, we usually remember it for a long time. Thus we frequently forget things that we have seen or heard in front of us, which we often have remembered well in childhood: nor does this come about for any other reason than that the usual things easily slip from the memory, but striking and new things remain longer in the soul. The rising, the passing, the setting of the sun no one marvels at, because they come about every day; but people marvel at the eclipses of the sun because they happen rarely, and they marvel more at eclipses of the sun than those of the moon because the latter are more frequent. Therefore he teaches that he is not aroused by a common nature and a usual thing, but is moved by novelty and significant business." Cf. Thomas Aquinas, *Summa theologiae* II-II, 49, 1, ad 2. Also consult Quintilian, *Inst. or.* XI, 2, 6 (ed. J. Cousin, Coll. Budé [Paris Les Belles Lettres, 1979], p. 208): "Quid? non haec uarietas mira est, excidere proxima, uetera meminit infantiae suae?"; St. Jerome, *Apol. adu. libros Rufini* I, 30 (P.L. 23, 422); Avicenna, *De anima* IV, 1 (ed. Van Riet, p. 43, 1–12); Averroes, *Compendium libri De memoria* (ed. Shields-Blumberg, pp. 71–72): "Et homo rememorat multociens quod sensit in puericia bona rememoratione, quia in puericia multum amat formas et miratur in eis; quapropter figitur in aspectu earum; quapropter difficile amittit eas"—

"And a man often remembers well what he sensed in boyhood, since in boyhood he loves the forms a lot and marvels at them; hence he is transfixed at their appearance; hence it is hard to for him to lose them"; Petrus Hispanus, *Scientia libri De anima* VII, 5 (ed. Alonso², p. 273, 15–22); Albert the Great, *Summa de homine*, Q.40, a.3, s.c.1 and ad 1m (ed. Borgnet, t. 35, p. 349b–350a); *De memoria* II, 3 (p. 111a).

11. The Latin of Moerbeke renders Aristotle's λίαν, "excessively," by the weaker Latin *multum*, "very."

12. Leonine ed., p. 114, lines 108–9.

According to Albert the Great, *De memoria*, 1. 4 (p. 104a), in the old decay of memory "comes about as it does in ruined buildings, in which a seal-impression does not take owing to their putrefaction: for all products of putrefaction are moist on the outside and dry within."

13. Leonine ed., p. 114, line 113 *premisit* ("advance the premise"): 450a28–29.

14. Here St. Thomas seems to be introducing a small-scale version of a scholastic "disputed question," where a batch of arguments against the proposed position is followed by another for it, concluding with a magisterial determination of the difficulty. For historical background see "The construction of an 'article'" in M.-D. Chenu, *Toward Understanding Saint Thomas*, translated with authorized corrections and bibliographical additions by A.-M. Landry and D. Hughes (Chicago: Henry Regnery, 1964), pp. 93–96.

15. Latin: "praesentialiter": For a brief discussion of presence and representation in Aquinas, see Edward Macierowski, "A Sacramental Universe: Rediscovering an Ancient Wisdom," *Caelum et Terra* 2, 3 (1992): 28–32, esp. pp. 31 and 32.

16. Note on #337 (line 140: "it was said"): Chapter 2, 450a14.

17. In the first chapter of Aristotle's *Categories*, the Greek word ζῷον is ambiguous. It can mean either an "animal," i.e., a living thing, or a "picture," i.e., some painted thing—whatever a ζωγράφος paints. Aquinas seems to have been aware of this ambiguity of the Greek term, for he contrasts the "painted" animal with the "true" animal. His gloss "painted" indicates that he takes the word here in the sense of "picture."

18. It will be useful to have a roadmap to keep three terms straight from here till the end of the chapter.

Aristotle's Greek	φάντασμα	εἰκών	θεώρημα
Moerbeke's Latin	*fantasma*	*imago*	*speculamen*
English	image	likeness	object of speculation

Note carefully that wherever Moerbeke has *fantasma* we have "image," and wherever Moerbeke has *imago* we have "likeness." We have disregarded etymology in favor of sense.

19. The Latin is *animalis veri*, literally "a true animal," i.e., an animal likely to produce a true judgment about it in one who knows it. Cf. *De veritate*, Q.1, a.1 (Leonine ed., vol. 22.1, p. 6, lines 177–184). Note the contrast between the "true" or "real" animal and the "painted" animal.

20. Here our translation "imagination or *phantasia*" inconsistently but unavoidably echoes Thomas's *imaginationis siue fantasie*. In this instance Thomas is

designating routinely the internal sense power of imagination. As noted earlier, however, Moerbeke's term *fantasma* for the product of the imagination is rendered consistently into English by "image"; Moerbeke's *imago*, which renders Aristotle's weighty Greek term *eikōn*, is always rendered by "likeness." Aristotle never uses the Platonic term εἰκασία for imagination, but only *phantasia* φαντασία; in like fashion, Thomas's use of the term "imagination" here has no special eikastic weight.

21. The phrase "marks an interest" renders *significat intentionem*.

22. As we have seen (Gauthier, p. 115, line 224) the notion of *intentio* in this text is marked by a special and explicit dependency on Avicennian doctrine. The Arabic term *ma'nà* underlying the Latin rendering *intentio* in psychological contexts such as those discussed above in Chapter 2 (see note 12) marks a non-formal feature that the soul grasps about a sensible object. A sheep grasps the *intentio* of a wolf by seizing upon its fear-value or its flee-ability, as it were, which is other than its shape, the color of its fur, the texture of its coat, its aroma, or even the smoothness or sharpness of its tooth. Aquinas elsewhere (*ST* I, 78, 4) argues that "if an animal were moved solely because of a sensible object of pleasure or pain, it would be necessary to suppose in an animal only the apprehension of the forms that the sense-power perceives, in which forms it suffers joy or distress. But it is necessary for an animal to seek or avoid things not only because they are agreeable or disagreeable to sense, but also because of certain other points of commodiousness and utility or of harmfulness. Thus a sheep runs away on seeing a wolf coming, not owing to any unfittingness of color or shape but as an enemy of its nature; and similarly a bird collects straw not because straw delights its sense but because it is useful for nest-building. It is therefore necessary for an animal to perceive such interests *(intentiones)*, which the exterior sense does not perceive. Moreover, there must be some other principle of this perception, since the perception of sensible forms comes from the immutation of a sensible <power>, but the perception of these interests does not." Aquinas recognizes four internal senses, namely, the common sense, the imagination, the estimative (in humans replaced by the cogitative), and the memorative. For a valuable historical survey of positions, see Harry A. Wolfson, "The Internal Senses in Latin, Arabic, and Hebrew Philosophic Texts," *Harvard Theological Review* 28 (1935): 69–133; reprinted in his *Studies in the History of Philosophy and Religion* edited by Isidore Twersky and George H. Williams (Cambridge, Mass.: Harvard University Press, 1973), vol. 1, pp. 250–314. Wolfson contrasts the "strict accuracy" of Albert the Great's reproduction of Avicenna's division with Aquinas's failure to copy accurately (pp. 120–22). George Klubertanz, S.J., *The Discursive Power* (St. Louis: Modern Schoolman, 1952), pp. 275–79, especially n. 56, suggests against Wolfson that Aquinas's objective was not historical but philosophical and that this involved "profoundly changing" (p. 277, n. 56) the meaning of his predecessors' terms. If such were in fact St. Thomas's objective, a method that considers principally the transmission of textual materials would require supplementation by a philosophical sensitivity to the possibility that these materials might be transformed deliberately.

23. The first occurrence of the term "immutation" is in Chapter 1.

24. Antipheron the Oreitan's name was garbled in the Latin tradition accord-

ing to Father Gauthier's note; Oreos was in fact a city on the Greek island of Euboea.

25. Cf. Ar., *EN* 2. 1 (1103b21–22): "Habits arise from similar operations."

26. According to Father Gauthier's note, in St. Thomas' day, the adage *multiplicata causa, multiplicatur effectus* was used in three senses: (1) 'If the causes become many, the effects become many.' Cf. Bonaventure, *Sent.* 4, d.27, a.2, q.1, contra 3 (ed. Quaracchi, v. 4, p. 679); Thomas, *Sent.* 3, d.8, a.5, arg.1, among other places. (2) 'If the cause becomes greater, the effect becomes greater.' Cf. Thomas, *ST* 1-2. 73. 6, s.c.1. (3) 'If the causes become many, the effect becomes greater.' Cf. Thomas, *Sent.* 2, d.32, q.1, a.3, arg.1; 4, d.5, q.2, a.2, qla 3, arg.1; *ST* 1-2. 52. 3, arg.1. Aquinas substitutes "is strengthened" here for "is multiplied."

27. Chapters 1 and 3.

28. Chapter 2.

Notes to Chapter 4

1. II, 1–3.

2. Gauthier cites other authors to the same effect: Adam of Bocfeld, *In De memoria,* 1a rec (Urb. Lat. 206, f. 201v); Albert the Great, *De memoria* II, 1 (p. 108–109; Borgh. 134, f. 221ra). Other accounts are provided in Anonymous, *In De memoria* (Milan Ambr. H 105 inf., f. 21rb); Adam of Bocfeld, *In De memoria,* 2a rec. (Vat. lat. 5988, f. 27vb; Bologna Univ. 2344, f. 55v).

3. II, 1, 449b15.

4. Aristotle, *Physics* VI, 7, 235b30–236a15.

5. See Gauthier's note to Aristotle's lemma at 451b5 for a discussion of manuscript variant readings. The first version cited is from an old translation; the other, by William of Moerbeke.

6. See below, II, 5–6; cf. II, 8, 453a9–14.

7. II, 5–7.

Notes to Chapter 5

1. "a memoria labuntur": cf. Pseudo-Cicero, *Ad Herennium,* III, xxii, 35, "e memoria elabuntur": "slip out of the memory."

2. Latin: "signa."

3. 451b10–16.

4. Note that for Aquinas recollection seems to presuppose the interruption of memory. Thus Averroes, *Compendium libri De memoria* (ed. Shields-Blumberg, p. 59, Versio Parisina): "reminiscencia est uoluntaria inuestigatio intentionis eiusdem cum fuerit per obliuionem amissa" (recollection is the voluntary search for the same notion when it was lost through forgetfulness); Petrus Hispanus, *Sciencia libri De anima* VII, 5 (ed. Alonso, 2nd ed., p. 270): "reminisci est motus requisitionis formarum et intentionum a memoria interuentu obliuionis lapsarum" (recollection is the movement of searching after forms and intentions that have slipped from the memory by the intervention of forgetfulness); Albert the Great, *De memoria* II, 1 (Borgh. 134, f. 220va): ". . . omnes concorditer dicunt quod rem-

iniscencia nichil aliud est nisi inuestigatio obliti per memoriam" (everyone unan-imously says that recollection is nothing but the search through memory for what has been forgotten).

Cf. the definition of *anamnēsis* in G. W. H. Lampe, *A Patristic Greek Lexicon* (Ox-ford: Clarendon, 1961), p. 113a, cited from Nemesius, *De natura hominis* 13 (Migne, *PG*, 40, 661B–C). "It is called 'recollection' when forgetfulness *(lēthē)* in-terrupts *(mesolabēsēi)* the memory. For recollection is the refreshment or recovery *(anaktēsis)* of a memory that has become feeble or evanescent *(exitēlou)*. . . ." The verb *mesolabeō* (Lampe, 846b) was originally a wrestling term, "grip around the waist," and thence came to mean intercept, interrupt, impede, separate, etc.

5. There is some resemblance of this passage to David Hume's famous doctrine of the "association of ideas": see *Enquiries concerning the Human Understanding*, ed. L. A. Selby-Bigge, 2d ed. (Oxford: Clarendon, 1902), section 3, par. 18–19: "To me, there appear to be only three principles of connexion among ideas, namely, *Resemblance, Contiguity* in time or place, and *Cause* or *Effect*." Cf. the fuller treat-ment in his *Treatise of Human Nature* (Oxford, 1888), Book I, section 4, "Of the connexion or association of ideas," pp. 10–13.

The epigraph to the present volume is of interest. Coleridge's claim about the order of treatment does not seem to be precise, or else he had some other passage of the *Parva naturalia* in mind. But his explicit claim that there are annotations to Aquinas in Hume's own hand calls for a closer doctrinal study comparing, con-trasting, and evaluating the two philosophers.

6. Latin: "ex intentione."

7. Following Gauthier's suggested reading *preter <intentionem>* at Leonine ed., p. 122, line 130.

8. 451b16–18.

9. Latin: "preter intentionem."

10. 451b16–25.

11. 451b16–25.

12. St. Thomas also gives a summary of his thought on the art of memory at *Summa theologiae* II-II, Q.49, a.1, ad 2, which can be tabulated as follows:

Latin	English	Remarks
"Et sunt quatuor per quae homo proficit in bene memorando."	There are four means whereby a man ad-vances in remembering well:	
"Quorum primum est ut eorum quae vult memo-rari quasdam simili-tudines assumat conve-nientes, nec tamen omnino consuetas; quia ea quae sunt inconsueta magis miramur, et sic in	The first of these is that he should get hold of some fitting but some-what unusual likenesses *(similitudines)*, since we marvel more at the un-usual and thus the mind is more intensely preoc-	Cf. Frances Yates, *The Art of Memory* (Chicago: University of Chicago Press, 1966), pp. 70–81. The first of the points made in the ST is not made here, but above at II, 2, next to the last

Latin	English	Remarks
eis animus magis et ve-hementius detinetur; ex quo fit quod eorum quae in pueritia vidimus magis memoremur. Ideo autem necessaria est huiusmodi simili-tudinum vel imaginum adinventio, quia inten-tiones simplices et spiri-tuales facilius ex anima elabuntur nisi quibus-dam similitudinibus cor-poralibus quasi alligen-tur; quia humana cognitio potentior est circa sensibilia. Unde et memorativa ponitur in parte sensitiva."	cupied with them; this is also why we are more likely to remember things we have seen in childhood. Discovering likenesses or images is necessary because sim-ple, spiritual notions *(in-tentiones)* more easily slip out of the soul unless they are tied down, so to speak, by some bodily likenesses; since human cognition is more pow-erful when dealing with sensible objects. Hence the power of memory is set within the sensitive part of the soul.	paragraph, Leonine lines 242–248 (cf. II, 3, lines 80–87). Here "likenesses" *(simili-tudines)* in the plural clearly refers to concrete images that are some-how like what is to be remembered or recalled rather than the abstract relation of likeness.
"Secundo, oportet ut homo ea quae memorit-er vult tenere sua con-sideratione ordinate disponat, ut ex uno memorato facile ad ali-ud procedatur. Unde Philosophus dicit in li-bro *De mem.* <452a13>: 'A locis videmur remi-nisci aliquando; causa autem est quia velociter ab alio in aliud veni-unt.'"	In the second place, a man must set out in or-derly fashion in his con-sideration the things he wants to remember, so that he may easily ad-vance from one object of memory to another. This is why Aristotle in the *De memoria* says: "We sometimes seem to recollect from places; the reason is that they go quickly from one to another."	Aquinas's second point in the ST is here in the *De memoria et reminiscen-tia* commentary put first.
"Tertio, oportet ut homo sollicitudinem apponat et affectum adhibeat ad ea quae vult memorari, quia quanto aliquid magis fuerit impressum animo, tanto minus elabitur. Unde et Tullius dicit in sua *Rhetor.* <ad	In the third place, a man must care about *(sollici-tudo)* and engage his feelings in *(affectus)* the things he wants to re-member, since the more something has been im-pressed upon the mind, the less it slips away.	The third point in ST is the second made here. St. Thomas gives a false MS reading: "sollicitu-do," instead of 'solitudo' (cf. note 20).

Latin	English	Remarks
Herenn., III, cap. 19>, quod 'sollicitudo conservat integras simulacrorum figuras.'"	This is also why Tully says in his *Rhetoric <ad Herennium>* that "care *(sollicitudo)* keeps the shapes of the images whole."	
"Quarto, oportet ut ea quae frequenter meditemur quae volumus memorari. Unde Philosophus dicit in libro *De mem.* <451a12>, quod 'meditationes memoriam salvant,' quia, ut in eodem libro <452a28> dicitur, 'consuetudo est quasi natura'; unde quae multotiens intelligimus cito reminiscimur, quasi naturali quodam ordine ab uno ad aliud procedentes."	In the fourth place, we must meditate frequently on the things we want to remember. This is why Aristotle in the *De memoria* says that "meditations preserve the memory" <451a12> and that "custom is a sort of nature" <452a28>; this is why we quickly recollect things we often think about, as though advancing in a natural order from one item to another.	There is nothing in the ST text corresponding to the fourth point made in the *De memoria* commentary about the starting point.

13. Reduction to some order: Aristotle, 452a2–4. Cf. Pseudo-Cicero, *Ad Herennium* III, 17–18, 30: "Item putamus oportere ex ordine hos locos habere . . ." (Again, we think we ought to have these places in orderly fashion); Cicero, *De oratore* II, 76, 353–354: ". . . inuenisse fertur ordinem esse maxume qui memoriae lumen adferet" (he is said to have discovered that it is mostly order that sheds light on the memory).

14. Second: cf. above, Leonine ed., p. 121, lines 39–40 and 44–47, Aquinas's last paragraph under 451b10. In *Summa theologiae* II-II, Q.49, a.1, ad 2, St. Thomas appeals to an erroneous MS reading of *Ad Herennium* III, 19, 31, calling for "care" *(sollicitudo)* rather than "isolation" *(solitudo);* the latter is the correct reading: "Item commodius est in derelicta quam in celebri regione locos conparare, propterea quod frequentia et obambulatio hominum conturbat et infirmat imaginum notas, *solitudo* conseruat integras simulacrorum figuras" (ed. Caplan, p. 210). It is more effective to prepare one's "places" or "topics" in an abandoned rather than in a crowded area, since having many men wandering about disturbs and weakens the marks of the images, whereas solitude keeps the

shapes of the likenesses coherent. One is reminded of Plato's *Phaedrus,* where the title character has gone out of the city to memorize a speech of Lysias. At any event, Albert the Great cites the text correctly in *De bono,* tr. IV, Q.2, a.2, arg.11 (ed. Col., t. 28, p. 247, 37–41).

15. Third: cf. above, Leonine ed., p. 122, lines 149–164 and Aquinas's citation of Aristotle, II, 3, 451a12–14 in *Summa theologiae* II-II, Q.49, a.1, ad 2. See also Quintilian, *Inst. or.* XI, 2, 40 (ed. Cousin, p. 218): "Si qui tamen unam maximamque a me artem memoriae quaerat, exercitatio est et labor. Multa ediscere, multa cogitare, et si fieri potest cotidie, potentissimum est: nihil aeque uel augetur cura uel neglegentia intercidit"—"But if someone wants from me the single greatest art of memory, it is practice and work. The most powerful thing is to get to know many things thoroughly, to reflect on many things, daily, if possible; nothing grows so well with care or fails so much by neglect."

16. Aristotle, above at 451b31–452a2; see below, II, 6, 452a12.

Notes to Chapter 6

1. The first point "above" is dealt with at II, 4, 451b6–10; the second at II, 5, 451b31–452a2.

2. 452a12.

3. 452a7.

4. *A. Po.* I, 15, 75a38–b20.

5. Cf. Gauthier's references at Leonine ed., p. 124, lines 39–47: Adam of Buckfield, *In De memoria,* 1a rec. (Urb. lat. 206, f. 202 rb, in mg. inf.): "a soul existing at rest often cannot recollect, but when it moves itself vehemently to apprehend a principle, running down from it to a consequence, then it recollects"; 2a rec. (Vat. lat. 5988, f. 28 rb; Bologna Univ. 2344, f. 56r, in mg. ext.): "he who does not have a ready starting-point does not immediately recollect when he wants to, but if he seeks out the starting-point, he will then be able to recollect, and has found the starting-point through which he can recollect the things that follow"; Albert the Great, *De memoria* II, 3 (p. 112a; Borgh. 134, f. 222 rb): "But it often happens that one who at first seeks and searches for something can in no way recollect it, but seeking later on he is able to find it and also does find it . . . and recollection comes into being."

6. 452a5–6.

7. 452a24.

8. 452a17.

9. The anonymous pseudo-Ciceronian *Ad Herennium* III, 16–19, 29–32 (ed. Caplan, pp. 208–12) is the source in question; see also Friedhelm L. Müller, *Kritische Gedanken zur antiken Mnemotechnik und zum "Auctor ad Herennium"* (Stuttgart: Franz Steiner, 1996) with a Latin-German bilingual appendix of the three capital sources.

For a survey by a historian of the Renaissance see Frances A. Yates, *The Art of Memory* (Chicago: University of Chicago Press; London: Routledge and Kegan Paul, 1966), which spends some time on Aquinas and Albert while marching from the ancient Latins and Greeks into Camillo, Lull, Bruno, and Fludd. Karl

Morgenstern's *Commentatio de arte veterum mnemonica* (Dorpat: I. C. Schünmann, 1835) is a 44-page collection of the ancient sources on the art of memory with appendices on later, mainly modern, authors; more discursive is Herwig Blum, *Die antike Mnemotechnik* in *Spudasmata*, Band XV (Hildesheim: Georg Olms, 1969). A brief essay on "mnemonic techniques" by philosopher Richard Sorabji is found in his introduction to *Aristotle on Memory* (Providence, R.I.: Brown University Press, 1972), pp. 22–34. Birger Gerhardsson, *Memory and Manuscript* (Uppsala, 1961; reprint, Grand Rapids: Eerdmans, 1998) discusses mnemonic techniques in Rabbinic Judaism on pp. 148–56. The medieval period is surveyed in Helga Hajdu, *Das mnemotechnische Schrifttum des Mittelalters* (Leipzig: Franz Leo, 1936; reprint, 1/2 Amsterdam: E. J. Bouset, 1967) whose 135-page coverage, including manuscript material, extends into the sixteenth century. Major medieval authors are examined by Janet Coleman in *Ancient and Medieval Memories: Studies in the Reconstruction of the Past* (Cambridge: University Press, 1992) with whole chapters devoted to Thomas Aquinas (pp. 422–64), John Duns Scotus, and William of Okham; also from Cambridge is Mary Carruthers, *The Book of Memory: A Study of Memory in Medieval Culture* (Cambridge: Cambridge University Press, 1990), with significant references to Aquinas. Fuller treatments are found in J. Castonguay, O.P., *Psychologie de la mémoire: Sources et Doctrine de la memoria chez saint Thomas d'Aquin* (Montréal: Les editions du Lévrier, 2ème éd., 1964), and in the second part of Marcos F. Manzanedo, O.P., *La imaginación y la memoria según Santo Tomás* (Rome: Herder, 1978), pp. 275–382. Magda B. Arnold, *Memory and the Brain* (Hillsdale, N.J.: Lawrence Erlbaum, 1984), especially chapters 9 and 10, finds Aquinas's account congenial. Touching only lightly on ancient and medieval authors by way of introduction, Paolo Rossi's *Clavis universalis: Arti della memoria e logica combinatoria da Lullo a Leibniz* (Milan: Riccardi, 1960; 2d ed., Bologna: Il Mulino, 1983) is not to be ignored.

Morris N. Young's comprehensive *Bibliography of Memory* (Philadelphia: Chilton, 1961) provides a foundation for the more practical mnemonic techniques taught in M. N. Young and W. B. Gibson, *How to Develop an Exceptional Memory* (Philadelphia: Chilton, 1962; reprint, North Hollywood: Wilshire, 1974). Alan Searleman and Douglas Herrmann's informative *Memory from a Broader Perspective* (New York: McGraw-Hill, 1994), working within the experimentalist paradigm of Hermann Ebbinghaus (1850–1909), p. 372, conclude: "Although technical mnemonics certainly work . . . , we do not generally recommend their use."

10. "by reason of . . . propinquity": cf. above II 5, 451b19–20.

11. "Thus, . . . is moist": Anonymous, *In De memoria* (Milano Ambr. H 105 Inf., f. 22 ra–rb): "for when milk is apprehended, there immediately comes about an apprehension of whiteness and *brightness,* and from what is white one easily comes down to air and from air to the moist. . . ." Adam of Buckfield, *In De memoria,* 1a rec. (Urb. lat. 206, f. 302v, in mg. inf.): "from milk we run down to white and from white to air, since in composition with the white the fiery nature thrives along with its intensely transparent medium *(dyafono),* i.e. air; and from air we descend to the humid, which is a quality proper to air. . . ." Albert the Great, *Summa de homine,* Q.41, a.1 (ed. Borgnet, t. 35, p. 352b2–5); *De memoria* II, 4 (p. 112b).

12. "and from the moist . . . the dry": Galen, *De complexionibus* I, 3 tr. Burgundio (ed. Burling, p. 12–13): "saying that winter is cold and wet, summer, hot and dry; autumn, cold and dry, yet they say that spring is the well-blended season at once both hot and humid." For further references on the blending of the seasons, consult Father Gauthier's annotation to lines 98–101 in the Leonine edition.

13. "as has been said": 452a13–17.

14. "the order of the Greek alphabet": ΑΒΓΔΕΖΗΘ with Η and Θ being transliterated by *I* and *T*. Students who use the technique of "conceptual mapping" may find this diagram in Aquinas familiar; others may consult, e.g., *The World Book Learning Library*, vol. 3: *Memory Skills* (Chicago, 1986), p. 79, where a triple-branched figure similar to our Figure 1 is introduced as an elementary study technique called a "cue tree." See the plates accompanying John B. Friedman's article "Les images mnémotechniques dans les manuscrits de l'époque gothique," in *Jeux de mémoire: Aspects de la mnémotechnie médiévale*, ed. Bruno Roy and Paul Zumthor (Montréal: U. Pr.; Paris: J. Vrin, 1985), pp. 169–84.

15. "said before": at 452a23.

16. 452a30.

17. "in a less customary way": At 452a29 the Greek text has *epi to synēthesteron:* "toward the more accustomed thing," which is correctly rendered in some of the Latin MSS by *in consuetius*. Other MSS read *inconsuetius:* "more unaccustomedly"; St. Thomas follows the reading *minus consuete* "less customarily." St. Albert, on the other hand, follows the correct reading in his *De memoria* II, 4 (p. 113b; Borgh. 134, f. 222vb2): "Therefore if recollection is sometimes moved through an old starting-point, i.e. customary from of old, then it is moved toward the recollectible thing that is more customary to it."

18. "such as monsters in the parts of animals": Aristotle, *De gen. an.* IV, 3–4, 769b10–771a14; 772b13–773a33. Thomas, *In II Sent.,* d.1, Q.1, a.1, ad 3; d.34, Q.1, a.3; *In III Sent.,* d.11, a.1 (ed. Moos, p. 359, n. 14); *De ver.* I, 23, a.2, lines 98–99; Q.24, a.7, line 130; *C.G.* III, 2 (Leonine ed., vol. 14, p. 6b5–6); *In Met.* VII, 8, in 1034b3–4.

Notes to Chapter 7

1. Latin *rationabile;* cf. Euclid, *Elements* V, def. 4: "Magnitudes are said to *have a ratio* to one another which are capable, when multiplied, of exceeding one another" (tr. T. L. Heath).

2. The Leonine text of Aristotle reads "for" *(enim)* at 452b13; our Greek MS tradition reports "consequently" *(oun)*.

3. The Leonine text of Aristotle at 452b13 reads "that" or "because" *(quia),* following the Greek MSS that read *hoti,* instead of those that read *hotan,* "when."

4. Cf. Aristotle below at 453a1.

5. Cf. Albert the Great, *De memoria* II, 5 (p. 114b).

6. *On the Soul* I, 8: 407a10–18.

7. *On Sense and What Is Sensed* I, 2: 437b10–438a3; I, 3:438a25–27.

8. Euclid, *Elements* VI, def. 1: "Similar rectileal figures are such as have their angles severally equal and the sides about the equal angles proportional" (T. L.

Heath tr.). Heath renders the Greek term *homoia* as "similar" and *analogon* as "proportional." In this chapter, Aquinas will be using Latin vocabulary that tracks Euclidean usage rather closely. Hence it is worth noting a couple of definitions from Euclid, that for *logos*, which will show up in Aquinas's vocabulary as "proportio" or "ratio," and that assigning the description *analogon*, which will appear chiefly in adjectival forms like "proportionales" or the adverbial form "proportionaliter." Here are the two key definitions from Heath's translation. Euclid, *Elements* V, def. 1: "A *ratio* is a sort of relation in respect of size between two magnitudes of the same kind"; ibid., def. 6: "Let magnitudes which have the same ratio be called *proportional*." For a more metaphysical view of analogy, see B. Montagnes, O.P., *La doctrine de l'analogie de l'être d'après saint Thomas d'Aquin* (Louvain: Publications Universitaires, 1963).

9. Gauthier cites Euclid, *Elements* I, Prop. 26 and the translation by Adelard of Bath under Prop. 29, that if a line meets two parallel lines, then the two "coalternate angles" will be equal. Euclid (I, Prop. 27) has the conditional pointing in the opposite direction: "If a straight line falling on two straight lines makes the alternate angles equal to one another, the straight lines will be parallel to one another" (Heath tr.).

10. Euclid, *Elements*, VI, Prop. 4: "In equiangular triangles the sides about the equal angles are proportional, and those are corresponding sides which subtend the equal angles" (Heath tr.). Gauthier's note quotes Adelard's Latin. Accordingly, the Greek, Latin, and English terms line up as follows: *analogon, proportionalia,* proportional; *homologoi, respicientia,* corresponding.

11. In this chapter the Latin word *proportio* is used as a synonym for mathematical ratio; there are also a couple of instances in this chapter where Thomas employs *ratio* in this sense.

12. Here the Latin uses the expression *tali ratione* to express the term "ratio."

13. Here *secundum hanc rationem.*

14. Restore the use of "proportion" to render *proportio* in the earlier portions of this chapter.

15. The Latin "loco eius" might also be rendered: "by means of its place," perhaps alluding to the mnemonic method of "places."

16. II, 3, 450b20 to 451a12, 15–16.

17. To be sure, a photocopy can be isomorphic with its original; but being a copy in this sense is not enough to induce either recollection. The Leonine edition here strongly echoes the vocabulary of "*eikōn-imago*-likeness" as discussed in Chapter 3: "Hoc est memorari intendere fantasmati alicuius rei prout est ymago prius apprehensi." Aquinas's point is that a phantasm or idea in and of itself is not enough to cause recollection: the phantasm or idea must be charged with eidetic intentionality.

18. Here Aquinas glosses the hitherto un-translated Greek term *metron* from 453a4.

Notes to Chapter 8

1. Some manuscripts gloss the word *questio* with the word *inquisitio*. *Inquisitio* better renders the notion of a search or a quest in the Greek word ζήτησις.

2. 449b6–8.

3. Gauthier's note at Leonine ed., p. 130, lines 8–9 cites several other medieval and modern interpretations of "preceding in time"; Aquinas's reference is to II, 7.

4. II, 2: 450a15–18.

5. Cf. above, II, 1.

6. *On the Soul* II, 2, 413a6–7, with Thomas, *In 2 De an.* 2 (Leonine ed., p. 76, lines 139–157).

7. See Gauthier's rich note in Leonine ed., p. 131, lines 63–65, citing Galen's *De complexionibus* I, 3. For a valuable study of the problem of the four humors or temperaments (sanguine, choleric, phlegmatic, and melancholic) focusing on the interpretation of Albrecht Dührer's famous wood-cut of Melancholia, see E. Panofsky, F. Saxl, and R. Klibansky, *Saturn or Melancholia: Studies in the History of Natural Philosophy, Religion and Art* (New York: Basic Books, 1964).

8. 453a18–19.

9. The phrase "corresponding movement" is used to bring out the force of the prefix *in-* in *incommotio*.

10. Aristotle, *De part. an.* IV, 10, 686b4–6; *De progressu an.* XI, 710a9–15. Alternative explanations are found in Aulus Gellius, *Noctes Atticae,* 2 vols., ed. Peter K. Marshall (Oxford: Clarendon, 1968), XIX, 13, 2–4, p. 581–82, and Isidore of Seville, *Etymologiarum sive Originum,* 2 vols., ed. W. M. Lindsay (Oxford: Clarendon, 1911), XI, 3, 7.

11. II, 3, 450b5–7.

12. Cf. Aquinas, *In II Sent.,* d.18, Q.2, a.3, ad 4; *Summa theologiae* I, Q.78, a.4; Q.85, a.1, ad 4; *In 2 De an.* 13, and the prologue to *De memoria; De malo,* Q.16, a.1, arg.4; *Summa theologiae* I-II, Q.74, a. 3, ad 1.

13. II, 1, above.

14. II, 2.

15. II, 4

16. II, 5–8.

BIBLIOGRAPHY

PRIMARY SOURCES

1. Latin Editions of St. Thomas Aquinas's Commentaries on *On Sense and What Is Sensed* and on *On Memory and Recollection*

Sancti Thomae de Aquino Opera omnia, Tomus 45.2; *Sentencia libri De sensu et sensato cuius secundus tractatus est De memoria et reminiscentia*, ed. R.-A. Gauthier. Rome: Commissio Leonina, Paris: Librairie Philosophique J. Vrin, 1985.

In Aristotelis libros De sensu et sensato, De memoria et reminiscentia Commentarium. Turin-Rome: Marietti, 1949.

2. Other Works of St. Thomas Aquinas Cited

Scriptum super libros Sententiarum Magistri Petri Lombardi Episcopi Parisiensis. 4 vols.: vols. 1 and 2 ed. R. P. Mandonnet; vols. 3 and 4 ed. M. F. Moos. Paris: Lethielleux, 1929–1947.

Summa theologiae (text of Pius V with Leonine variants), 5 vols. Ottawa: Commissio Piana, 1941.

[English translation: *Summa Theologica*. Trans. English Dominican Fathers. 5 vols. Allen, Texas: Thomas More Publishing, 1981.]

Sancti Thomae de Aquino Opera omnia, Tomus 1.1; *Expositio libri Peryermenias*, ed. R.-A. Gauthier. Rome: Commissio Leonina, Paris: Librairie Philosophique J. Vrin, 1989.

[English translation: *Aristotle On Interpretation: Commentary by St. Thomas and Cajetan*. Trans. Jean T. Oesterle. Milwaukee: Marquette University Press 1962.]

Opera omnia, Tomus 2; *In Aristotelis libros Physicorum*. Rome: Commissio Leonina, 1884.

[English translation: *Thomas de Aquino: Commentary on Aristotle's Physics*. Trans. R. J. Blackwell et al. New Haven: Yale University Press, 1963.]

Opera omnia, Tomus 22: *Quaestiones disputatae de veritate*. Rome: Commissio Leonina, 1970–76.

[English translation: *On Truth*. Vol.1 trans. R. W. Mulligan, Vol.2 trans. R. W. Schmidt. Chicago: Regnery, 1952–54.]

Opera omnia, Tomus 24.1; *Quaestiones disputatae de anima*, ed. B. C. Bazán. Rome: Commissio Leonina, Paris: Les Éditions du Cerf, 1996.

[English translation: *Questions on the Soul.* Trans. James H. Robb. Milwaukee: Marquette University Press, 1984.]

Opera omnia, Tomus 24.2; *Quaestio disputata de spiritualibus creaturis*, ed. J. Cos. Rome: Commissio Leonina, Paris: Les éditions du Cerf, 2000.

[English translation: *On Spiritual Creatures.* Trans. M. C. Fitzpatrick and J. J. Wellmuth. Milwaukee: Marquette University Press, 1949.]

Opera omnia, Tomus 40A; *Contra errors Graecorum*, ed. H.-F. Dondaine. Rome: Commissio Leonina, 1969.

Opera omnia, Tomus 43, pp. 243–314; *De unitate intellectus.* Rome: Commissio Leonina, 1976.

[English translation: *On the Unity of the Intellect against the Averroists.* Trans. Beatrice H. Zedler. Milwaukee: Marquette University Press, 1968.]

Opera omnia, Tomus 45.1; *Sentencia libri De anima*, ed. R.-A. Gauthier. Rome: Commissio Leonina, Paris: Librairie Philosophique J. Vrin, 1984.

[English translations:

Commentary on Aristotle's De anima. Trans. Kenelm Foster and Silvester Humphries. Notre Dame: Dumb Ox Books, 1994.

A Commentary on Aristotle's De anima. Trans. Robert Pasnau. New Haven and London: Yale University Press, 1999.]

Opera omnia, Tomus 47; *Sentencia libri Ethicorum*, ed. R.-A. Gauthier. Rome: Commissio Leonina, 1969.

[English translation: *Commentary on the Nicomachean Ethics.* Trans. C. I. Litzinger, O.P. 2 vols. Chicago: Henry Regnery, 1964.]

Opera omnia, Tomus 50; *Super Boetium De Trinitate*, ed. Pierre-M. J. Gils; *Expositio libri Boetii De ebdomadibus*, ed. Louis J. Bataillon and Carlo A. Grassi. Rome: Commissio Leonina, Paris: Librairie Philosophique J. Vrin, 1985.

[English translations:

Faith, Reason, and Theology. Questions I–IV of his Commentary on the De Trinitate of Boethius. Trans. Armand Maurer. Toronto: Pontifical Institute of Mediaeval Studies, 1987.

The Division and Method of the Sciences. Questions V and VI of his Commentary on the De Trinitate of Boethius. Trans. Armand Maurer. Toronto: Pontifical Institute of Mediaeval Studies, 1986.

An Exposition of the "On the Hebdomads" of Boethius. Trans. Janice L. Schultz and Edward A. Synan. Washington, D. C.: Catholic University of America Press, 2001.]

S. Thomae Aquinatis. *In duodecim libros Metaphysicorum Aristotelis ad Nicomachum Expositio*, ed. 3, R. M. Spiazzi. Turin: Marietti, 1949; reprint, 1964.

3. Other Latin Sources

Albert the Great. *B. Alberti Magni Opera Omnia.* Ed. August Borgnet. Paris: Vivès, 1890–99. Vol.9, pp. 1–96, *De sensu et sensato;* pp. 97–119, *De memoria et reminiscentia.*

Augustine. *De civitate Dei,* ed. B. Dombart, A. Kalb, CCSL 47, 48. Turnhout: Brepols, 1955.

[English translation: *City of God.* Trans. Gerald Walsh, S.J., et al. Nbew York: Doubleday, 1958.]

———. *De Trinitate,* ed. W. J. Mountain, CCSL 50, 50A. Turnhout: Brepols, 1968.

[English translation: *On the Holy Trinity.* Trans. A. West and W. Shedd. In Nicene and Post Nicene Fathers of the Church. Vol.3. Grand Rapids, Michigan: Wm. B. Eerdmans, 1976.]

Cicero, Marcus Tullius. *Rhetorici libri duo qui vocantur De inuentione.* Bibliotheca scriptorum Graecorum et Romanorum Teubneriana. M. Tulli Ciceronis Scripta quae manserunt omnia, 2. Ed. E. Stroebel. Stuttgart : B.G. Teubner 1977.

———. *De inventione,* in *Cicero in Twenty-eight Volumes,* XX, tr. H. M. Hubbell. The Loeb Classical Library. Cambridge: Harvard University Press; London: W. Heinemann Ltd., 1923–1979.

Pseudo-Cicero. *Ad C. Herennium de ratione dicendi (Rhetorica ad Herennium),* in *Cicero in Twenty-eight Volumes,* I, tr. H. Caplan. The Loeb Classical Library. Cambridge: Harvard University Press; London: W. Heinemann Ltd., 1923–1979.

Quintilian. *The Orator's Education,* 5 volumes. Tr. D. A. Russell. The Loeb Classical Library. Cambridge: Harvard University Press; London: W. Heinemann Ltd., 2001.

4. Greek Sources

Aristotle, *De sensu and De memoria.* Text and translation, with introduction and commentary, by G.R.T. Ross. Cambridge: The University Press, 1906.

Aristotle, *Parva naturalia.* A Revised Text with Introduction and Commentary by Sir David Ross. Oxford: Clarendon Press, 1955.

Aristotelis Parva naturalia Graece et Latine. Ed. P. Siwek. *Collectio philosophica Lateranensis* 5. Romae 1963.

[English translation: *The complete works of Aristotle : the revised Oxford translation.* 2 vols. Ed. Jonathan Barnes. Princeton, N.J.: Princeton University Press, 1984. *Sense and Sensibilia,* transl. J. I Beare; vol.1, pp. 693–713. *On Memory,* transl. J. I. Beare; vol.1, pp. 714–20.]

Commentaria in Aristotelem graeca, v. 3. Ed. Paulus Wendland. Berlin: G.

Reimer. Alexander, *In librum de sensu commentarium*. Pars 1 (1901). Themistius (Sophonias), *In parva naturalis*. Pars 6 (1903).

[English translation: Alexander of Aphrodisias, *On Aristotle's "On Sense Perception"*. Transl. Alan Towey. Ithaca: Cornell University Press, 2000.]

5. Arabic Sources in Latin Translation

[For the Arabic original of Averroes's epitome of Aristotle, see the edition of Helmut Gätje, *Die Epitome der Parva Naturalia des Averroes*, I. Text (Wiesbaden: 1961), pp. 40–41.]

[Latin translation: *Averrois Cordubensis Compendia librorum Aristotelis qui Parva Naturalia vocantur*, ed. A. L. Shields and H. Blumberg. *Corpus Commentariorum Averrois in Aristotelem, Versionum Latinarum*, Vol.7. Cambridge (Mass.), 1949.]

[English translation: *Epitome of Parva Naturalia*, translated from the original Arabic and the Hebrew and Latin versions by Harry Blumberg (*Corpus Commentariorum Averrois in Aristotelem, Versio Anglica* Vol. VII, published at Cambridge, Mass. by The Medieval Academy of America, 1961). A useful paraphrase of Blumberg's version checked against the Latin version edited by Shields can be found by Janet Coleman, *Ancient and Medieval Memories: Studies in the reconstruction of the past* (Cambridge University Press, 1992), ch. 18, "Averroes: *The 'Epitome' of the 'Parva Naturalia'; the 'De Memoria'*, pp. 401–15.]

[For a critical edition of the Arabic original of the Avicennian psychological treatise that was translated into medieval Latin: *Avicenna's De Anima (Arabic Text), being the Psychological Part of Kitâb al-Shifâʾ*, ed. R. Rahman. London: Oxford University Press, 1959.]

[Latin version: *Avicenna Latinus. Liber de Anima seu Sextus de Naturalibus*. Ed. S. van Riet. Louvain: I, 1972 (I–III); II, 1968 (IV–V).]

[No English translation as of 2004.]

Avicenna Latinus. Liber de Philosophia Prima sive Scientia Divina. Ed. S. van Riet. Louvain: I, 1977 (I–IV); II, 1980 (V–X); Lexiques I–X, 1983.

SECONDARY SOURCES

Arnold, Magda B. *Memory and the Brain*. Hillsdale, N.J.: Lawrence Erlbaum, 1984.

Ashley, Benedict. "Aristotle's *De sensu et sensato* and *De memoria et reminiscentia* as Thomistic Sources". University of Notre Dame Thomistic Institute: July 14–21, 2000. http://www.nd.edu/Departments/Maritain/ti00ashley.htm.

Austin, J. L. *Sense and Sensibilia*. Oxford: Oxford University Press, 1962.

Bermon, Emmanuel, ed. *Revue de philosophie ancienne* 20 (2002), No.1: *Thème: Les Parva naturalia d'Aristote*.

Blum, Herwig. *Die antike Mnemotechnik,* in *Spudasmata,* Band XV. Hildeseim: Georg Olms, 1969.

Boyle, Leonard. "The Setting of the Summa Theologiae of St. Thomas—Revisited." In *The Ethics of Aquinas,* ed. Stephen J. Pope. Washington, D.C.: Georgetown University Press, 2002.

Carruthers, Mary. *The Book of Memory: A Study of Memory in Medieval Culture.* Cambridge: Cambridge University Press, 1990.

Castonguay, J., O.P. *Psychologie de la Mémoire: Sources et Doctrine de la* memoria *chez saint Thomas d'Aquin,* 2ème ed. Montréal: Les Éditions du Lévrier, 1964.

Chenu, M.-D. *Towards Understanding St. Thomas.* Trans. A. M. Landry and D. Hughes. Chicago: H. Regnery, 1964.

Coleman, Janet. *Ancient and Medieval Memories: Studies in the Reconstruction of the Past.* Cambridge: Cambridge University Press, 1992.

Decaen, Christopher A. "The Viablity of Aristotelian-Thomistic Color Realism." *Thomist* 65 (2001): 179–222.

Dewan, Lawrence. "St. Albert, the Sensibles, and Spiritual Being." In *Albertus Magnus and the Sciences,* ed. James A. Weisheipl, pp. 291–320. Toronto: Pontifical Institute of Mediaeval Studies, 1980.

Dod, Bernard G. "Aristoteles latinus." In *The Cambridge History of Later Medieval Philosophy: From the Rediscovery of Aristotle to the Disintegration of Scholasticism 1100–1600,* ed. Norman Kretzmann, Anthony Kenny, Jan Pinborg; assoc. ed. Eleonore Stump. Cambridge: Cambridge University Press, 1982.

Everson, Stephen. *Aristotle on Perception.* Oxford: Clarendon Press, 1997.

Festugière, A. M. "La place du 'De anima' dans le système aristotélicien d'après S. Thomas." *Archives d'Histoire Doctrinale et Litteraire du Moyen Age* 6 (1931): 25–46.

Frank, R. M. "Meanings Are Spoken of in Many Ways: The Earlier Arab Grammarians," *Le Muséon: Revue d'études orientales* 94 (1981): 259–319.

Friedman, John B. "Les images mnémotechniques dans les manuscripts de l'époque gothique." In *Jeux de mémoire: Aspects de la mnémotechnie médiévale,* ed. Bruno Roy and Paul Zumthor, pp. 169–84. Montréal: Les Presses de l'Université de Montréal; Paris: J. Vrin, 1985.

Gauthier, R.-A. *Magnanimité.* Paris: J. Vrin, 1951.

Huber, Carlos, S.J. *Anamnesis bei Plato* (Pullacher philosophische Forschungen, VI). München: Max Hueber, 1964.

Hume, David. *Enquiries concerning the Human Understanding,* ed. L. A. Selby-Bigge. Oxford: Clarendon, 2d ed., 1902.

———. *Treatise of Human Nature,* ed. L. A. Selby-Bigge. Oxford: Clarendon Press, 1888.

Klein, Jacob. *A Commentary on Plato's Meno.* Chapel Hill: University of North Carolina Press, 1965.

Klubertanz, George. *The Discursive Power.* St. Louis, Mo.: Modern Schoolman, 1952.

Lakein, Alan. *How to Get Control of Your Time and Your Life.* New York: Penguin, 1973.

Lampe, G. W. H. *A Patristic Greek Lexicon.* Oxford: Clarendon, 1961.

Lewis, C. S. *Studies in Words.* Cambridge: Cambridge University Press, 1990.

Lindberg, David. "Medieval Latin Theories of the Speed of Light." In *Roemer et la vitesse de la lumière. Table Ronde du Centre nationale de la recherche scientificque, Paris, 16 et 17 juin 1976,* ed. René Taton, pp. 45–72. Paris: J. Vrin, 1978.

Litt, Thomas. *Les corps célestes dans l'univers de saint Thomas d'Aquin.* Philosophes Médiévaux 7. Louvain: Publications Universitaires; Paris: Béatrice-Nauwelaerts, 1963.

Lohr, Charles H. "The Ancient Philosophical Legacy and Its Transmission to the Middle Ages." In *A Companion to Philosophy in the Middle Ages,* ed. Jorge J. E. Gracia and Timothy B. Noone. Oxford: Blackwell, 2003.

Macierowski, Edward. "A Sacramental Universe: Rediscovering an Ancient Wisdom," *Caelum et Terra* 2, 3 (1992): 28–32.

Mahoney, Edward P. "Metaphysical Foundations of the Hierarchy of Being According to Some Late-Medieval and Renaissance Philosophers." In *Philosophies of Existence Ancient and Modern,* ed. Parviz Morewedge. New York: Fordham University Press, 1982.

Malcolm, Norman. *Memory and Mind.* Ithaca, N.Y.: Cornell, 1977.

Mansion, A. "Le commentaire de saint Thomas sur le *De sensu et sensato* d'Aristote: Utilisation d'Alexandre d'Aphrodise". In *Mélanges Mandonnet,* vol. 1, pp. 83–102. Bibliothèque thomiste 13. Paris: J. Vrin, 1930.

Manzanedo, Marcos F., O.P. *La imaginación y la memoria según Santo Tomás.* Rome: Herder, 1978.

Modrak, Deborah K. W. *Aristotle: The Power of Perception.* Chicago: University of Chicago Press, 1987.

Montagnes, Bernard. *La Doctrine de l'analogie de l'être d'après saint Thomas d'Aquin.* Louvain: Publications Universitaires; Paris: Béatrice-Nauwelaerts, 1963.

[English translation: *The Doctrine of the Analogy of Being according to St. Thomas Aquinas.* Trans. E. M. Macierowski. Milwaukee: Marquette University Press, forthcoming in 2005.]

Müller, Friedhelm L. *Kritische Gedanken zur antiken Mnemotechnik und zum "Auctor ad Herennium."* Stuttgart: Franz Steiner, 1996.

Noone, Timothy B. "Scholasticism." In *A Companion to Philosophy in the Middle Ages,* ed. Jorge J. E. Gracia and Timothy B. Noone. Oxford: Blackwell, 2003.

O'Brien, D. "The Effect of a Simile: Empedocles' Theories of Seeing and Breathing." *Journal of Hellenic Studies* 90 (1970): 139–79.

Owens, Joseph. "Aquinas as Aristotelian Commentator." In *St. Thomas Aquinas on the Existence of God: Collected Papers of Joseph Owens, C.Ss.R.,* ed. John R. Catan. Albany: State University of New York Press, 1980.

———. *Cognition: An Epistemological Inquiry.* Houston: Center for Thomistic Studies, 1992.

———. *The Doctrine of Being in the Aristotelian Metaphysics.* 3rd ed. Toronto: Pontifical Institute of Mediaeval Studies, 1978.

———. "Judgment and Truth in Aquinas." In *St. Thomas Aquinas on the Existence of God.*

Panofsky, E., F. Saxl, and R. Klibansky. *Saturn or Melancholia: Studies in the History of Natural Philosophy, Religion and Art.* New York: Basic Books, 1964.

Pegis, A. C. *St. Thomas and the Problem of the Soul in the Thirteenth Century.* Toronto: Pontifical Institute of Mediaeval Studies, 1934.

Perler, Dominik, ed. *Ancient and Medieval Theories of Intentionality.* Studien und Texte zur Geistesgeschichte des Mittelalters 76. Leiden-Boston-Cologne: Brill, 2001.

Pritzl, Kurt. "On Sense and Sense Organ in Aristotle". In *Realism: Proceedings of the American Catholic Philosophical Association 59 (1985),* ed. Daniel O. Dahlstrom, pp. 258–74. Washington, D.C.: American Catholic Philosophical Association, 1985.

Ryan, John K. "Aquinas and Hume on the Laws of Association." *New Scholasticism* 12 (1938): 366–77.

Searleman, Alan, and Douglas Herrmann. *Memory from a Broader Perspective.* New York: McGraw-Hill, 1994.

Smyth, H. W. *A Greek Grammar for Colleges.* New York: American Book Company, 1920.

Sorabji, Richard. *Aristotle on Memory.* Providence, R.I.: Brown University Press, 1972.

Steneck, Nicholas H. "Albert on the Psychology of Sense Perception." In *Albertus Magnus and the Sciences,* ed. James A. Weisheipl, pp. 263–90. Toronto: Pontifical Institute of Medieval Studies, 1980.

Torrell, Jean-Pierre. *Saint Thomas Aquinas.* Vol. 1: *The Person and His Work.* Trans. Robert Royal. Washington, D.C.: Catholic University of America Press, 1996.

White, K. "St. Thomas Aquinas and the Prologue to Peter of Auvergne's 'Quaestiones super De sensu et sensato.'" *Documenti e Studi sulla Tradizione Filosofica Medievale* 1 (1990), pp. 427–56.

Wippel, John F. *The Metaphysical Thought of Thomas Aquinas: From Finite Being to Uncreated Being.* Washington, D.C.: Catholic University of America Press, 2000.

Wolfson, Harry A. "The Internal Senses in Latin, Arabic, and Hebrew Philosophic Texts," *Harvard Theological Review* 28 (1935): 69–133. Reprinted in

Wolfson, *Studies in the History of Philosophy and Religion*, ed. Isidore Twersky and George H. Williams. Cambridge, Mass.: Harvard University Press, 1973.

Woschitz, Karl M. *Elpis-Hoffnung: Geschichte, Philosophie, Exegese, Theologie eines Schlusselbegriffs*. Wien: Herder, 1979.

Wright, W. *A Grammar of the Arabic Language*. Cambridge: University Press, 1896–1898.

Yates, Frances. *The Art of Memory*. Chicago: University of Chicago Press, 1966.

Young, Morris N. *Bibliography of Memory*. Philadelphia: Chilton, 1961.

Commentaries on Aristotle's "On Sense and What Is Sensed" and "On Memory and Recollection" was composed in Meridien, and designed and produced by Kachergis Book Design, Pittsboro, North Carolina; and printed on 60-pound Glatfelter Natural and bound by Edwards Brothers, Lillington, North Carolina.